BY JEREMY McCARTER

★

Young Radicals

Hamilton: The Revolution
(with Lin-Manuel Miranda)

Bite the Hand That Feeds You:
Essays and Provocations by Henry Fairlie
(editor)

Young Radicals

YOUNG RADICALS

In the War for American Ideals

JEREMY McCARTER

RANDOM HOUSE NEW YORK

u|n

Published in the United States by Random House, an imprint and division
of Penguin Random House LLC, New York.

RANDOM HOUSE and the HOUSE colophon are registered
trademarks of Penguin Random House LLC.

LIBRARY OF CONGRESS CATALOGING-IN-PUBLICATION DATA
NAMES: McCarter, Jeremy, author.
TITLE: Young radicals : in the war for American ideals / Jeremy McCarter.
DESCRIPTION: New York : Random House, 2017. | Includes
bibliographical references and index.
IDENTIFIERS: LCCN 2016055051| ISBN 9780812993059
(hardback : acid-free paper) | ISBN 9780679644545 (ebook)
SUBJECTS: LCSH: Radicals—United States—Biography. | Political
activists—United States—Biography. | Bourne, Randolph Silliman,
1886–1918. | Eastman, Max, 1883–1969. | Lippmann, Walter, 1889–1974. |
Paul, Alice, 1885–1977. | Reed, John, 1887–1920. | Idealism, American—
History—20th century. | World War, 1914–1918—Social aspects—
United States. | United States—Politics and government—1901–1953. |
BISAC: HISTORY / Modern / 20th Century. | BIOGRAPHY &
AUTOBIOGRAPHY / Cultural Heritage.
CLASSIFICATION: LCC HN90.R3 M22 2017 | DDC 322.4/20973—dc23
LC record available at https://lccn.loc.gov/2016055051

Printed in the United States of America on acid-free paper

randomhousebooks.com

2 4 6 8 9 7 5 3 1

First Edition

Book design by Liz Cosgrove

This book is dedicated to

OSKAR EUSTIS,

true believer, democratic dreamer,
fighter of the good fights

We must march, my darlings, we must bear the brunt of danger,
We, the youthful sinewy races, all the rest on us depend

— WALT WHITMAN

Contents

Introduction

This is a story about hope and what comes after hope, and despair and what comes after despair.

It's about what happens when the world, which had seemed to be spinning rapidly in the direction of peace and social progress, falls to pieces. It's about reaching out to grasp the new America that seems to be drawing near—freer, more equal, more welcoming—and having America try to break your hand.

Maybe you know the feeling.

For six years, I tried to imagine how it felt to live through the 1910s, when Americans saw their faith in progress and their hope for their country surge as they have rarely surged before or since, only to see many of their dreams broken by the violence and repression that accompanied American entry into World War I. Lately I find it easier to make that imaginative leap. In fact, as I type this in late January 2017, in the bewildering early days of a new presidential administration, it's no leap at all.

The dislocation of World War I isn't what drew me to this subject:

It was the dreamers who found themselves dislocated. In Greenwich Village, just before the war, a lively, funny, kaleidoscopic bohemia thrived. Mainly young and mostly broke, artists and writers and activists incubated all sorts of rebellions. They helped to shape the rise of modernism in painting and poetry and theater, socialism in politics, and a dazzling array of social advances—in women's rights, in means of expression, in the final sweeping away of Victorian strictures. They gave vivid expression to a spirit that young Americans across the country could feel in those years—not merely a sense of motion, because society is always moving, but *acceleration*. Encountering their stories during college, I was struck by how much more vibrant their hopes for America seemed than anything I was hearing amid the cool technocratic triumphalism of modern liberalism. Those rebels expected life to be as vivid as the fauvist colors they wore.

In 1917, when Woodrow Wilson sent the country to fight Germany, the vibrant prewar atmosphere vanished more quickly than anyone had thought possible. America's first taste of foreign war on such a scale was enough to drive it mad. Yet the young radicals—some of them, anyway, the bravest of them—persisted. They didn't surrender their hopes. They didn't retreat to a college quad. The country grew more dangerous, but they kept striving to bend reality in the direction of their ideals. Why?

That was the large and tantalizing question that impelled me to start writing this book in the winter of 2011. And it kept me writing for nearly six years, because it presented so many other tantalizing questions. Where do idealists come by their galvanizing visions of a better world? Why do they give up health, safety, comfort, status to see those visions made real? How do they reckon with failure—or, more rarely, with success? The pattern recurs throughout our history, but rarely in so compact a form as the World War I years. Life changed so much and so quickly, in ways good and bad, that idealists traveled the entire arc of inspiration, struggle, hope, despair, and final reckoning not over the course of a long lifetime, but in eight or nine frenetic years.

Many formidable studies of that era exist. They systematize, they contextualize, they explain. They are what drew me to the subject in the first place. But this book about ideals and the people who fight for them has a different aim. For while ideals are vast abstractions, they are also as personal as a handprint. I want to express myself, and you want to express yourself, but we don't mean the same thing by "free expression." If we both struggle on its behalf, we will do so for our own personal reasons, and we will pay for it in different ways. The only way to understand ideals and the people who fight for them is to watch the story on the individual scale, where you can register personal desires, personal choices, and personal consequences. The story has to be told in close-up, not panorama.

Yet no single close-up, however detailed, can capture the vitality of that era. No individual could experience all or even most of its commotion. The right number of protagonists in this story—or, to put it more clinically, the proper sample size for this experiment framed up in the laboratory of history—lies someplace between "one" and "many." But where?

While puzzling over this question, I had the same experience that so many Americans did in the early twentieth century: I found enlightenment in William James. The great philosopher, from his perch in Cambridge, did more than anyone else to shape the intellectual climate of that era: its delight in variety, its enthusiasm for change, its conviction that the only idealists worth admiring are those who strive to realize their ideals *in the world*. James believed that in the absence of a single divine Truth to guide us, we navigate our way through life pragmatically. We pick out patterns, we try to impose order on multitudinous facts, we experiment. He illustrated his point with a metaphor from astronomy: "We carve out groups of stars in the heavens, and call them constellations."

This book, then, is the story of a constellation. It describes the exploits of five young radicals whose ideals led them to travel a similar trajectory across the sky of their era. Why five, instead of four or six? I can only cite a master who preceded me, who selected his subjects not according to a formal plan, but "by simple motives of convenience and of art." I picked them because they evoke what's distinctive about their era and what resonates in ours. I thought the choices that each of them made would shed light on the choices of the others. I thought they would be good company.

They are Walter Lippmann and John Reed, Harvard classmates and friends, who passed each other on the path to and from socialism, to and from active political engagement; the editor Max Eastman, who chased a dual life of poetry and propaganda through many misadventures; the militant suffragist Alice Paul, who was determined to win freedom for women using all the resources at her disposal, including her own health; and Randolph Bourne, the prophet-essayist who saw what even his fellow radicals couldn't see—not in his time, and not in ours.

Some of them were friends and some were rivals and some were friends-turned-rivals, but they were never a self-identified group. (The stars "patiently suffer us" to yoke them together, James wrote, "though if they knew what we were doing, some of them might feel much surprised at the partners we had given them.") Instead, these five share some salient characteristics. All launched their way onto the American scene around 1912, when they were in their twenties: venturesome young Americans growing up in a venturesome young country. All distinguished themselves by having a bolder, fiercer, more radical vision for American life than most of their contemporaries. All faced dangerous obstacles to the realization of that ideal, but chose to persist all the same.

That act of choosing is the most important trait that binds them. For if we're going to understand why idealists fight for their ideals, it helps to study idealists who have good reasons *not* to fight. All five of these young radicals attended college, all were white, none were poor. They didn't need the trouble they brought on themselves. They *chose* to run risks for their ideals—not just at the beginning but again and again through their lives.

I admire their courage and their vision; I regret their lapses of judgment and failures of nerve. Above all, and especially in the last few weeks, I feel toward them a sense of kinship. It is a very American feeling. After all, it is one of the principles of our nation (as of this writing, anyway) that Americanness isn't a function of race or religion or country of origin, but a willingness to join in a common national project, to uphold certain democratic ideals. In each generation, new conditions make us interpret those ideals in new ways. We are always reconsidering what equality means, how freedom may be used, and what we owe to one another. But the ideals themselves persist. When we take to the streets today, the slogans on our signs might be new, but the values expressed by those signs are very old, and they bear the traces of battles that the young radicals waged. We inherit their ideals as surely as I've got my grandfather's cheekbones.

The echoes of the 1910s in our current predicament are awfully ominous: The young rebels who carried such high hopes into 1917 were heading into some of the darkest, most despairing years in American history. But their story should give us a little consolation—or at least some perspective.

The war for American ideals was under way before the crises of that decade, and it continued after they ended. It'll certainly (well, almost certainly) outlive us, too. A different outcome in the 2016 presidential election would have changed the kinds of fights we'd be having, but we'd still be having them. The need to keep fighting about the meaning of America's ideals is, itself, an American ideal. We face the same question that the young radicals faced, not just once but every day: whether to get into the fight, and how.

I. COMMENCEMENT,

OR FIVE DREAMS FIND THEIR DREAMERS (1912–13)

Not a victory is gained, not a deed of faithfulness or courage is done, except upon a maybe; not a service, not a sally of generosity, not a scientific exploration or experiment or textbook, that may not be a mistake.

—WILLIAM JAMES

Anythink Commerce City

7185 Monaco Street
Commerce City, CO 80022
303-287-0063
Tues and Thurs., 11AM-7PM
Wed, Fri, Sat, 9:30AM-5:30PM
Sun and Mon, Closed

Date: 1/23/2019 Time: 2:42:16 PM

Items checked out this session: 2

Title: Young radicals : in the war for Amer
Barcode: 33021030264318
Due Date: 02/13/19

Title: Law 101 : everything you need to kno
Barcode: 33021032087501
Due Date: 02/13/19

Page 1 of 1

... where anything is possible.

Chapter 1

The future arrives on New Year's Day, 1912. Walter Lippmann arrives with it.

The brisk young man strides into the city hall of Schenectady, New York. Black-haired, dark-eyed, rounded with baby fat: You might think him handsome, if he did anything that invited you to notice his looks. But he doesn't. He has no time.

The future arrives that day because a socialist has become Schenectady's mayor. Other American cities have elected socialist mayors—even larger cities, such as Milwaukee—but they have tended to be in the upper Midwest, a region tainted by alien enthusiasms for Lutheranism, social democracy, and beer. Schenectady, by contrast, is an old city Back East. If Mayor George Lunn can make socialism work here, it will mean a new chapter in the life of America's cities. A journalist tracing the rapid spread of socialism that year says that Schenectady has an outsize significance because it "well reflected in miniature the economic and industrial problems that press upon the whole country for solution."[1]

For Lippmann—arranging his desk outside the mayor's office, making it just so—one problem presses harder than the rest: "the control of politics and of our life by great combinations of wealth." The richest 1 percent of the population has about 40 percent of the wealth. In an era before Social Security, workers' compensation, and effective limits on child labor, that disparity leaves an enormous underclass of poor families. Most Americans are one missed paycheck away from disaster.[2]

Socialists don't agree on what to do about this. Some are ready for direct action, sabotage, dynamite. That's not where Lippmann turns first. His socialism draws from the British Fabians: H. G. Wells, Sidney and Beatrice Webb, George Bernard Shaw. He wants to see socialists win elections and use their new authority to get rid of wasteful, plutocratic systems that make the rich richer.

Ruminating on the Fabians is not something that mayoral secretaries tend to spend a lot of time doing, but Lippmann is no ordinary secretary. Terrible at stenography (or so he claims) he receives delegations, takes part in planning sessions, and writes speeches—this last task being more impressive than it might sound, considering the texts that Reverend Lunn used to deliver before a congregation.[3]

Two months into Schenectady's socialist era, Lippmann extols their early gains in an article for *The Masses*, a new socialist monthly published in New York City.

"The budget is done, and a splendid piece of work it is," he enthuses.

(*The Masses* is not a very exciting magazine.)

Mayor Lunn and his allies have funded more training for mothers, better inspection of the milk supply, and a system for stockpiling ice for cheap distribution in the summer. All of it—even the new playgrounds—will cost less than the old administration's programs, because of great improvements in coordination and efficiency.[4]

In other words, socialism in practice has begun, in a modest way, to bear out socialism in theory. Which means it has begun to back up the argument that Lippmann has been making to a prosperous businessman who is sharply skeptical of socialism: his dad.

"It is not the fantastic dream of unpractical men; it is not the cry of the 'have-nots' against the 'haves'; it is not a thing which may work or may not," he insisted to Jacob Lippmann a few years earlier, in the first flush of his zeal. "It is rather a hard-headed, sound, scientific business proposition, based on the theory that 'united we stand, divided we fall,' which is the next, logical, and practically inevitable phase of industrial society."[5]

It's all going according to plan—for him, for Schenectady, for socialism. He is tasting the pleasure—and is any pleasure sweeter?—of winning an argument with the old man. So why is he uneasy?

Day after day, sitting at his desk, he watches men arrive looking for their share of what he calls "this new heaven on earth which socialism promised them." They are cold and hungry and out of work—dozens of them, hundreds of them. What can the mayor do for them?

Not much, Lippmann laments to a friend. Not nearly enough. "Inspect them a little closer for disease—give them a municipal skating rink and a concert! Tabulate a few more statistics of unemployment!"[6]

In his letters to Mom and Pop, Lippmann can expound socialism in tones so steady that they wouldn't rattle a teacup. But make no mistake: His convictions have been tempered in flame. During his sophomore year at Harvard, a working-class suburb of Boston was devastated by a fire. Lippmann was one of the students who answered the call to help people in what was left of Chelsea. For the first time in his well-upholstered life, his abstract apprenticeship in socialist thought—all those pamphlets and manifestos—rose before him in three desperate dimensions: the smell of charred tenements, the crying widows, the children without homes. Those people had no government to help them, no resources at all.

Now Schenectady is going to fail them, too?

He starts listening a little more attentively to his older colleagues in those staff meetings. He notices that their talk is not quite as idealistic as it used to be. He hears timidity, a lack of reflection, phrasemaking. Worse than all the rest, he watches his colleagues console themselves— *congratulate* themselves—by saying they are scratching out their little victories at the expense of powerful special interests. He wishes that were true! He once spent a year helping the great muckraker Lincoln Steffens investigate Wall Street's control of American life, particularly the tangled web of financial corruption in city governments. It taught him that the enemy of progress is rarely a small band of wicked pluto- crats: It is a system that encompasses and draws its sustenance from everyone, even those who think themselves virtuous.

A sinister cabal isn't the barrier to enacting the socialist policies that would help those poor families, he comes to see: It's "the unwatered hinterland of the citizens of Schenectady."[7] If they really wanted social- ism, if they were ready for it, they'd be getting it. But they're not.

The gap between hope and reality brings him quickly to a crisis: Can he condone this sham exercise in socialism, let alone continue to be a part of it? For the first time in his overachieving life, he finds him- self in a predicament with no clear way out.

What is to be done?

On one hand, he feels that he should stay on the job, make the best of it, and trumpet whatever success they attain, because he is a walking advertisement for socialism's future. A lot of comrades have banked a lot of hope in him. He is an officer of the Intercollegiate Socialist So- ciety. He landed the Schenectady job because Morris Hillquit, one of the founders and leaders of the Socialist Party of America, recom- mended him to the mayor-elect. To quit would be an admission that he has failed.

On the other hand, the prospects for failure are growing by the day. Lunn was elected as a protest against the corruption of the old admin- istration. Once he starts focusing on reelection, he'll have to water down his socialism even more. Soon Lippmann's job will force him to say and do things that are flatly false to his convictions.

In trimming his sails that way, he would be false to something even deeper than his socialism: his vast hope for his time. Everywhere Lippmann looks, he sees untapped resources, latent possibilities, a country with the capacity to leap ahead. He is a socialist because he thinks that central planning, informed by social science, offers Ameri- can society the quickest possible route to an enlightened future. In an undergraduate magazine, he offered his view of what was unprecedented about the twentieth century: "Its shaping lies in our hands; for the first time in history an enlightened nation may consciously prepare the future to suit its own purposes." That essay brought an unexpected visitor to his dorm-room door: the great philosopher William James, then in semiretirement, who had crossed Harvard Yard to express his admiration. Lippmann considered James to be the greatest living American, and getting to spend time with him the greatest thing that happened to him in college.[8]

This crisis in Lippmann's young life reveals something new in his makeup: resourcefulness. Given a choice between two unpalatable options, he devises a third. It is a two-step plan—as logical and thorough as everything else he puts his mind to.

First, he quits. In early May, he cleans out his desk in city hall. He says his goodbyes. He returns to his parents' home on the Upper East Side of Manhattan, wincing at what must have been a slow, sly paternal smile.

Second, a few weeks later, in the pages of *The New York Call*, the country's leading socialist publication, he writes a blistering attack on the failures of Mayor Lunn and his administration.

In "Schenectady the Unripe," Lippmann explains why the city had betrayed everybody's radical hopes: The citizens hadn't been converted to socialism, which meant a socialist mayor would only let down the cause. But Lippmann offers this high-minded theoretical explanation amid a hailstorm of personal judgments: "untrained," "immature," "impotent."[9]

The rebuttal from comrades is swift and severe. It comes first from Morris Hillquit, who is, after all, doubly implicated in Lippmann's attack: He is a special adviser to Lunn's administration, which means that Lippmann is insulting his work, and he is the party elder who vouched for Lippmann in the first place, which means that "Schenectady the Unripe" is a mess of Hillquit's own making. He chastises his young comrade in the *Call* for the "singular reticence" he showed while in Schenectady, implying that Lippmann had simply given up.

Lippmann declines to be chastised, not even by a man of Morris Hillquit's stature. He hits back hard, alluding to their "delightful conversations," some of which happened in Hillquit's own home: "I certainly have not forgotten how sympathetic he was, how much he agreed, *and how little he did.*"[10]

The essay and the combative exchange boost Lippmann's profile in radical circles. He seems even more committed to socialism than anybody realized. Or is it the opposite?

America is "bursting with new ideas, new plans and new hopes," he writes later that year. "The world was never so young as it is today, so impatient of old and crusty things."[11]

When he returns from his attempt to kick-start the future, he is twenty-two years old.

Chapter 2

John Reed prowls the docks, laughing with the sailors, chatting up the whores. The big Irish cops know him there, as do the Chinese in Chinatown and the Jews on the Lower East Side. He rides the elevated trains up and down the avenues, hitching up his pants, shouldering into places he doesn't belong. For a snack, he'll sometimes eat a grapefruit—tearing it in half, wolfing down the insides, then wringing the rind like a rag, tilting his chin back so the juice runs down his throat.[1] Overtaken at last by fatigue, or morning light, he romps home to ramshackle Greenwich Village, the air around Mrs. Vanderbilt's stables sweet with horse manure.

In the grungy apartment that he shares with three friends, he writes down what he has seen and heard on his adventures. Then he tries to sell it.

Reed is a writer, or would like to be. A full year of scratching away in the depths of New York journalism has yielded a couple of bylines and a fat stack of rejections. Lincoln Steffens, a friend of his father, helped him get a low-level editorial job at *The American Magazine*. It doesn't pay much, but it's enough to keep afloat in the Village. When the city's leaders stretched a grid of numbered streets and avenues across Manhattan in 1811, they decided that the little roads in that odd angle of the island were already too crooked and unreasonable to bother straightening out. There's no cachet to the place when Reed moves in: It's just cheap. But that's attraction enough for poor immigrants, painters, poets, agitators, and cranks of all kinds.

They are all waiting for inspiration to strike. For Reed, it strikes in the spring of 1912.

He comes up with "one of the biggest stories that has been sprung around these parts in half a century," as he tells a friend.[2]

But before any editor can accept it, he has to write it. And in order to do that, he needs to marshal an array of qualities that his twenty-four years on the planet haven't heretofore revealed: discipline, focus, a capacity to sit still.

Reed knows that he is the wrong guy for in-depth analysis. So he's lucky that the *right* guy is not only a friend, but a friend with time to pitch in, for he has just quit his job in Schenectady and come home to New York.

Reed asks for Walter Lippmann's help, and Lippmann gives it.[3] Probably it's in both their interests. Walter is a big part of the story that Jack wants to tell.

Jack is tall and muscular, disheveled and floppy haired—"nothing but a bundle of fine nerves, bulging energy, overweening vanity, and trembling curiosity, with an egotistical ambition to distinguish himself as a poet," according to Steffens.[4] These are the qualities that alerted him to his big story in the first place.

He has learned that his alma mater, Harvard, is trying to tamp down political activity on campus and restrain the unruly tendencies of the student body. Jack doesn't like that one bit. As he looks back on his years in Cambridge, and looks around at his life in Manhattan, he sees the same restless spirit at work: "an influx of revolutionary ideas, discontent, criticism and revolt."[5] He wants to grab that spirit, pin it down, and describe it at length, preferably in the pages of a high-paying national magazine.

Reed gives his classmate a lot of the credit for letting that spirit rush through the college. When Lippmann co-founded the Socialist Club during their sophomore year, he made politics a burning issue on campus for the first time. "The meetings of the club were more alive than anything that had been seen around Harvard for years," Reed recalls. The club's members didn't just sit around sifting doctrines. They worked to see their ideals made real in the world, "to see their theories *applied*—not merely academically discussed—applied to the world, to themselves, to *Harvard*."

In other words, they were troublemakers. Reed loves troublemakers. It's one reason why, when Lippmann paid a visit to the Western Club, Reed stood, bowed, and half-satirically declared, "Gentlemen, the future president of the United States!"[6]

Now, in a shabby walk-up in Greenwich Village, Lippmann explains to Reed what he has done and why. He sits for interviews, recommends sources, reads drafts. The project is a chance to talk about the experiences they have shared, such as writing for the literary magazine and studying with the much-loved English instructor Charles T. Copeland, known to all as "Copey."

They shared one other experience at college, but they probably don't talk about it: the sensation of being an outcast, of feeling terribly alone.

Jack had come from Portland, Oregon, an unfashionably remote hometown. Four years of prep school in New Jersey had left him big and loud and rough around the edges—"not entirely good form," in Lippmann's words. Lippmann *was* good form, having grown up on East Eightieth Street, summering in Europe, and knowing which spoon to use first, but he was consigned to Harvard's margins, too. He is a Jew.

The result of Reed and Lippmann's labors is even less practical than the theories that Reed used to hear in those meetings. "The Harvard Renaissance," in its finished form, runs twenty thousand words. No magazine is going to publish a story so long from a writer so young. Reed sends it out anyway, being as outsized in hope as in everything else.

For a while, his every waking thought is about that manuscript. Then he stops thinking about it altogether. A message arrives from the other end of the continent: *Come home right away.*

On July 2, 1912, a Portland newspaper devotes much of its front page to the astounding news from the Democratic National Convention. The reform-minded governor of New Jersey, Woodrow Wilson, has defied every prediction and secured the presidential nomination on the forty-sixth ballot.

Down toward the bottom of the page, three little lines note that Charles J. Reed has died.

Jack made it home in time to tell his father goodbye. Even separated by a continent, their affection had been large and genuine. "I think and talk of you every day, and love you and am proud of you every hour," C.J. had written to his son a few months earlier.[7]

Jack had given C.J. and Margaret Reed ample reasons *not* to be proud: the scrapes with school officials, the dustups with the law, the picaresque trip to Europe, which yielded accounts of ugly American behavior, a French fiancée, and a little book Jack wrote and illustrated for their amusement: *Songs from a Full Heart and an Empty Head.*

It falls to Jack, as the older of the two Reed boys, to help his mother sort through the chaos of the family finances. Their fortunes have tumbled a long way since his childhood, which he spent in a big house, tended by servants. While he was away at school, C.J. had agreed to become a U.S. marshal, and helped break up a timber fraud ring. His work led to a string of convictions and the friendship with Steffens, who reported on the investigations. But C.J. found himself ostracized by the Portland establishment he'd defied. For a time, Jack's father spent all day going door-to-door, trying to sell life insurance.[8] His health declined and never recovered.

"My father worried himself to death—that's all," Reed tells a friend after his death. "He never let any of us know, but he was harassed into the grave. Money!"[9]

C. J. Reed had fought wrongdoing, even among his friends and associates, and taken the consequences. Could Jack say that he had been doing the same? With "The Harvard Renaissance" rattling in his ears, it would have been impossible to pretend that he had.

For in those twenty thousand words about the bold radicalism of Lippmann and his comrades, Reed had omitted his own role. He liked watching Lippmann stir up trouble, but he never joined the Socialist Club. He had other priorities, such as writing musicals, playing water polo, and being a cheerleader for the football team. Reed had no socialist convictions—no real political interest of any kind. ("Curse me if you will for a Selfish Plutocrat," he wrote to his friends from a trip to London. "I had every chance to mingle with the Socialists of England, and I chucked them all to see Pavlova dance!")[10] The one time he tried to get involved in campus politics, the result was a debacle. During senior year, a routine election for class offices had turned into a bitter campus-wide fight. The forces of "the Yard" (that is, the less wealthy students who lived in dorms on Harvard Yard) had squared off against "the Street" (that is, the sons of privilege who lived in the fancy apartments on Mount Auburn Street). Lippmann was the principal spokesman for the Yard: He didn't want to win friends among the aristocrats; he wanted to curtail their privileges. Reed, stupidly, self-servingly, took sides with the Street. In his desire to win the aristocrats' favor, he broke off his friendship with a classmate even less popular than he was.

Of the pair, Reed and Lippmann, who had acted more like the late C. J. Reed? And who had acted like the plutocrats who spurned him?

In 1912, in Portland, in mourning, Reed feels the tug of two desires. There's the impulse that everybody can see: to write plays and poems, play pranks, maybe even get rich. There's another one that nobody can see, because it's churning too deep inside. But his father had known it was there, and feared it. Before C.J. died, he asked Steffens to keep political convictions from destroying his son's life the way they had his own.

"He is a poet, I think; keep him singing," he said. "Let him see everything, but don't—don't let him get like me."[11]

Steffens tried. He had extricated Jack from his foolish French engagement, helped him get that magazine job, and stood him small loans when he needed them—as long as he used the money for something capricious, not for paying a bill. Now he tries to lighten Jack's sorrow, and make him "feel free and the world wide-open."[12]

Reed is pretty sure the opposite is true. What is he supposed to do? If he stays in Portland, he can help his mother and younger brother in their sadness. But he can't stay in Portland—there's nobody to talk to, he'd go crazy in a year. But why go back to New York? "The Harvard Renaissance" has found no buyers, as he should have known it wouldn't. The commercial magazines are so much tamer and more conventional than Reed's tastes: How can he ever break through?

Like Lippmann losing heart in Schenectady, Reed has no precedent to consult and no light to guide the way. The predicament captures the spirit of 1912 better than all the ink he'd spilled on the college radicals.

Three months later, Jack Reed rides a train hurtling back to Manhattan.

He returns to Greenwich Village bearing a peculiar product of his time away—a literary effort full of paradoxes. In a time of sorrow, he wrote of joy. Lonely in his hometown, he put words in the mouths of faraway friends. Having failed to describe the radical spirit of his generation seriously and journalistically, he tried it comically and in verse: He wrote an epic poem about his neighborhood, "A Day in Bohemia":

> We are free who live in Washington Square,
> We dare to think as Uptown wouldn't dare,
> Blazing our nights with arguments uproarious;
> What care we for a dull old world censorious
> When each is sure he'll fashion something glorious?
> Blessed art thou, Anarchic Liberty
> Who asketh nought but joy of such as we!

Eaten up by his family's financial cares, Reed dreamed his way back to a place that had little use for money: that shabby apartment he shared with three friends. (It was three doors east of Macdougal Street, where NYU Law School stands now.) He described the decrepitude of the place—cockroaches, cats shrieking in the backyard mud, Italians screaming in tenement windows across the way—but he makes them seem like enormous advantages for young people trying to get free.

> The dust it flies in at the window,
> The smells they come in at the door,
> Our trousers lie meek where we threw 'em last week
> Bestrewing the maculate floor.
> The gas isn't all that it should be,
> It flickers,—and yet I declare
> There's pleasure or near it for young men of spirit
> At Forty-Two Washington Square!
>
> But nobody questions your morals,
> And nobody asks for the rent,—
> There's no one to pry if we're tight, you and I,
> Or demand how our evenings are spent.
> The furniture's ancient but plenty,
> The linen is spotless and fair,
> O Life is a joy to a broth of a boy
> At Forty-Two Washington Square!

Reed's poem depicts the place on a typical Tuesday morning, when he and his friends wake up late and rush off to their jobs—in his case, at *The American Magazine*. After work, when he meets some fellow bohemians for tea, he finds fresh targets for satire: the poet who writes no poetry, the anarchist who gets nervous when there are no cops to protect him. Just as he admired Lippmann's socialists because they applied their ideals, Reed praises only the artists who actually produce art.

After a cheap dinner at Paglieri's (the only kind he and his friends can afford), they reconvene at 42 Washington Square—"Parnassus Flats," he calls it, mock heroically—and a stream of guests begin to arrive. Most of them are artists of one stripe or another, like his college classmate, the poet Alan Seeger, or the hobo poet Harry Kemp. One visitor is unlike the rest:

> LIPPMANN,—calm, inscrutable,
> Thinking and writing clearly,—soundly, well;
> All snarls of falseness swiftly piercing through,
> His keen mind leaps like lightning to the True;
> His face is almost placid,—but his eye,—
> There is a vision born to prophecy!
> He sits in silence, as one who has said:
> "I waste not living words among the dead!"
>
> Our all-unchallenged Chief! But were there one
> Who builds a world, and leaves out all the fun,—
> Who dreams a pageant, gorgeous, infinite,
> And then leaves all the color out of it,—
> Who wants to make the human race, and me,
> March to a geometric Q. E. D.—
> Who but must laugh, if such a man there be?
> Who would not weep, if WALTER L. were he?

In those verses, Reed still sounds like the careless, callow boy who sucked up to aristocrats, a prankster making fun of his buttoned-up friend. But the poem culminates in something new: a raucous argument in which everybody noisily agitates for this or that creed. Lippmann, for instance, demolishes somebody's anarchism and makes the case for socialism. Reed laughs about it, but he still treats the radicals' debate as the culmination of the story he has been trying to tell:

> Now with an easy caper of the mind
> We rectify the Errors of Mankind;

Now with the sharpness of a keen-edged jest,
Plunge a hot thunder-bolt in Mammon's breast;
Impatient Youth, in fine creative rage,
With both hands wrests the quenchless torch from Age;
Not as the Dilettanti, who explain
Why they have failed,—excuse, lament, complain,
Condemn real artists to exalt themselves,
And credit their misfortunes to the elves;—
But to Gods of Strength make offertory,—
And pit our young wits in the race for glory!

A long comic poem is no place to announce a road-to-Damascus conversion, and anyway Reed hadn't made one. But the young man who wrote these lines was coming around to principled revolt. "The Harvard Renaissance" described rebels in the third person; "A Day in Bohemia" describes them in the first. The observer is becoming a participant.

"A Day in Bohemia" goes a long way toward doing what "The Harvard Renaissance" failed to do: making Reed's reputation. As it passes from hand to hand, it also helps to give the still-amorphous Village a legend. Week after week, young people who dream of a liberated future, as Lippmann and Reed do, keep showing up, having heard a rumor of freedom.

The mélange of political, social, and cultural dissidents would never accept a king, but in Jack Reed they have discovered something better: part crown prince, part jester.

Chapter 3

The story of Max Eastman's wayward life—the story of a shy academic becoming the death-defying champion of a cause, of a son of two ministers turning into a shameless pagan, of an apolitical country-boy poet growing up to be hailed as "the founding father of the twentieth-century American left"—this story begins on a summer day in 1912, when the mail arrives.[1]

Eastman opens an envelope and inside finds a torn sheet of drawing paper. It reads, in its entirety: "You are elected editor of The Masses. No pay."

What could it mean?

Max is familiar with the magazine. A socialist is bound to be, even if you want to avoid it, which he would have been happy to do. *The Masses* is a year-old monthly magazine edited by Piet Vlag, a long-nosed, dark-eyed Dutchman who worked in the cafeteria of the Rand School. One brief look into its pages is enough to see leaden editorials, pages crammed with text, and stagy illustrations of manly hands gripping blazing torches. Walter Lippmann's paean to Schenectady's budget, published a few months earlier, had been on the racy end of its spectrum.

Max can't understand why the dozen signatories to the note would offer him a subscription, let alone make him editor.

Is it a mistake? A joke?

Max's eye drifts to one signatory in particular: Art Young. The roly-poly artist is one of the foremost political cartoonists in America and a fervent socialist, though neither trait is evident to people who meet him. (Young favors slouchy suspenders and a laconic drawl. "Nothing is funnier than a man who is boiling mad. Especially a fat man," he would explain in his memoir. "Perhaps that is one reason why I usually hold my anger in leash.")[2]

The previous winter, Eastman met Young at a banquet honoring the visiting socialist dignitary Jack London. Max told Young he wanted to serve the socialist cause. That's why he'd quit his job teaching alongside John Dewey in the Columbia philosophy department. He was paying his bills by making speeches, but he found the work demeaning—especially since the success of his cool, understated presentations on behalf of woman suffrage was leading to offers to speak about subjects farther afield. The closer he got to being a mere entertainer, the queasier he felt.

The simplest explanation for the letter is that Young misunderstood what Eastman said that night. Max wants to help socialism, but he needs to make a living. He can't take a job that doesn't pay. And anyway, an editing job doesn't suit his introvert's temperament. The job would wreak havoc on his life.

Although, now that he thinks about it (standing there, peculiar letter in hand), what is his life? Something needs to change—and badly. Maybe havoc is the answer.

That summer, Max and his wife, Ida Rauh, have traded their apartment in Greenwich Village for a summer sublet in Waterford, Connecticut. She is pregnant with their first baby, which was reason enough to flee the city heat. The quiet means less to Ida, who likes noise and bustle and people, than to Max, who doesn't. He had hoped the solace would help him finish a book that would modernize—and, who knows, revolutionize?—the enjoyment of poetry. He calls it *The Enjoyment of Poetry.*

But he is trying to write about enjoyment without feeling any joy. His marriage had been a mistake, he has come to feel. Ida is brilliant and idealistic: Like Max's sister, Crystal, she is one of the first female lawyers in New York. In fact, he has Ida to thank for converting him from somebody who mocked socialism to a fervent believer. Still there is a deep part of his soul that she can't reach. It is rooted in western New York, where he grew up, not the city, where they live. It doesn't kindle to the social causes that Ida and many of their friends work for. It wants to write poems. It wants to play.

Could *The Masses* be the change that he needs?

No. Clearly, no.

Eastman decides that he will look up Art Young and decline the magazine's offer when he gets back to the city. That is due to happen in early September, when Ida will give birth, and Max will become a father. He doesn't feel too joyous about that, either.

"Come up and meet the bunch anyway," says Art Young a few weeks later, when Max returns to New York.

Now a man who was settled in his convictions, or even had a grown-up willingness to hurt somebody's feelings, would have held firm. He would have insisted that his "no" was final, and that there was no need to attend a *Masses* meeting, for there was nothing left to discuss.

Max Eastman is not that man. His motto is *Anything to avoid a harsh scene.*[3]

And so one night in mid-September—shortly after the birth of his son, Daniel, toward whom he feels pretty warmly, actually, warmer than he expected to—Eastman finds himself climbing flights of stairs to the studio of Charles A. Winter, the art editor of *The Masses,* and Alice Beach Winter, his wife.

Eastman looks around at the bunch; the bunch blinks back. Then they start to talk. And what they say surprises him.

How have such fascinating people produced such a dull magazine? Here are men and women of formidable achievements—in painting, in poetry, in criticism—who range freely over social, political, and artistic questions, not just dreary cooperative socialism. In their talk around the Winters' big table, in the easy connections they draw between this and that protest against the old ways of doing things, he detects a new spirit: "a sense of universal revolt and regeneration, of the just-before-dawn of a new day in American art and literature and living-of-life as well as in politics."[4]

He likes them. And after a season of feeling starved for affection, he likes that they like him.

Something is spread across the table that Eastman has never seen before: the guts of a magazine. Here are long columns of text, bits of headlines, and graphics of different shapes and sizes. Charles Winter thought that Eastman might like to see the process by which drawings and stories and poems are arranged on a page of the magazine.

Max is fascinated. He has never heard of this. "Pasting up the dummy," Winter calls it.

He suggests Max give it a try.

Within moments, Eastman is enthralled; within minutes, he is obsessed. The process, he discovers, combines two joys: "the infantine delight of cutting out paper dolls or keeping a scrapbook with the adult satisfaction of fooling yourself into thinking you are molding public opinion."[5] He discovers that he is a genius at pasting up dummies.

The savvy radicals must exchange delighted glances as their gangly, fair-haired, twenty-nine-year-old visitor plays with the scissors and paste pot: He had walked into a trap. What he didn't know when he opened that letter, and might have not realized until that night, is that The Masses was effectively dead.

After a year of publication, The Messes (as Vlag had called it in his thick Dutch accent) had worn out the patience of the life insurance executive footing the bill. Vlag patched up a merger between the magazine and a women's socialist publication in Chicago without asking his contributors' opinions, then moved to Florida. Art Young and the other artists had wanted to continue without Vlag. To do so, they would need an organizer: someone to handle the dirty work, the drudgery, the grown-up stuff. That, it turns out, is why Young had proposed Eastman for editor—not because Max showed any particular socialist promise. Young had read to the group an article Max wrote about organizing the Men's League for Women's Suffrage. In a funny, self-deprecating way, Eastman explained how he rounded up socially prominent men by assuring them they wouldn't have to do anything. The organization's sole function was to exist.[6]

A thriving radical organization in which most of the work is done by one man: That sounded right to the artists of *The Masses*.

It will all be cooperative, the bunch assure him that night in the Winters' studio. Everybody will pitch in.

Eastman must know that it isn't true. All his frustrations about finding the right balance between political agitation and poetic expression will multiply. His life needs to change, but editing a failing socialist magazine isn't the way to do it. He would be a fool or a masochist to agree.

His first issue of *The Masses* appears two months later. It is an "experimental" number, he explains to readers: a demonstration to potential supporters of what the magazine could become. In an editor's note, he explains the company's financial plight and frankly asks for loans.

To make sure those readers feel maximum inspiration to give, Eastman tries to dazzle them with a magazine unlike any that have been produced in the radical press in America. He makes it bolder, funnier, more vivid. He puts color on the cover and makes the text less dense. He takes big swings, none bigger than the magazine's political orientation, which he changes completely.

Earlier in the year, after a decade of continuous growth, the Socialist

Party had split. On one side are the yellows: people like Lippmann and the party's leaders, who concentrate on winning elections and steady reforms. On the other side are the reds, who countenance using violence to combat the violence they suffer at the hands of capitalists. In a letter to *The New York Call,* his first public utterance as a socialist, Eastman criticizes the moderate leaders of the party who expelled the labor leader Bill Haywood (who is very, very red). But he doesn't pick a side—he says that both approaches should be allowed to coexist.

That broad-minded approach, a resistance to doctrinal purity, is Eastman's most distinctive contribution to the magazine. Ida had converted him to socialism by convincing him that Marx's theory of class struggle wasn't dreamy utopian thinking, or a creed that demanded unthinking fealty, but a close kin to the hardheaded experimental approach to life he'd learned from John Dewey. ("Ida," he had exclaimed, "that's a perfectly wonderful idea!")[7] Eastman's love of variety extended beyond socialist disputes. "*The Masses* shall be hospitable to free and spirited expressions of every kind—in fiction, satire, poetry, and essay," he promises.

In essence, he wants the magazine to reflect the kind of freewheeling radicalism he heard in the Winters' studio: frank, wide-ranging, unafraid. He declares his eagerness to publish things that a moneymaking magazine beholden to advertisers and middle-class mores wouldn't touch. To make sure nobody misses the point, he devotes the middle two pages of his experimental issue to an enormous Art Young illustration that depicts the New York press as a whorehouse. A rich man labeled "Big Advertisers" pays an editor to have access to the ladies within: ladies who are really the men working at a newspaper in incongruously slinky dresses.

Eastman's rejuvenated magazine attracts notice in radical circles, some of it outraged (one friend tells him that Young's drawing is "vulgar beyond anything I have ever seen in an American magazine")[8] but all of it useful. They need to make a splash to have a chance.

A few weeks after the issue appears, the bunch reconvenes to see how the experiment has gone.

It has not gone well.

Eastman's plea for support has yielded a puny twenty dollars. Despite agreeing that everybody would hit up their rich friends for money, nobody has raised a dime.

For Eastman, the verdict brings relief: He doesn't have to agonize over whether to accept the burden, because there is no burden to accept. *The Masses* looks to be finished.

Except that in 1912, radical circles are compact, and strange collisions occur. Shortly after the dispiriting meeting with the staff, Eastman runs into Inez Milholland: fierce suffragist, radical activist, ex-girlfriend.

She says nice things about his foray into magazine journalism. She hopes he'll keep it up.

Max confesses that it's impossible: The money isn't there.

"Have you tried Mrs. Belmont?" she says.

Max points out that the august lady, an ex-wife of a grandson of Cornelius Vanderbilt, is not likely to back a magazine making an explicit case for revolution—not blood-in-the-streets revolution, but workers' control all the same.

"What of it?" says Inez. "You're a militant—that's all that matters."[9]

And she's right. At dinner in Alva Belmont's palatial home on Madison Avenue, Eastman persuades her that the fight for economic justice is not so different from the militant suffragettes' fight for the vote in England—the cause that Belmont supports and wants to bring to America. He leaves with a big enough pledge to keep the magazine alive.

Eastman can feel momentum building now. He's not sure that he likes it. The last time he felt momentum, it carried him into an unhappy marriage.

He wants to be a poet. He doesn't want to keep raising money. He definitely doesn't want to spend all his time corralling contributions from writers and artists who receive no money for their work, or turning down work that they volunteer, which feels even worse.

In this gloomy mopey mood one morning, Eastman gets a phone

call. A writer wants to submit some stories for his consideration. He insists on doing so in person. Eastman has barely prepared himself when the visitor arrives: a nervous young man who paces and fidgets and does everything he can to avoid making eye contact.

Eastman takes the manuscripts and sends their author away. It's the last straw: He is going to get out of this nerve-jangling editing racket for good.[10]

Then he reads the stories.

They are bold and stylish. They confront heavy subjects with a light touch. The best story of the bunch is about a prostitute who is taken on a world tour by a john, only to return home to New York and go back to her old life—an old-fashioned story somehow updated and made radical, without losing human interest. No commercial magazine would touch such a story.[11] And so Max grabs paper and a pencil, and scribbles a note to its author.

"Your things are great," he writes to John Reed.

Eastman tells Reed he's going to run one of the stories in the next issue, and asks him to write more: "Some of us have got to do a turn every month until the magazine gets going."[12]

Eastman has made a lot of claims on behalf of *The Masses,* especially about its willingness to publish great work that a commercial magazine wouldn't tolerate, without entirely believing that such work exists. John Reed leads him to consider, with a jolt, that the things he has been saying *might actually be true.*

As soon as Eastman can manage it, he moves the magazine's office from Nassau Street, in dreary Lower Manhattan, to Greenwich Village. The magazine's arrival in 1913 is another milestone for the neighborhood's burgeoning rebellion. Like the Liberal Club, Polly's Restaurant, and a dozen little teahouses and bookstores, it creates a meeting point, a beacon.

But *The Masses* isn't just *in* Greenwich Village—it is of, by, and for the Village. Every few weeks, Eastman, Reed, the artists, and the writers get together to decide what should appear in the next issue. Somebody reads a story or poem out loud; everybody shouts what they think of it. It's not just the people on the masthead. Friends are welcome to show up and shout along.

Walter Lippmann joins one of the early meetings, even though shouting isn't his style. He has been seeking a form of socialism that's more effective than the approach that proved so dismaying in Schenectady. The meeting yields no revelations, but it does leave him admiring Eastman's "beautifully tempered mind."[13]

Other guests are less impressed. Hippolyte Havel, irascible anarchist cook at Polly's Restaurant, joins them one night and can't believe what he sees.

"Bourgeois!" he screams at them in his thick Czech accent. "Voting! Voting on poetry! Poetry is something from the soul! You can't vote on poetry!"[14]

Havel is on the staff of an anarchist magazine, somebody points out. Surely they take votes.

"Yes!" Havel replies. "But we don't abide by them!"[15]

In truth, the process is not quite as democratic as it seems: Eastman makes a lot of the decisions on his own after the meetings break up. He exerts himself to make sure that a certain provincialism he detects around the Village—an enthusiasm for revolt that's too easy, too fashionable—doesn't distort what he's trying to do. But the magazine still remains an index of radical causes. It defends the militant suffragettes in England and Margaret Sanger's crusade to publish information on what she has just labeled "birth control." It sticks up for striking workers in the face of violent repression. Eastman publishes his wish that the racist night riders who are trying to drive black families out of Georgia will inspire a Toussaint-Louverture figure to rise and lead an armed resistance.[16]

Given the choice between two positions, the magazine habitually picks the more incendiary one. But it also runs beautiful images simply because they're beautiful, and jokes because they make the contributors

laugh. The cover of one issue is a John Sloan illustration of a sumptu-
ously wealthy couple in an opera house box, above the caption "The
Unemployed." There's a notably modern tone in the way the magazine
talks about itself. An ad for the mundane job of circulation manager
says: "A small salary, a large commission, and a BIG CHANCE FOR THE
FUTURE are waiting for the right man."

Some of Eastman's comrades aren't happy with this laughing tone.
Isn't there a class war on? Aren't there ramparts to climb, converts to
win?

Max never denies it.

"We could strengthen our propaganda value by toning down our
expression of life," he concedes to one prominent comrade. "But it just
isn't politic propaganda, it *is* life to which the venture is primarily dedicated. I can't help it. That is deeper in me than the desire to be useful."[17]

Horace Traubel, one of the last of Walt Whitman's comrades, grasps
what many of Eastman and Reed's contemporaries miss. He understands that *The Masses* does more than *agitate* for change: It *embodies*
change. It is a message sent back from the freer world it is trying to
create: "a vehement red-paint signal post."[18] To Eastman, Traubel's note
of praise feels like a send-off from Whitman himself.

In spite of their awkward first encounter, Eastman and Reed become friends. They're a study in fruitful contrasts: Max, running cool, a
little shy, devoted (as Art Young puts it) to "truth, polemics, tennis, and
swimming"; Jack, running hot, talking loud, playing endless pranks
(one day he carries the office safe out to the sidewalk "just to give you
boys something to do"—they have to call the fire department to get it
back).[19] Working together, they create something new.

One day in early 1913, Reed shows Eastman a little something he
has written, an attempt to articulate the principles that animate their
work. Eastman likes the general idea, but not Reed's execution. Jack
still has no grasp of socialist theory, so he makes a mess of the terminol-
ogy. Max rewrites it:

This magazine is owned and published cooperatively by its editors. It has no dividends to pay, and nobody is trying to make
money out of it. A revolutionary and not a reform magazine; a
magazine with a sense of humor and no respect for the respect-
able; frank, arrogant, impertinent, searching for the true causes;
a magazine directed against rigidity and dogma wherever it is
found; printing what is too naked or true for a moneymaking
press; a magazine whose final policy is to do as it pleases and
conciliate nobody, not even its readers—there is a field for this
publication in America.[20]

Max and Jack's statement runs at the front of every issue after that.
It is a manifesto for their magazine—but also for their neighborhood
and their young era.

Chapter 4

Ten months after Walter Lippmann blasted his city-hall comrades, five months after John Reed wrote his bohemian epic, three months after Max Eastman launched his kaleidoscopic *Masses,* the spirit that the young radicals all felt stirring finds its boldest expression yet.

On March 3, 1913, eight thousand women march up Pennsylvania Avenue. Some walk, some ride horses, some stand on parade floats. Thick crowds line the route, gawking. The nation's capital has seen plenty of processions before this one, martial celebrations of battlefield triumphs. This is something new—something audacious. Women are marching to secure something they haven't yet won.

The order of the procession, the choice of music, even the marchers' clothing have been chosen to reinforce an argument in motion.[1] A banner spells it out in letters a foot high:

WE DEMAND AN
AMENDMENT TO THE

CONSTITUTION OF THE
UNITED STATES
ENFRANCHISING THE
WOMEN OF THIS COUNTRY

The urgent tone of the sign is unusual; so is what it requests. For a generation, suffrage work has concentrated at the state level. The strategy has won votes for women in nine states, particularly in the new states of the West. Still: It's slow, expensive, and labor-intensive. It would be faster to win the vote through a federal amendment—the strategy that Susan B. Anthony had devised forty years earlier—but her successors have deemed it unrealistic. In 1913, young Americans are tired of that word, "unrealistic." They know progress is possible—they have grown up surrounded by it. Now they want more of it, and more quickly. Women want the vote *now*, and they are taking to the streets as they never have before to say so.

They make the demand boldly but they do it without rancor. The parade culminates in a grand allegorical pageant on the steps of the Treasury, in which one hundred women and children depict suffrage not as a break with tradition, but as a fulfillment of the best American ideals.

The parade and the pageant deliver a single, stirring, affirmative message: It all flows together seamlessly. Or would have, anyway, if the government's arrangements for the parade didn't reflect in miniature its support for women's rights: slow, lax, either inattentive or actively hostile.

As Inez Milholland, mounted beautifully on horseback, leads the parade toward the pageant, crowds on both sides of Pennsylvania Avenue begin to creep into the street. The police don't stop them. The suffragists' beautiful banners need to be squeezed or abandoned altogether. Soon the route is blocked completely.

Then the fighting begins.

The parade devolves into a mob scene, a melee. Hundreds of women are pushed, grabbed, knocked down. Ambulances begin to fill up. Reporters' pencils fly.

A mile away, the doors of Union Station swing open. Woodrow Wilson steps through. He is cheered by students from Princeton, the college he'd left less than three years earlier to begin a career in politics—a career that was about to reach its zenith. Having outdueled not only former president Theodore Roosevelt but also the sitting president, William Howard Taft, he had been elected president. He would take his oath of office the next morning.

With his wife, Ellen, the president-elect steps into a waiting car. The Princeton boys cheer again as he pulls away.

The broad avenues of Washington are decked in patriotic bunting for his inauguration. But Wilson doesn't get to see those roads. With the center of the city descending into chaos, his motorcade is shunted to the backstreets, which are deserted.

"Where," he is reported to have said, "are the people?"[2]

Wilson has an old-fashioned belief in individual culpability. If a large organization breaks the law, for example, you send its president to jail. And so when an aide explains that a woman suffrage parade has pulled focus from what should have been his triumphant arrival in the capital, it would be in character for him to wonder: *And just who is responsible for that?*

Alice Paul was born on January 11, 1885, the eldest of four children in a Quaker family. Some of the Paul family customs were very traditional: At home, a handsome farm outside Moorestown, New Jersey, they sprinkled their speech with "thy" and "thou." But some of their ideas were very advanced, such as the one about the equality of the sexes, and the one about the necessity of exerting yourself to make the world a better place—by, for instance, organizing a monumental suffrage parade in the heart of the nation's capital on the eve of a new president's inauguration.

Paul excelled at Swarthmore, which was an extension of home: Her grandfather had helped to found the school a few decades before. But she soon swung out into the wider world, seeking to fix it. She was in England to learn about the latest social reform ideas when, in 1907, she saw a suffragette being heckled viciously but not backing down. This was Christabel Pankhurst, daughter of Emmeline: the leader of militant suffrage agitation in England, and everywhere else. Paul had found an ally and friend.

People who met Alice Paul often remarked on her physical fragility: She was diminutive and soft-spoken, with delicate hands and large gray eyes. But she possessed a remarkable capacity for making decisions and acting on them. A fellow radical described her as being "swift, alert, almost panther-like in her movements."[3] This facility for setting her mind on a task—even a very difficult task—and committing her body to follow made her a great ally to the Pankhursts.

She reasoned things out. The inequality of the sexes, particularly where political power was concerned, was a great injustice. That injustice could be rectified only by changing the minds of the country's leaders. Those leaders would respond only to a shift in public opinion. So if giving a speech would compel attention, mount the soapbox. But if the speech failed and it became necessary to break a window, then find a rock. But don't throw it with any undue or hasty passion, merely the settled certainty that a great good lies on the other side of a small wrong.

The English authorities had their own remorseless logic, not so different from Creon's in *Antigone*. If it is a crime to break windows, then this meddlesome American girl must be arrested for breaking windows. And if she refuses to pay a fine, she must be sentenced to a filthy, stinking jail. And if she refuses to eat there, because a hunger strike is another tactic in her foolish crusade, then she must be secured to a table and force-fed so she doesn't die.

In November 1909, in Holloway prison, Alice Paul suffered this ordeal fifty-five times.[4]

Her friends put her on a boat home to America after that, hoping her family could restore her to health. When she was able to stand and walk and reach the back of a room with her voice again, she went on-stage at Cooper Union and told her story. Inez Milholland was by her side. Asked why she had fought and suffered so much for the cause, she quoted a line she had seen scrawled on a prison wall: "Resistance to tyranny is obedience to God."[5] That's not from *Antigone*, but could be.

At twenty-seven, she looked around and wondered why American suffragists lacked the fire of her English friends. She joined the National American Woman Suffrage Association, the most prominent such organization in the country. Discovering that NAWSA had let its activities in Washington lapse, she asked to work on its congressional committee, and soon found that she *was* the congressional committee. With no money, an outdated mailing list, and a dilapidated office, she and her friend Lucy Burns dreamed up an idea for a suffrage parade. It was an implausible notion, but Paul decided it would be done.

Savvy veterans of the suffrage movement knew that Paul was asking for trouble. A federal amendment to the Constitution would be ratified only if several southern states approved. That meant having to contend with the color line; it meant catering to southern prejudices. Initially Paul welcomed the full participation of black women: She always denied any personal prejudice. Yet as the march date approached, she grew more concerned about the hostility from onlookers—Washington was, after all, a southern town, racked with racial tensions—and the possible defection of marchers themselves.

"As far as I can see," she concluded, "we must have a white procession, or a negro procession, or no procession at all."[6] In an attempt at compromise, black women were invited to march separately from white women—at the back of the parade.

To Ida B. Wells-Barnett, the anti-lynching crusader and founder of the first suffrage organization for black women—a civil-rights champion since before Alice Paul was born—this was not compromise, this was cowardice. She insisted on marching with her fellow Illinois delegates or not at all. When she was refused, she disappeared. She re-emerged while the parade was under way, stepping out of the crowd to take her rightful place in the Illinois delegation.[7] Paul took fire from white and black women alike for this. But it staved off the boycott she had feared, and it meant that the headlines could focus on the violence that marchers of all races suffered when the parade broke down. On the day of Wilson's inauguration, several newspapers run split front pages: the president's swearing-in on one side; calls for a congressional investigation into the suffragists' mistreatment on the other. Paul had insisted on holding the parade on March 3 to maximize press coverage—a gamble that paid off beautifully.

The movement has come a long way since the days when Susan B. Anthony would get so excited to see suffrage mentioned in the newspaper that she would call other suffragists over to see it.[8] Paul's publicity coup has put the idea of a federal suffrage amendment back into the minds of millions of Americans. But have they reached the one mind that matters most?

Fourteen days after the parade, Alice Paul and President Wilson sit opposite each other in the White House.

She is part of a five-woman delegation from NAWSA, paying their first visit to the new president. They don't know what to expect. Having spent less than three years in elected office, Wilson lacks much of a track record on suffrage. He was born and raised in the South, which suggests that he could be an obstacle to progress, but he is also a political scientist who has written beautifully about democracy, and who seems genuinely devoted to his three daughters, which suggests that he might be an ally.

Paul and her fellow delegates sit in a row of chairs, facing the president. The arrangement suggests a group of pupils being examined by their teacher. If someone at the White House arranged the seats that way specifically to intimidate the women, he succeeded.[9]

Paul speaks first.

Drawing on her training in English politics, she skips the lofty idealistic pleas about women's equality and gets down to practicalities. Women already possess millions of votes, she tells him. One-eighth of the electoral college is chosen by states where women vote. One-fifth of the Senate comes from suffrage states, and one-ninth of the House. And so Paul presents him with a straightforward request: They want him to include in his first message to Congress a call for a constitutional amendment giving women the vote.

Paul's colleagues—all older than she is—add other points of view. One mentions the benefits of suffrage to families; another quotes one of his political science books back to him: If he would just change "men" to "women" in his arguments about democracy, she says, he would be making the case for them.[10]

President Wilson is polite but noncommittal. He has no opinion on suffrage, he tells them. He has never given the subject any thought. Anyway, in these crucial early days of his presidency, there are other issues he wants to focus on: currency reform, tariff reform.

"But, Mr. President," interjects Paul, "do you not understand that the Administration has no right to legislate for currency, tariff, and any other reform without first getting the consent of women to these reforms?"

Wilson is taken aback.

"Get the consent of women?" he asks.[11]

That idea seems not to have occurred to him.

After a pledge to give the subject his full consideration, the president bids the suffragists good day. They return to the NAWSA office, which hums and roars after the torpor of a few short months ago.

In one respect, Wilson told them the truth. He really does have a lot of legislative priorities—goals that he begins achieving with astonishing speed. Wilson uses the friendly Democratic majorities in both houses to throw the government into gears that nobody knew existed. He wins his fights for tariff reform, currency reform, and even the creation of the Federal Reserve. Wilson reinvigorates his office, delivering his crucial speeches to Congress in person, something no president has done since Thomas Jefferson.

When Wilson's first State of the Union address comes and goes without any endorsement of a suffrage amendment, Paul decides to stay hopeful. She is confident that "events will prove President Wilson a friend of woman suffrage."[12] Her colleagues marvel at how she never admits the possibility of defeat—or seems to tire, or to lose her nerve. She is proving to be as adept and inventive a leader as the president is. She and Lucy Burns start a new organization, the Congressional Union for Woman Suffrage, to raise funds for the federal amendment fight. She even starts her own magazine, *The Suffragist*.

Later that year, NAWSA holds its annual convention in Washington. "There is no possible excuse for further delay," she tells an enormous crowd, her low voice resounding through the hall. "This should be the last convention it will be necessary to call to agitate the question of 'votes for women.'"

She is bold, but far from alone: A thousand women cheer every word.[13]

Chapter 5

A federal government in overdrive, a percolating bohemia, a surging suffrage movement, a Socialist Party learning its strength. This is only a partial list of the dynamic forces energizing and destabilizing American life in 1913. Immigrants have been arriving in near-record numbers every year: eight hundred thousand, a million, more. Cars begin to connect villages and towns that were not connected before, and won't get disconnected ever again. An art exhibition doesn't just give audiences new things to see, but a new way of seeing.

"Many tall buildings, skyscrapers, fell down yesterday in the city of New York," writes one journalist after the opening of the Armory Show of modern art, startling Americans with Picasso, Braque, Duchamp, Matisse. "Immense conflagrations, terrifying and exciting fires burst out all over the city. But it was in the mental and moral city that these events happened."[1]

To young radicals, the upheaval of 1913 is reason for joy. They know their physics: It's easier to move a body that's already in motion. Or, as

Walter Lippmann puts it in his first book, *A Preface to Politics*, which is published that year: "The dynamics for a splendid human civilization are all about us. They need to be used."

High on the list of those dynamics is a startling new porousness in America's political, cultural, and social spheres. "It seems as though everywhere, in that year of 1913, barriers went down and people reached each other who had never been in touch before," according to Mabel Dodge, who would know. She does more than almost anybody to spur this phenomenon along.[2]

At the suggestion of the ubiquitous Lincoln Steffens, she begins hosting a weekly salon in her sumptuous all-white living room at 23 Fifth Avenue, just north of Washington Square. Uptown and downtown mingle on equal footing: labor leaders and painters, anarchists and poets, feminists and spiritualists. For most attendees, the scattershot quality of those conversations is thrilling—but there are exceptions.

"You have a chance to do something really creative here, Mabel," fumes Lippmann, a regular visitor. "Do try and *make* something of it instead of letting it run wild. Weed it out and *order* it."

But Mabel does not want to order it. She likes Walter, but she doesn't always *listen* to Walter. (She teases him for his baby fat, calls him "Buddha.") She considers herself a chosen instrument of Fate, and does not wish to probe too deeply into its workings.[3]

"Fate" is not something a lot of people take seriously in 1913, a year when science is riding high. Still, when you consider a certain pivotal night in that year, when Mabel says the exact right thing, at the exact right moment, to the exact right people, thereby giving rise to the defining event of the era—the fullest manifestation of the young radicals' aggressive hopes for their country—when you consider the unlikelihood of all that, you have to wonder: Maybe Mabel Dodge really *is* the instrument of Fate.

On the momentous night in question, she ventures forth to a not-quite-meeting-not-quite-party in a sparsely furnished apartment on the wilder side of Washington Square Park. The main attraction of the evening is Big Bill Haywood, mountainous one-eyed leader of the Industrial Workers of the World and lately a habitué of the Village (he has been sleeping with the hostess of the not-quite-party). Haywood begins to describe the latest IWW action for a crowd that includes socialist leaders, novelists, a sculptor, a couple of journalists, a transcendentalist, and Mabel.[4]

Across the river, in Paterson, New Jersey, twenty-five thousand silk workers have gone on strike to protest their deteriorating working conditions and the lack of an eight-hour day. Haywood thinks it could be the sequel to the IWW's victory the previous year in Lawrence, Massachusetts, but the New York press refuses to cover it, so the city's workers don't know what's happening.

This is when Fate, or science, or an angel of radical causes, loosens Mabel's tongue.

"Why don't you bring the strike to New York and *show* it to the workers?"

Haywood swings his great eye around to comprehend her. What does she mean?

She means a pageant like Alice Paul's. Let New Yorkers experience what's happening in Paterson by re-creating the strike in three dimensions. Let them see the actual picketers, hear the actual speeches by Haywood and the other leaders.

"Well, by God! There's an idea!" exclaims Big Bill. "But how? What hall?"

"Madison Square Garden!" she says. "Why not?"

With the exceptions of St. Patrick's Cathedral and maybe the floor of the stock exchange, that is the most ludicrous answer Dodge could have given. A pageant at the Garden would be enormous, expensive, monumentally difficult—

"I'll *do* it!" cries a voice.

Somebody laughs. "Well, if anyone can do it, you can, Jack."[5]

John Reed slides over and introduces himself. He says he'll go to the picket line to assess the situation, then report back.

A few nights later, Lippmann is at the Harvard Club when a telegram arrives. It's from Paterson. NOTHING TO DO FOR 20 DAYS. HAPPY AND HEALTHY. JACK.[6]

Reed's friends are more amused than alarmed by his arrest for mouthing off to a cop near the picket line. Lippmann sees it as further proof that Jack's actions are motivated chiefly by "an inordinate desire to be arrested." Eastman begins referring to him as the magazine's "jail editor."[7] It's a vintage Reed caper, all right—except that across the river, something serious is under way.

Amid the roaches and lice and indescribably vile odors of the Passaic County jail, as Reed chain-smokes to fight the smell, he gets an education in solidarity. He watches the jailed strikers huddle around Haywood, drawing reassurance from his mountainous presence as much as from what he says. He listens to the workers, who are mainly immigrants, sing labor anthems in a half dozen tongues. He marvels at their defiance. They tell him that the owners and the churches are against them, but so are many socialists and even other unions. Haywood's IWW, which embraces unskilled as well as skilled workers, and which doesn't shy from a fight, gives these men virtually their sole support.

When Reed emerges after four days in "the democracy of the jail," he hasn't become a convert to socialism, but he is more passionately committed than ever before to fighting alongside these workers—and all workers like them.[8]

"Think of it! Twelve years they have been losing strikes—twelve solid years of disappointments and incalculable suffering," he writes in *The Masses.*

"They must not lose again! They can not lose!"[9]

He throws himself into Mabel's scheme.

For three furious weeks in 1913, Reed and his radical friends join hands with IWW leaders and the workers themselves in a common project: a living demonstration of the alliance that has been dreamed about for as long as there has been a class struggle.

A thousand workers are going to take part in Reed's pageant. Jacket off, megaphone in hand, he marches to and fro in the rehearsal hall, barking directions. He addresses them in Italian, Hebrew, and several other languages that he doesn't speak. Lippmann and Dolly Sloan—the business manager and, aside from Eastman, the only competent book-keeper at *The Masses*—help with organization and fundraising. Max himself comes to New Jersey and gives speeches to rile up the strikers, sometimes twenty-five thousand at a time. Margaret Sanger, pioneer of birth control, finds host families around New York for the children of strikers, so they can maintain their picket lines and still have time to rehearse. Reed gets his Harvard classmate Robert Edmond Jones, soon to be the leading set designer in America, to design the scenery.

They'll have just one performance, one chance to get it right.

On the morning of June 7, 1913, those thousand strikers take ferries across the Hudson, then march up Fifth Avenue. When night falls, the tower above Madison Square Garden blazes to life: The letters "IWW" shine forth in red electric lights ten feet high. Fifteen thousand people pile into the building to watch. The sheriff is there, too, praying for a reason to shut the whole thing down.[10]

On a stage that's nearly a city block wide, the strikers perform scenes of Reed's devising. The picket line, the shooting of a striker by a private detective, his funeral procession—all are enacted by the enormous en-semble. The crowd scenes feature speeches by Haywood, Carlo Tresca, and Elizabeth Gurley Flynn—the same speeches they had delivered in Paterson. One reporter says that Tresca's fiery address "outdid Marc Antony's funeral oration."[11]

Reed also finds room for songs, several of which feature lively 1913-ish juxtapositions. An Italian worker sings a folk song backed by a chorus of German women; Reed sets IWW chants to the melodies he knows by heart: Harvard football fight songs. It ends with everybody, cast and audience alike, standing to sing the "Internationale." Mabel marvels at the "terrible unity" that has been created: "I have never felt such a high pulsing vibration in any gathering before or since," she will say many years later.[12]

The papers praise Reed's triumph, even as they denounce the unsavory radicalism of the IWW. It is, even now, an epochal creative achievement. It is a proof of concept of a kind of people's art, the joint project of workers and intellectuals, and is acknowledged as such: "A new social art was in the American world, something genuinely and excitingly new."[13]

Reed makes it through the performance, then collapses. The strain of writing, directing, and producing the event—of being the conduit for a vast amount of political and cultural communication—has overtaxed even his formidable powers. A few days later, Mabel spirits him off to Europe, bound for her villa in Florence, where Reed will ostensibly be the tutor to her son.[14]

The true purpose of the trip is consummated on their first night in Paris.

"I thought your fire was crimson," he whispers to her in bed, "but you burn blue in the dark."[15]

It's another exciting union of 1913.

The merry spirit of that year flares quickly, but it doesn't last long. The young radicals might enjoy the progress they're making, but they are antagonizing powerful interests who are not eager to see their power go away.

The reprisals arrive before the year is out.

When Alice Paul reports on the activities of her congressional committee at the NAWSA convention, she also describes the work of her freshly created Congressional Union, which raises funds for the amendment push. She is proud of both; she expects the national leaders to be pleased.

Instead, a past president of NAWSA, the formidable Carrie Chapman Catt, rises to complain that she is "more or less razzle-dazzled" by the Congressional Union's financial and organizational independence.[16] Who is Alice Paul to start a new suffrage organization? How little does she think of the older, larger group? Where is all the money going?

The week after the convention, Paul is addressing a group of suffragists-in-training when she collapses, too. Her doctor concludes that her ailment is "not organic." In other words: She is cracking up. He advises her to stop working and go home to New Jersey to recover her strength.[17]

During the next few weeks, the leaders of NAWSA maneuver to isolate Paul. They do not like the idea of an upstart organization, with ties to the disreputable Pankhursts, being tangled up in its operations.

Paul doesn't mean to lead an insurrection. She looks for some way to remain within the fold. But after a disastrous summit with Anna Howard Shaw, the president of NAWSA, Paul and Burns are cast out.

They can go on fighting for suffrage if they like, but they'll do it alone.[18]

A week after Paul comes to grief at the NAWSA convention, Eastman picks up an evening newspaper at the corner of Broadway and Eighth. He is surprised to see his own name. Apparently he is under indictment for criminal libel.

A few months earlier, he and Art Young had attacked the Associated Press, accusing it of intentionally concealing news of the war around the Paint Creek mines of West Virginia. Eastman had heard the story from the labor leader Mother Jones herself. Young had drawn an AP executive pouring a vial marked "Lies" into a pool marked "News." Eastman wrote an accompanying editorial, proclaiming that "truth is for sale to organized capital in the United States."[19] In other words, they delivered the standard one-two *Masses* punch. The only difference is that their target decided to punch back.

Eastman and Young are arrested. They pay their bail. They plead not guilty. And then they wait. Criminal libel is a serious charge. They could be facing two years in jail.

Max has been craving more time to write poems: Two years in prison isn't what he had in mind.

———

In Florence, basking in Mabel Dodge's embraces, Reed eventually stirs himself from bed long enough to send a letter. "For God's sake write and tell me whether the Paterson strike is finished or not," he tells Lippmann.[20]

Yes, it is finished—and it has failed.

The strikers had gone back to work without their demands being met. The pageant broke new ground creatively, and produced new tools for labor agitation, but it didn't raise the money it was supposed to raise. The IWW never regains the power and prestige it had amassed the year before.

Have their bold hopes been naïve? Lippmann faces the question squarely in *A Preface to Politics:* "Are we perhaps like a child whose hand is too small to span an octave on the piano?" He doesn't answer the question directly, but he doesn't need to. His confidence radiates from the book like the sun breaking through the clouds. "Experience itself will reveal our mistakes; research and criticism may convert them into wisdom," he declares.[21]

A fortunate young man speaks for a fortunate young generation—one that hasn't experienced a general war and has been told it never will, one that trusts that progress is automatic, in spite of the occasional setback. Their optimism carries them into a new year, rich with possibilities: 1914.

Chapter 6

Your letter made a great impression on me, because it so closely touched my own experience. I know the bewildering, cramping effect of not having anyone to talk to or understand.[1]

During Randolph Bourne's sophomore year at Columbia, one of his professors liked one of his essays enough to share it with a friend at *The Atlantic Monthly*. The magazine published it, and five more of Bourne's pieces in the years that followed.

Because he had a such a personal style—authoritative but conversational, erudite but intimate—many readers felt that he was speaking directly to them. This was particularly true of the young, for they were both his audience and his subject.

Many men and women wrote to Bourne after reading his essays. He often wrote back, and sometimes the exchanges became friendships. Of all the letters that he sent, none were more frequent or more revealing than the ones he wrote to Prudence Winterrowd.

In December 1912, in the middle of Bourne's senior year, Winterrowd wrote to chide him for his essay "The Excitement of Friendship."
She admired its lovely insights into his life—how Bourne felt alive only
when with a friend, how he made friends instantly or not at all—but
objected to his juvenile remark about the "fatal facility of women's
friendships." He accepted her correction, and a friendly exchange
began.

When she described the religiosity and suffocation of life in
Shelbyville, Indiana, he found a kindred spirit, for he had lived through
the same trials when trying to escape Bloomfield, New Jersey: its an-
cient Anglo-Saxon stock, its stifling Presbyterian mores, the unread
row of so-called great books arrayed behind glass. He recommends
books to speed her liberation: Maeterlinck, Bergson, Dewey, and, above
all, his beloved William James, who inspires him to face the perplexing
world: "He has settled so many of my own worries that I preach him as
a prophet."[2]

Bourne knows that books are not enough. Personality needs company. He suggests in January 1913 (in the letter quoted at the top of
this chapter) that she come to New York for college. There might have
been more to his invitation than spiritual guidance. Even for a writer as
naturally informal as Bourne, his letters to Winterrowd are conspicuously charming.

"You know, I have no acquaintance who is so thoroughly Jamesian
in style as yourself, with so much zest and sweep of life," he tells her.[3]

Is he making a high-minded effort to encourage a protégée—or is
he flirting?

> If you are going to come next year, I only wish I knew that I was
> going to be here. You write so awfully well, that if a letter is "a
> miserable travesty on a personal conversation," as a certain ob-
> scure essay writer recently said [that is, Bourne himself, in "The
> Excitement of Friendship"], the idea of that personal conversa-
> tion quite thrills me with anticipation.

This college year is the jumping-off place for me. I have no idea where I shall be next year. Academic study is a little too much of an invitation to dawdle, and every now and then it strikes me as an effective waste of time in a world where there are as many things to be done and done at once. And never was there a less qualified person to do them![4]

When Bourne writes that letter to Winterrowd on February 5, 1913, the calendar is bearing down on him. Commencement is less than four months away. He is uneasy because he knows what it's like out there. He had a brilliant high school career, but his mother could not afford Princeton. (His feckless father, never mentioned and never seen, had left him and his sister years earlier.) Bourne worked in a piano roll factory for a few miserable years until he secured a scholarship to Columbia. He will be twenty-seven when he graduates, and needs to begin again.

This fear about his prospects leads him to publish a collection of his essays. *Youth and Life*, which appears in March 1913, includes all of the essays he published in *The Atlantic* and some he wrote to fill out the book. Assembled in one place, they leave the reader with a strong impression of their author. Here is a young man with the fortitude to test every value, venture every hazard, refuse to brook any social injustice or stale convention. Here is not just an explainer, but an exemplar and a champion—someone committed to taking the world as a series of adventures, of new ideas and experiences that must be tested, all adding up to a vision of "The Experimental Life."

Except that, as Bourne confesses to Winterrowd, this impression isn't true.

I look sometimes at my book and think—"What a divine caricature you are of the personality of R.S.B.? Who would recognize in you there the puny, timid, lazy, hypochondriacal wretch who really wrote those words of courage and idealism?" And then, instead of straining heroically to reach those lofty levels, I go out and do some foolish thing or waste a day or put off my work, or have a day-dream or mope about how my friends are getting ahead of me, and I'll never be able to learn regular habits of work, or accomplish anything worthwhile.

After I had written 'The Handicapped', a girl friend wrote me the most ecstatic letter saying I had been living on the mountains. I was stunned and humiliated. What an awful lie, I thought! As I saw the valleys where I had dwelt and the silly avoidable misery I had suffered owing to my little faith and I could not reply to her without shame. That is 'Youth and Life' from one who was never young, and has only partly lived.[5]

Bourne calls the "I" of his essays a caricature, not a lie, because there is a great deal of truth in it. His essays really do capture how he thinks about the world. But they omit more than they reveal.

"The Handicapped," which Bourne cites in his April 10 letter to Winterrowd, describes how the world looks from the perspective of one lacking the physical capabilities of the people around him. But the essay never explains what the predicament is.

A childhood illness stunted Bourne's growth and twisted his spine. It nearly killed him, and left him a hunchback. He can walk—he takes distinctive birdlike steps—but he doesn't run. He can play the piano—and does so, regularly and beautifully—but lacks the wherewithal to play the organ. Even in his letters to Winterrowd, which reveal so much about the state of his heart and mind, he never describes his deformities, or the fact that he stands only five feet tall.

His condition, though, is the key to his philosophy, his personality.

If he lacks confidence, as he tells Winterrowd, it's because people never showed any confidence in him.

If he makes friends instantly or not at all, as he wrote in "The Excitement of Friendship," it's because most people spurn him on sight. (After publishing Bourne's first essay, the editor of *The Atlantic* invited him to the Century Club for lunch—only to cancel shortly after Bourne arrived, as he couldn't bear to be seen with one so deformed.)[6]

If he fears going back to the working world, as he laments again and again, it's because he remembers too keenly how it feels to be told "You can't expect us to create a place for you," and "How could it enter your head that we should find any use for you?"

His deformity renders him "a man cruelly blasted by the powers that brought him into the world, in a way that makes him both impossible to be desired and yet—cruel irony that wise Montaigne knew about— doubly endowed with desire." This yearning "colors all his appreciations, motivates his love of personality, and fills his life with a sort of smoldering beauty."[7]

Above all, his deformity fuels his radicalism. He knows he must try to make the world more hospitable to "the unpresentable and the unemployable, the incompetent and the ugly, the queer and crotchety people who make up so large a proportion of human folk." The people like him.

Here is a picture of the preacher if you will accept it. The photographer chose the pose, I didn't, but I fell for it in spite of the jeers of my friends, who do not appreciate my dignity always in just the way they should.

I have been mixed in my mind lately concerning my future, and have been coquetting with a Fellowship which has been tentatively awarded me. It would give me enough to study abroad upon, and thus I could realize one of my earliest ambitions. On the other hand I have been living here in such a kindly sheltering circle of friends that it chills me, especially in the night-time, to think of exposing myself to a foreign world, and putting my friendship-forming capacities to so cruel and new a test. The experimental life calls, it is true, especially when the sun is bright and warm, and I comfort myself with the feeling that my friends will be here when I come back, and they cannot change very much in a year. If you are to come here next winter, though, it discourages me to think that I would not be here to aid your assimilation, and immerse myself in that flood of good talk which I know we are saving up for each other.[8]

In the photo that Randolph encloses in his April 28 letter to Prudence, he sits casting a level gaze toward the right edge of the picture. He is dressed formally, in clothes that seem too bulky for his delicate hands. The bulkiness, of course, is his hunched back, which layers of clothing could conceal, a little. But there is no masking the oddness of his expression. His face looks like a collage—like cubism. The head is too small for the body. The eyes don't line up. The mouth seems too big, and too full, for the eyes. His brown hair, short on the sides, spikes strangely on top.

With this picture, sent half a year into an intimate correspondence, Bourne continues to perpetrate a lie. At the moment of his birth, a doctor botched the job of delivering him, forceps mangling his face and skull. Randolph tells Prudence that the photographer chose the pose, but in truth, it had been the only option: Had he turned another inch or so, the camera would have revealed his warped left ear.

All these letters—even these photos—reveal only glimpses of a complicated young man. Bourne is right to compare a letter to a whiff of stale smoke for someone craving a cigarette. They tell us that Bourne ultimately decides to accept that Columbia fellowship, and spends a year studying social conditions in Europe. They tell us that Prudence Winterrowd takes his advice and enrolls at Barnard while Bourne is away. And they tell us how prickly the exchange soon becomes. Bourne complains to a friend that she has taken a liberty by addressing him as "Dear Randolph." Such a "swoop to the personal" makes him "very uncomfortable," he says—even though he has been calling her "Dear Prudence" for months.[9] They go on trading letters; they even meet, a couple of years later, when she sees him in a restaurant. But she feels that she disappoints him. Some things work better on the page.

Bourne's letters help us feel why his friends loved him so much: his quick, ironic mind; his romantic streak, his free-ranging curiosity. But they can't answer the questions about his unlikely life that matter most.

Did you really feel, as you claimed, that if your deformities were
    the cause of your radicalism, that they were not a heavy
    price to pay?
At the end, when you knew it was too late for you, did you still
    think the experimental life was the only one worth leading?
If you had known how your story would end, and how quickly,
    would you still have fought the way that you did?

II. THE WORLD IS ON FIRE AND THERE IS TINDER EVERYWHERE

(1914–16)

A war is a true point of bifurcation of future possibilities. . . . Communities obey their ideals; and an accidental success fixes an ideal, as an accidental future blights it.

—WILLIAM JAMES

Chapter 7

Walter Lippmann pushes through the crowds of frantic Belgians, the shouting men, the sobbing women, desperate for news. He scours the bulletin boards. They tell him nothing he doesn't already know.

He needs to reach Switzerland. He has to find his mother and father, who are trapped in Switzerland. But the trains have stopped running. The tracks are washed out, sunk beneath a sea of young German men with guns.

Credit has collapsed. Store shelves are empty. Bank lobbies are filling up. Lippmann knows hardly a soul. If he is going to find a way out of Brussels, he'll need to do it alone.

It is July 30, 1914—a Thursday. Austria-Hungary has declared war on Serbia, seeking retribution for the assassination of Archduke Franz Ferdinand on the streets of Sarajevo. Russia has mobilized to defend its ally, Serbia. It means that Germany is likely to mobilize against Russia, and maybe against France. And if that happens, God help the Belgians.

Lippmann finds a late-night boat for England. Exhausted and disbelieving, he scrambles aboard. Among bright boys he has always been the brightest. Now he is a refugee like the rest.

Eighteen hours later, Randolph Bourne blunders into history. He and a Columbia friend are on their way to Vienna for a socialist conference when his quick birdlike steps carry him into the crowded heart of Berlin.

Kaiser Wilhelm II appears on a balcony above Bourne's head. He bristles with medals, martial and stern. The crowd erupts.

"A momentous hour has struck for Germany," he declares. "The sword has been forced into our hands!"

Bourne can't comprehend it, not just because he stands only shoulder-high in that throng. He has spent the past year admiring European towns and their arrangement, the various national cultures and their expressions. These studies led him to write an essay *stating outright* that no general war was possible. Now the kaiser has issued an ultimatum to Russia to halt its mobilization against Austria-Hungary. The plain meaning of his words is war.

The next afternoon, Bourne is walking on Unter den Linden when he hears that Czar Nicholas II has defied his cousin the kaiser. Russia has let the deadline pass without answering the German ultimatum.

"Krieg! Krieg!" scream patriots all around Bourne.

He flees Berlin that night. Heading north, he hopes to slip away to Scandinavia before the borders close. Back home, newspapers have begun to marvel at the bizarre prospect of American citizens being stranded on a continent spiraling into war.

Bourne finds a boat packed with Russians and Swedes. He and his friend squeeze aboard. It turns out to be the last one to get away.

He feels that the heavens have fallen.[1]

The next morning, a Sunday, Lippmann awakens to learn that Germany has followed through on its ultimatum and declared war against

Russia. That means Germany will also be at war with France, which had mobilized the day before in support of Russia.

Lippmann and his friends, mainly young British radicals, stare at one another, struck dumb, trading what he calls "idiotically cheerful remarks."

That afternoon, in Trafalgar Square, he shoulders through another crowd. The British people are chanting, shouting, pleading with their leaders not to follow the European powers into war. Lippmann shares their feeling of desperation, but he doubts there is any way to forestall the war. There seems to be nothing—absolutely nothing—for him to think, say, or do.

Months earlier, he had read John Reed's account of the Mexican Revolution, and puzzled at his friend's description of feeling bored in the midst of battle. In London, skidding on the edge of war, Lippmann finally understands what Reed was getting at: the torpor of sustained adrenaline.

Public opinion seems trivial, democratic hope nothing more than "a flower in the path of a plough."[2]

In Trelleborg, under a cold Swedish rain, Bourne and his friend seek a dry place to spend the night.

Without warning, a mob of raucous young men appears, barreling his way. They have guns and wear uniforms.

Bourne has no time to run. The narrow street offers nowhere to hide. He flattens himself against a wall and braces for impact.

The soldiers storm by.

Bourne checks himself. He thinks he is unharmed. He raises his umbrella and continues to walk. In France, earlier in the year, he had bought a dark student cape, a stylish way to conceal his humped back, at least a little. He notices that it is getting wet—but why?

He looks up at his umbrella.

It has been pierced by a soldier's bayonet.

He keeps walking.

On August 4, 1914, Tuesday night, Lippmann paces back and forth on the House of Commons terrace, the Thames on one side, the stone walls of Parliament on the other. He and his friends cling to their scant hopes.

When Big Ben strikes eleven, those hopes give way: Germany has made no answer to Britain's demand that it respect Belgium's neutrality, which means that a state of war begins. The conflict now stretches all the way from Siberia to the Irish Sea. If you include the colonies of the belligerents, it stretches much farther than that.

There is no precedent for what the reckless and miscalculating leaders of Europe have done. At the height of prosperity and interconnectedness, after half a century without a general war, they have consigned the planet to flames.

For the young radicals, the war is a shout to tell them something is wrong with their view of life. The world that they had begun to remake has revealed itself to be different from anything they imagined. The long peace that Lippmann had taken for granted was only "a brief spell of exceptionally fine weather," he now sees. Bourne can't fathom the event that "outraged all our preconceived notions of the way the world was tending."[3]

Unlike Lippmann and Bourne, who just manage to slip away from the catastrophe—Bourne will call these last few days "the toddlings of an innocent child about the edge of a volcano's crater"—most Americans are not immediately menaced by the war.[4] The United States has no obligation to join the fighting, and anyway it hardly has an army with which to do it. The Atlantic Ocean looks wide in 1914.

Still, the war becomes a fact in every life, a cloud that never moves. Bourne and Lippmann arrive independently at the same course of action: They have more thinking to do. They each want to understand the feeling of surprise and dread that propelled them out of a war zone, and try to explain it to the perplexed American public.

Luckily for them, they have a venue in which to do it. Each of them has a new magazine waiting for him in New York, if he can find a way home.

It is, in fact, the same magazine.

Dark cape slung over his shoulders, Bourne climbs the front stairs of the townhouse, knocks, and waits. He is standing outside a quiet brownstone on a quiet block: 421 West Twenty-first Street is ten minutes and a world away from the merry melee of Greenwich Village.

The door swings open. Inside, Bourne can see a remarkably handsome reception room, and, beyond that—is that a *dining room*?

What kind of magazine *is* this?

No untidy mounds of paper, no sharp metallic smell of ink; typewriters clacking peacefully in the distance, if they clack at all. Bourne might arrive in time to see the table being set for lunch, which is prepared and served each day by Etienne and Lucy, the married couple who live in the basement, tending the corporeal needs of the thinkers grappling with their bold thoughts above.

No, even though it is still a few weeks away from publishing its first word, *The New Republic* is not like any other magazine.

Bourne and Lippmann were aware of each other before this October day that marked the beginning of their collaboration. In their college days, Lippmann sent a note to Bourne complimenting one of his earliest published essays: "Your damnation of Orthodoxy is that of a friendly voice."[5] In fall 1913, they had a chance encounter in London. Bourne thought enough of their serendipitous lunch at the Cheshire Cheese to write his mother a letter about it; Lippmann never mentioned it.

And now here they are: *colleagues*. The twenty-eight-year-old Bourne and twenty-five-year-old Lippmann are two of the youngest members of the core staff of this bully new magazine of political and social renewal. Which is not to say that they were going to have equal status in their new joint venture, or equal say in its direction, or equal success.

The man who hired them is Herbert Croly, a prim forty-five-year-old political scholar. His book *The Promise of American Life* introduced a new argument about contemporary politics: that the federal government needed new powers to restore the freedoms that had been lost to enormous corporate entities. The message had appealed to Theodore Roosevelt, who tapped its ideas for his "New Nationalism," and to Willard and Dorothy Straight, who put up their money (Wall Street for him, inheritance for her) to start a magazine.

Lippmann was one of the magazine's first prospects. Croly approached him just as the boy wonder of socialism was souring on socialism in all its forms. "I confess I see no more hope in Max Eastman's views than I do in Mayor Lunn's," he wrote to a friend in 1913. "The difference seems to be that political socialists are born stupid while our amateur proletarians and I.W.W. camp-followers cultivate stupidity as a virtue." In other words, the mediocrities in Schenectady might not realize how feckless they were, but shrewd radicals like Eastman ought to know better than to wallow in "romantic proletarian humility." Lippmann grasped at once that Croly's magazine would give him the chance to develop the very thing that his former comrades lacked: "a constructive message."[6] And if it would bring him closer to Roosevelt, his first political idol, so much the better.

Croly was glad to hire Bourne, too, though he wasn't quite sure why. A referral from one of Bourne's professors, Charles Beard, had led Croly to say he was "sure we can find a place for a good deal of your work." He told Bourne that the magazine would be "radical without being socialistic."[7] Bourne would have preferred radical *and* socialistic, but a guaranteed salary of $1,000 a year gave him more than enough reason to stop worrying about the hazy nature of his job.

"I am only hoping to be really big enough for the opportunity," he told a friend.[8]

In October, when Bourne gets his first look at the place, the office is thrumming with last-minute preparations for the magazine's debut. The war upended months of meticulous planning, forcing a lot of quick improvisation. Among other things, the editors have to justify this project in a world very different from the one they expected to inhabit. There are plenty of gifted essayists on that staff, but Croly entrusts the assignment to Lippmann.

"Who cares . . . to edit a magazine—to cover paper with ink, to care about hopes that have gone stale, to launch phrases that are lost in the uproar?" he asks in the debut issue. "What is the good now of thinking?"

Showing a flair for paradox, Lippmann argues that wartime, when the labor of thought seems most futile, is the moment when thought is most necessary: "It is the only force that can pierce the agglomerated passion and wrong-headedness of this disaster." The world's only salvation lies in exercising control over the "hidden forces" that have led civilization astray. "For while it takes as much skill to make a sword as a ploughshare, it takes a critical understanding of human values to prefer the ploughshare."[9]

Bourne tries to do his part, too. He submits story after story for consideration. Some are gratefully accepted; more are declined, occasionally with stinging notes from the editors. He tries to stay positive. "I feel as if I were attending an incomparable school of journalism," he says.[10]

Through it all, he gravitates to Lippmann. Because Lippmann has editorial duties, he has an office on the third floor, overlooking Twenty-first Street. Bourne climbs the stairs to talk politics with him—and to marvel at his productivity. It almost seems that he sets his mind like a clock.

"Well, I do in a way arrange in my mind what I am going to do in the morning," Lippmann tells him.[11]

Bourne has a complicated ego. He hasn't outgrown the self-lacerating streak he displayed in his undergraduate letters. ("I never overcame a difficulty in my life, but wilted at the first rebuff, or sat back and philosophized about it," he tells a friend that year.)[12] The sight of Lippmann breezing through his heavy workload might easily fill Bourne with envy, but instead it does the opposite. Around the time of the magazine's launch, Lippmann publishes *Drift and Mastery*, a dazzling book that contends that modern life has grown unjust, wasteful, and alienating because no conscious effort is being made to organize the positive forces in life. Its optimism and its marvelously fluid style recall Bourne's *Youth and Life*—a comparison that would please Bourne. He calls *Drift and Mastery* "a book one would have given one's soul to have written."[13]

Bourne's first published contribution to the magazine, about the state of education, receives a nice response from readers.[14] But Bourne aims higher. He has big ideas, even though some aren't yet ripe for the hostile environment of a *New Republic* editorial meeting.

In France, he had begun to ponder the way that the radical impulses of his era—feminism, socialism, internationalism—didn't just echo one another, but might also *reinforce* one another, "slowly linking the chains of social consciousness, and thus transforming the individual persons, the individual groups, lifting them to a higher level, giving them a more abundant sense of sympathy and unanimity." Such a union, he thought, might build to something like a secular version of the "Beloved Community" that the American philosopher Josiah Royce had described a few years earlier: an ideal community bound by the loyalty of each to all, and infused with grace.[15]

It's too complicated for him to express in those early days, when his editor seems more interested in having him stop using so many clichés in his submissions. But even in those perplexing first months of war, young people have their aspirations. Some of them take human form. As he tells a friend soon after the magazine's first issue: "I am wishing I could write like Walter Lippmann."[16]

Chapter 8

Alice Paul asks the reporters to leave the room. She waits until they are gone.

Before her sit a dozen women, members of the Congressional Union's advisory board. They have just finished listening to Lucy Burns recount the year and a half of agitation that has brought them, along with several dozen other suffragists, to Alva Belmont's Newport cottage for the weekend: the petitions and classes and marches and newsletters and nonstop pleading for funds, all in the service of asking the men who run the country one persistent question: *Will you let women vote?*

Paul has asked the reporters to leave because she wants women to start asking a *new* question. It comes in two parts.

"The point is, first, who is our enemy," she says, "and then how shall that enemy be attacked?"

This is not the customary Newport chitchat—but it is precisely in tune with a world that has just plunged into war. It is August 30, 1914.

The first answer is easy: The enemy of the suffrage cause, and therefore of American women, is the Democratic Party. Since March 1913, it has controlled the presidency and both houses of Congress: It could have voted for suffrage anytime it wished. Instead, a party caucus had voted its explicit opposition to a federal suffrage amendment. Some individual Democrats are friendly to suffrage, but none of them cared enough for the cause to bolt the party over it. A few of them had been ready to do so for the issue of beet sugar.[1]

As for the second question—how to attack—Paul proposes they reverse the course of their agitation. Instead of chasing the power women *don't* have, they should deploy the power they *do* have. Paul wants to send Congressional Union organizers to the nine states where women can vote, and persuade them to oppose every Democrat running for a national office in the midterm elections, which are ten weeks away.

"We, of course, are a little body to undertake this—but we have to begin," she tells them. "We have not very much money; there are not many of us to go out against the Democratic Party. Perhaps this time we won't be able to do so very much, though I know we can do a great deal, but if the party leaders see that some votes have been turned, they will know that we have at last realized this power that we possess and they will know that by 1916 we will have it organized."

She invites responses from her listeners, some of the most accomplished and brilliant women of their time: Crystal Eastman, linchpin of so many radical causes; the leading social reformer Florence Kelley; and their hostess, Alva Belmont, among others. These savvy women know that they aren't the first activists to try holding the party in power responsible for disenfranchising women. The suffragettes had tried it in England, and it had led to violence in the streets. Paul says she doesn't want the same to happen here. Their fight is strictly political.

Nevertheless, a political fight is still a fight. And fighting is something that well-bred ladies in Newport cottages aren't supposed to do—and maybe *shouldn't* do, at least not in August 1914. Suffrage has become a mainstream issue. A strategy as combative as Paul's risks voiding all the progress of the last few years, pushing their cause back to the fringe. It's a particularly fraught moment to oppose President

Wilson. In the same week that Europe careened into war, his wife, Ellen, had died. Paul would assail him at the precise moment that Americans are rallying to his side.

She calls for a vote anyway. It is unanimous.

The women do as Paul requests, and keep the plan secret, which ensures maximum shock value when the new campaign is announced.

One astounded reporter describes it this way: "The Suffragists have declared war on the Democratic Party."[2]

A few weeks later, amid great fanfare, and snapping of photographs, and flapping of purple, gold, and white pennants, the organizers depart Washington, bound for the nine suffrage states.

Paul doesn't go with them. Even with access to the Belmont fortune, the Congressional Union needs constant fundraising, and only she and Lucy Burns seem able to do it very effectively. Anyway, Paul has never been fond of stages, soapboxes, pulpits. Her charisma is potent, but it works quietly. Already, in the second year of her leadership, she is showing an extraordinary capacity to make women work themselves ragged to satisfy her.

One of her lieutenants, Doris Stevens, describes how she motivates even those who do not wish to be motivated.

"Miss Paul," somebody would say, "I have come to tell you that you are all wrong about this federal amendment business. I don't believe in it. Suffrage should come slowly but surely by the states. And although I have been a lifelong suffragist, I just want to tell you not to count on me, for feeling as I do, I cannot give you any help."

Paul listens, waits, then replies, "Won't you please sit down right here and put the stamp on these letters? We have to get them in the mail by noon."

"But I don't believe—"

"Oh, that's all right," she says, setting down a chair. "These letters are going to women probably a lot of whom feel as you do. But some of them will want to come to the meeting to hear our side."[3]

Once they join her, women (for she permitted only women to join her) don't find the work easy. There is no smoking in the public areas of the Congressional Union office, because Paul thinks smoking reflects poorly on the cause. There is little hand-holding for their pains, beyond the knowledge that they are serving a worthy ideal.

"She often forgets to thank you when you say yes; for she has apparently assumed that you will say yes," according to one colleague. "She does not argue with you when you say no—but you rarely say no."[4]

The fixity of purpose makes life difficult; the difficulty compounds over time. Her health is a constant worry to her friends. She works too hard and too much. In addition to being the Congressional Union's chief strategist and fundraiser, she is editing *The Suffragist* that fall, because the previous editor, the journalist Rheta Childe Dorr, has resigned. She couldn't abide Paul's insistence on having things her own way.

Paul's absolute single-mindedness also leads her to take stands that permit, or even perpetuate, great evil. In the South, white supremacists oppose suffrage because they fear that enfranchising women will create more pressure to enfranchise black people. Simple brutal math tells Paul that she needs some of these people to secure a constitutional amendment. So she does not hesitate to soothe their fears.

In the same season when she is conducting her morally elevated, politically savvy western campaign, she publishes an editorial that declines to comment on "methods of preventing the Negroes from exercising the right of the franchise," a prim euphemism for literacy tests and other vile measures for disenfranchising African Americans. In fact, the editorial argues, woman suffrage would actually be *another means of sustaining white supremacy:* "The enfranchising of all women will increase the relative power of the white race in a most remarkable way."[5]

Paul courts white supremacists even though black women make significant contributions to suffrage: Ida B. Wells-Barnett through the Alpha Suffrage Club; Mary Church Terrell through the National Association of Colored Women. She does it even after W.E.B. Du Bois complains that suffragists who "try and work for democracy for white people while being dumb before slavery for blacks" risk alienating white and black supporters alike.[6]

When Alice Paul says that suffrage is the most important issue of her time, she means it. A colleague suspects that she has promised herself to think or read nothing unconnected to suffrage until the House and Senate pass it, the president signs it, and thirty-six state legislatures approve.[7]

By October 1914, people far beyond the nine suffrage states are following Paul's progress. "A new idea and practice in American politics is being experimented with, an idea highly interesting to watch," editorializes a newspaper in Boston.[8]

Throughout the West, Congressional Union organizers arrange mass meetings, circulate petitions, and spend long days knocking on doors. Many voting women respond warmly to the appeal; many Democratic officeholders are furious; Paul views both reactions as a sign of success. When a congressman shows up at the office and pleads with her to stop campaigning against him, it just makes them fight harder.

"Although we have repeatedly been to the Capitol to visit Senators and Congressmen within the past two years, it was not until we announced our election plans that they began to visit us," *The Suffragist* notes. "When they find that we will not be moved from our plan of campaign they will then turn to the Democratic leaders and try to induce them to show a more friendly attitude toward suffrage."[9]

Stories about the Congressional Union campaign often share the front page with news of atrocities in Europe. The contrast helps the cause. For when half the world is savaging the other half, the purportedly unladylike agitation of the suffragists doesn't seem quite as shocking. In the *New-York Tribune,* under the headline "Militants," one suffragist writes: "So far no one has said that the destruction of the architectural treasures of Louvain by German men proves that no man is fit for the ballot."[10]

The Congressional Union needs this attention, but it also drives up the stakes. With so many people watching the campaign—which is supposed to demonstrate women's power and solidarity—what happens if they fail?

Paul is too savvy to leave the outcome to anything as unreliable as voters' whims. She publishes an editorial in *The Suffragist* surveying all the literature that has been distributed, the rallies that have been held, and the Democrats who have been discomfited, and on the basis of all that gratifying evidence, she declares victory for the campaign.[11]

The election is still three weeks away.

Chapter 9

The sensible, self-preserving thing to do when the war breaks out is to run away from it, as Bourne and Lippmann do. John Reed, being neither sensible nor self-preserving, runs *toward* it.

He reaches Paris in September. Twenty miles away, a million French and British troops are making a desperate final stand, trying to stop the German army that has already ravaged Belgium from marching down the Champs-Élysées. His love of action, his brain full of *Boy's Own* adventure stories, make him frantic to reach the front lines. Also it's his job.

Metropolitan magazine has sent him to Europe as a war correspondent, a profession that Reed has rapidly ascended. The previous fall, he had pushed his way into the middle of the Mexican Revolution. He had ingratiated himself with the rebels who followed Pancho Villa—"the Mexican Robin Hood," Reed called him—even though those peasants had no reason to tolerate a Yankee, let alone befriend one. He had danced with them, drunk with them, sung under the stars with them; he rode into battle by their sides. The stories of their exploits were sensational enough to make Reed famous: A typewriter company began to feature him in its ads.[1]

But in Paris, none of his Mexico tricks work. He can't get near the battlefield through any official method or even any unofficial method. Desperate for a story, Reed finally sneaks into the war zone. It had worked when he waded across the Rio Grande. This time, the authorities catch him, arrest him, and, as a condition of his release, make him promise to never do it again.

How do you write about a war you can't see?

He is stuck in Paris, which he calls "the city of the dead." Flags hang limp and streets are empty, except for tiny flocks of children wearing black armbands. He writes an article that he knows is no good, and asks his editor not to publish it.[2] Jack is blocked, stymied, stewing. He starts drinking and doesn't stop. He is joined on his debauch by a ragtag bunch of friends: the sculptor Arthur Lee and his German wife, Freddy; the painter Andrew Dasburg; other reporters. They reconstitute a gruesome version of Greenwich Village's bohemian swirl.

Reed sees battles, but they're bar fights. He witnesses damage, but it's the kind he inflicts on himself.

The Allies win the Battle of the Marne. They dig their trenches deeper. Everybody seems to be sinking into the mire.

In New York, Mabel Dodge is stewing, too. She knows that Reed's trouble runs deeper than writer's block or lack of a press pass. She doesn't like it, and she determines to fix it. A year after the torrid start of their romance, she remains besotted with him, in a complicated way. (She was unhappy when Reed dedicated his Mexico book to his mother: "I, myself, obscurely, wanted to be his mother.")[3]

From her all-white apartment on Fifth Avenue, she peppers him with one transatlantic letter after another, trying to prop him up, to keep him from settling for merely commercial success, to boost his spirits the way she had during the frantic weeks before the Paterson Strike Pageant.

Sensing that her message isn't having the desired effect, she calls in reinforcements. Unfortunately, as the war in Europe is even then demonstrating, sometimes alliances make a problem worse.

She asks Walter Lippmann for help in her usual way: imperiously.

"Now can you write him a letter and *tell* him he's *not* to go on being mediocre? He would feel it *deeply* from you.

"Drive it home."[4]

She knows how much it meant to Reed when Lippmann praised his Mexico stories. ("It's kind of embarrassing to tell a fellow you know that he's a genius. I want to hug you, Jack," Lippmann had written. "Incidentally, of course, the stories are literature, but I didn't realize that till afterwards. They were so much alive with Mexico and with you.")[5] But Lippmann has become a very busy man since then. He is trying to launch a magazine. He has little time for pep talks.

He tries to calm Dodge down.

"You are, I think, unnecessarily worried about Jack," he writes to her on *New Republic* stationery. "He is merely feeling the same helplessness that every imaginative person must feel. This war makes us all ridiculously inadequate . . . and a little humility is the beginning of wisdom."[6]

Lippmann may be full of book knowledge, but he has only a sliver of Dodge's ability to read people. She is right to be alarmed about Reed. Adrift in Paris, he begins to self-destruct.

Soon Reed needs help, too. Guess where he turns to find it.

"My dear Walter," Reed writes to Lippmann. "Without any preamble whatever, I must tell you that Freddy Lee and I have fallen in love with each other, and that we know that we must have each other for good."

This brief burst of bizarre news (for Freddy is married to their friend Arthur—all of them are friends) is followed by a barrage of demands pushier than Mabel's: to comfort the heartbroken Mabel; to reassure

Freddy, who is being treated badly by her husband; to intercede with his editor, so that he can have a month off to nurse Freddy through an illness; and to let the magazine know that he would be drawing on them for money but would pay it back when he could.[7]

Walter has no time for this. But Mabel isn't done with him, either. She copies him on telegrams to Jack; shares samples of her heartsick, terrible poetry; forwards Reed's letters for him to scrutinize.[8]

"You must see in it that either Reed and I are both wrong or both right or one is wrong and the other right," she asks of one such letter. "Which is it anyway?"[9]

Lippmann has had enough.

"I have been very much embarrassed by the number of letters and messages you've sent me," he writes to her. "They've come at the rate of more than two a day, plus telephones, automobiles, and messengers. I can't respond to all that, and you'll have to understand me that I mean to be good friends with you, but that all this is too much for me. It is not pleasant to write this to you."[10]

Lippmann has plenty of affection for both of his friends, but the frivolity of Greenwich Village, and the people who play there, seem more and more ridiculous to him, more remote from his life. He has responsibilities; he has work to do; there is a war on. Like Prince Hal, he is ready to turn his back on Falstaff and all his pranks, and turn his gaze to the palace.

Perhaps his efficient brain, so averse to waste, makes a logical connection. If he is supposed to be working for the magazine but is instead mired in Reed's messy life, then Reed's messy life should be pressed into service for the magazine.

A few days after his pointed letter to Dodge, Lippmann writes an even more pointed profile of his friend. He calls it "Legendary John Reed."

Lippmann's tale begins at Harvard, with Reed's career as a football cheerleader. It was a "sensational triumph," Lippmann calls it, in a tone that's not quite praise. He surveys some of Reed's later adventures, including his various incarcerations, then addresses himself to Jack's naïve, shabby politics:

> For a few weeks Reed tried to take the *Masses'* view of life. . . .
> He made an effort to believe that the working class is not com-
> posed of miners, plumbers, and working men generally, but is a
> fine, statuesque giant who stands on a high hill facing the sun.
> He wrote stories about the night court and plays about ladies in
> kimonos. He talked with intelligent tolerance about dynamite,
> and thought he saw an intimate connection between the cubists
> and the I.W.W. He even read a few pages of Bergson.

Lippmann offers a sincere tribute to Jack's writing from Mexico: "All his second-rate theory and propaganda seemed to fall away, and the public discovered that whatever John Reed could touch or see or smell he could convey." But he is only setting his friend up for another blow: "He did not judge, he identified himself with the struggle, and gradually what he saw mingled with what he hoped. Wherever his sympathies marched with the facts, Reed was superb."

Then he really pours it on:

> By temperament he is not a professional writer or reporter. He is
> a person who enjoys himself. Revolution, literature, poetry, they
> are only things which hold him at times, incidents merely of his
> living. Now and then he finds adventure by imagining it, oftener
> he transforms his own experience. He is one of those people who
> treat as serious possibilities such stock fantasies as shipping be-
> fore the mast, rescuing women, hunting lions, or trying to fly
> around the world in an aeroplane. He is the only fellow I know
> who gets himself pursued by men with revolvers, who is always
> once more just about to ruin himself.
>
> I can't think of a form of disaster which John Reed hasn't
> tried and enjoyed. He has half-spilled himself into commercial-

ism, had his head turned by flattery, tried to act like a cynical war correspondent, posed as a figure out of Ibsen. But always thus far the laughter in him has turned the scale, his sheer exuberance has carried him to better loves.

There's affection in those paragraphs—in Lippmann's finale, too: "In common with a whole regiment of his friends I have been brooding over his soul for years, and often I feel like saying to him what one of them said when Reed was explaining Utopia, 'If I were establishing it, I'd hang you first, my dear Jack.' But it would be a lonely Utopia."[11]

Still, "Legendary John Reed" remains a mystifying story to write, let alone to publish, about a friend in such distress.

Lippmann knows Reed well enough to describe him vividly: This article is one of the handful of definitive accounts of his personality. But there's one crucial thing about Reed that Lippmann doesn't understand. Even Reed doesn't understand it in 1914. He will need more time, more maturity, and more sobriety to grasp why he failed in the face of the war.

Eventually Jack will realize that all the stories he had covered so brilliantly before reaching Paris—labor battles in places such as Paterson and Ludlow, the Mexican peons fighting for their rights—had the same essential subjects: "drama, change, democracy on the march made visible—a war of the people."[12] But the European war offers none of these things: no ideals, no spontaneity, no clear right and wrong. Both sides, he thinks, are engaged in nothing nobler than the "ruin of the spirit as well as of the body, the real and only death."[13]

Though Lippmann mocks Reed for his lack of commitment, the opposite is closer to the truth. *Lippmann* is the one who has proven so deft at easing away from his socialism, closing the door on his bohemian playmates, and embracing the progressivism of Herbert Croly and Teddy Roosevelt.

"I don't love any idea sufficiently to worry ten minutes if someone compelled me to abandon it," he tells Justice Oliver Wendell Holmes, Jr., one of his more conspicuous admirers.[14]

Reed, not Lippmann, is the one who will confess, in an unpublished exercise in self-reflection, "The War has been a terrible shatterer of faith in economic and political idealism."[15]

In spite of all his struggles that fall, Reed manages to tell a superb story. He doesn't write it—he lives it. It's about the confusion, sorrow, and despair that this new kind of war inflicts on any idealist who gets near it. Nobody, not even his closest friends, gets the message.

Chapter 10

Dispatching John Reed to the front lines—their vicinity, anyway—is only one of the ways that American magazines scramble to respond to the war. The conflict is so new, so vast, and so bewildering that each publication tries to help readers make sense of the military developments however it can. Even *The Masses*.

The magazine's first wartime issue includes an item titled "Apology":

> We shall refrain from explaining in detail the movements of the armies and navies of the warring nations this month, as the man whose cousin was once in the militia is out of town, and the man who owns a yacht is indisposed. This puts us at a disadvantage with the magazines which have "military experts" on their staff, but we must ask our readers to bear with us.[1]

War hasn't changed Max Eastman's view of *The Masses*. It still needs to represent a freer, more joyful life, not just argue the case for one. That means it's vital, even amid a darkening violent world, not to let the war take over. It's important to keep running stories and poems and pictures about nothing, and jokes just because they're funny, and to send up the pompous conventions of other magazines—as well as their own. In fact, in one regard, that task has gotten easier, because 1914 brings them a prematurely middle-aged magazine to abuse. Eastman rarely misses a chance to mock "those mighty young bronze beasts who edit the *New Republic*."[2]

This is all good fun, but the war does confront *The Masses* with a direct challenge to a deeply held ideal—one they can't laugh off.

Less than a decade earlier, the socialist leaders of the Second International had pledged that the workers in their respective countries would refuse to fight in a capitalist war. Solidarity to their comrades would supersede nationalistic sentiment and attachment to a bourgeois government. It had all seemed very clear. Yet in the opening days of the war, German socialists voted for war credits, British socialists began to sound as martial as munitions magnates, French socialists grabbed their bayonets.

Eastman can't pretend this is a small matter. In 1912, when a socialist congress reiterated the pledge, he hailed it in an editorial as "an epoch in the martial history of the world."[3] And his critics don't let him forget that he has vowed, since his very first issue, to shun dogma and undertake "a continuous re-testing of the theories which pertain to the end we have in view."

Two years earlier, when Lippmann had cracked his shin on the shortcomings of socialism in Schenectady, it had helped push him toward progressivism. (It also meant that Lippmann spared himself the need to explain why socialism failed to prevent the war. Eastman can't abide Lippmann's lucky timing or his smug superiority: "I always wanted the sky to fall on Walter Lippmann and make him suffer," he writes. They remain pretty friendly.)[4]

Eastman declines to toss out his socialist convictions. On the contrary. He musters his defense in a couple of smoothly argued editorials.

War simply had come too soon, he says: Only when socialism is strong enough to fight capitalism at home can it stop capitalism's wars.

To those who say that socialism has been shown up, he responds that *capitalism* has been shown up, and the timid measures to sand down its worst edges shown useless. "You see here the true nature of the thing over which you have been smearing your tincture of reform."[5]

He praises what he calls the "noble mutinies and patriotic treasons" of individual socialists in the warring countries—heroic episodes that are, he maintains, stifled by censors.[6]

Above all, he insists that whatever difficulties the war might pose, the future still looks bright.

"I do not believe a devastating war in Europe will stop the labor struggle," he writes. "I believe it will hasten the days of its triumph. It will shake people together like dice in a box, and how they will fall out nobody knows. But they will fall out *shaken;* that everybody knows."[7]

In other words, do not despair about that hole in the ceiling. It is, in fact, a skylight.

For a man who leads a conspicuously merry magazine, Max Eastman does not feel very merry. Even the abrupt finish of the criminal libel case against him (charges dropped, bail returned, no explanation given—a mystifying end to more than a year of dread) cheers him only briefly.[8]

In early 1914, he began making four visits a week to a new kind of doctor, one who claimed that people could ease their mental difficulties by *talking* about them. These appointments with an early practitioner of Freudian analysis presented Eastman with a stream of possible diagnoses for the sadness and worry that had beset him since his youth, when a psychosomatic ailment hit him so strongly he had to wear a back brace. Homosexuality, mother fixation, the Oedipus complex, inferiority complex, narcissism, exhibitionism, autoeroticism: They all sound plausible to Max.[9]

Eastman tries to improve his predicament. To ease the burden of the magazine, he hires Floyd Dell, a sharp literary critic who is also a masterful associate editor. And he starts paying himself a little salary, so he won't have to give so many speeches for money.

His misbegotten marriage to Ida Rauh proves more difficult to fix. She is brilliant, and beautiful, and talented, and he loves her, and they make each other miserable. After Max makes a full confession of a half infidelity, they have an argument rivaling anything unfolding on the western front. It leaves them agreeing that Max will live part-time in a separate studio in Greenwich Village. Which makes things better, for a while.[10]

Still the deepest source of his dismay persists. To write poetry, he thinks, is to engage with the world. It's why he reveres Shelley and Aeschylus: poets who led energetic lives in addition to writing verses. Yet here he is, a young and reasonably healthy man, having no exposure to the greatest war in all of history. Eastman feels as strong a compulsion to see the war for the sake of his poetry as Reed did for his job as a war correspondent. So he decides to expose his supersensitive nerves to the concussive horror of the western front.

By this point, in early 1915, Europe has witnessed many ill-judged advances on all sides. Eastman's trip ranks high on the list. Like Reed a few months earlier, he can't get anywhere near the battlefields. The most action he witnesses is hearing the air-raid sirens blare that a zeppelin attack is imminent, and watching officials scream at the citizens of Paris to take cover, and seeing those citizens rush to the rooftops, as one, to get a better view.

All the while, Eastman is tormented by what Dr. Jelliffe might identify as an overactive superego. He is playing catch with another American one day when the glares of *les citoyennes* (who wonder why two able-bodied men aren't at the front, fighting the Germans) drive him to make a guilt-stricken visit to the Red Cross hospital. He feels that he should inquire about volunteering for the ambulance service.

He doesn't do any volunteering—the difficulty in scheduling saves him—but he does get a poem out of what he sees at the hospital.

Today I saw a face—it was a beak,
That peered with pale round yellow vapid eyes
Above the bloody muck that had been lips
And teeth and skin. A plodding doctor poured
Some water through a rubber down a hole
He made in that black bag of horny blood.
The beak revived; it smiled—as chickens smile.
The doctor hopes he'll find the man a tongue
To brag with, and I hope he'll find it, too.

Max is pleased enough with the result to publish it in *The Masses*. Only later will he admit that the poem is a fraud. He hadn't seen the horrors he described while at the hospital: He had written about some photos he had seen in the waiting room.

Eastman leaves Paris morose. In London, his gloom only grows. George Bernard Shaw, the most famous radical alive, agrees to meet him, and dazzles him with an interview. For some reason that even Eastman can't puzzle out, he never bothers to write what would be a blockbuster account of their meeting.

Having failed to generate any interest in the greatest war in history and the most charismatic writer alive, he similarly fails to raise any interest in the prettiest prostitute in Leicester Square. He hires her, only to send her away, with apologies for her wasted time.[11]

"The principal impression I bring from Europe is that the war is not interesting," Eastman writes when he gets home to the Village. He acknowledges that the new modern modes of killing have their novelties. "It is startling, and indeed appalling, to have a ton of metal dropped on you from twenty-six miles away after describing a trajectory seven miles high. It has a flavor of the gigantic miraculous—it suggests the Hippodrome. But as a mode of human conflict it lacks the dramatic elements of an ordinary fist-fight."

What he doesn't say is that proximity to the horrors of the European war have given him a queasy sense of being spiritually out of place. The high spirits of *The Masses* had seemed vulgar there. "In the face of this wholesale dying, a religion of abundant living, though it be the last and only honest cosmic justification for any human thing, is an impertinence."[12]

Eastman might be irritated by Walter Lippmann, but Lippmann has diagnosed his problem as precisely as any shrink could. For idealists with conspicuous talent and a desire to fix the world, for women who have secured the vote and can take part in self-government, for young people unshackled from Victorian social strictures—even for a young country growing stronger while the old world falls apart—the deepest dilemma of all is one that Lippmann posed in *Drift and Mastery:* What do you do with your freedom when you get it?

Chapter 11

President Wilson puts the telegram on his desk, stands up, retrieves his hat.

He walks out of his office. He has told no one where he is going, or even that he is leaving, but he walks right out of the White House.

On May 7, 1915, he walks alone, at night, in the rain.[1]

On Sixteenth Street, heading north, there is little to distinguish him from the other soggy pedestrians. His only remarkable feature, his imposing jaw, is down, near his chest. Probably nobody recognizes him; certainly nobody grasps his anguish. But then they never do.

"I have the uncomfortable feeling that I am carrying a volcano about with me," he told Ellen during their courtship, many years before. He dislikes these sensations, the tug of lust or anger or pride so powerful that it could knock him off the plane of reason, the one that the scholarly gentleman seems (but only seems) to occupy without strain.

There is, in fact, a lot of strain.

When Ellen died in 1914—during that nightmare week that saw him sitting next to her bed, holding her hand, reports arriving that Europe had begun its self-annihilation—he felt that volcano beginning to stir. Her death left him overwhelmed with despair, having lost his only real confidante; with guilt, because his ambition had led them to trade the serenity of Princeton for the killing strain of Washington; and bafflement: *He* was the one in precarious health (the stroke that had cost him part of his vision, the recurring stomach trouble); *she* was the one who was gone.

These emotions could not be indulged. His temperament wouldn't permit it, even if his job would. When a British diplomat sent condolences, Wilson thanked him for his kind words at what he called "this time of supreme trial when I am to discover whether I am master of myself or not."[2]

This all-powerful sorrow, this fear about passion so tremendous that it could destroy reason, carried from his private life into his public proclamations. Soon after Ellen's funeral, late one August night, he sat down at his typewriter and composed a message to the American people, a plea for self-mastery on a national scale: "We must be impartial in thought as well as in action."[3]

Maybe this wasn't Wilson's private sorrow carrying into politics: Maybe he was just thinking of Proverbs: *He that is slow to anger is better than the mighty; and he that ruleth his spirit than he that taketh a city.* Wilson's father was a Presbyterian preacher. This verse must have supplied many a sermon during his churchly youth, those years when he willed himself to curb his young man's desires, to show the rectitude befitting a minister's son.

There is a church on Wilson's rainy walk. It is a mile north of the White House, at the corner of Sixteenth and Corcoran streets: a Swedenborgian congregation, relatively new, done up in handsome gray limestone. He turns when he sees it; he doesn't go in.

The neutrality that Wilson requested came relatively easy to the American people. Four months after the shooting started, he could boast that the United States remained "at peace with all the world," and insulated from "a war with which we have nothing to do." His personal equanimity proved more difficult to sustain.

One day in late 1914 he had received a delegation of black leaders. These men had campaigned for him, insisting to skeptics that in spite of his southern heritage, he meant it when he promised they could count on him "for absolute fair dealing and for everything by which I could assist in advancing the interest of this race in the United States."

William Monroe Trotter, an editor from Boston, asked why his administration had instituted segregation in some government departments: humiliating, degrading measures that sabotaged the surest route to a middle-class life for black families at the time—and in spite of a half century of peaceful cooperation in those departments.

Wilson cut him off. "If this organization is ever to have another hearing before me it must have another spokesman. Your manner offends me."

Trotter asked why, how.

"Your tone, with its background of passion."

"But I have no passion in me, Mr. President, you are entirely mistaken; you misinterpret my earnestness for passion."

Trotter raised the specter of the black voters who had supported Wilson in 1912 turning against him in 1916, but the reference to politics enraged Wilson even more. He accused Trotter of trying to blackmail him. Furthermore, anybody who sought the presidency was "a fool for his pains," asking for burdens that were "more than the human spirit could carry."[4]

By the time Wilson showed them out forty-five minutes later, the volcano had scorched everything in sight. The newspapers dwelled for days on Wilson's bad temper, his bigotry, his appalling belief—heretofore concealed—that segregation was *a benefit* to black people.[5]

The gap between his speeches, which rang with the language of freedom and democracy, and his private beliefs, which were conspicuously racist even by the standards of 1914, made him look like a hypocrite. Of course, even then, Americans knew all about the chasm between people's ideals and their actions. Few knew it better than Trotter, who believed himself to be a descendant of Thomas Jefferson and one of Jefferson's slaves.[6]

It is still raining when Wilson reaches the corner of Fifteenth and Corcoran. On a walk like this one a few weeks after his interview with Trotter—a walk he had taken through Midtown Manhattan, at the behest of Colonel Edward Mandell House, the political operative who has replaced Ellen as his most trusted confidant—he had grown so despondent about his personal and professional crises that he wished somebody would shoot him.

Nobody had shot him then, and nobody shoots him now. And so there is nothing to remove the burden placed on him by the telegram he received that night, the one that sent him walking in the rain, the one that told him that no prior challenge to his self-mastery, or the country's, compared to what lay ahead.

He turns in the only direction that duty will allow him to turn: to the right, bound for home.

The next morning, banner headlines tell the American people the news that had shaken the president so badly the night before. They express the outrage and horror that later generations would feel about Pearl Harbor and the 9/11 attacks: a loss of life made all the more horrifying because it happened in a previously unthinkable way.

The passenger ship *Lusitania,* near the end of a transatlantic crossing from New York, has been attacked without warning by a German submarine. More than a thousand civilians—men, women, and children—have died in the cold waters off the Irish coast. The "war with which we have nothing to do" has just claimed 128 American lives.

Some Americans seek a military response—not just Theodore Roosevelt, who has been feeling belligerent for months, but even the smooth-talking and subtle Colonel House. "We are being weighed in the balance, and our position amongst the nations is being assessed by mankind," he tells Wilson.[7]

Most Americans don't want to fight. "We have everything to lose and nothing to gain by taking part in it," Walter Lippmann tells *The New Republic*'s Paris correspondent. "It would only mean that the last great power was engulfed in the unreasonableness of it all."[8] But he realizes with a sense of dread that no matter what the American people might think, or even what the Constitution might say, the grieving widower in the White House holds the choice between peace and war. One bellicose speech would put an end to a century of American isolation, and put its small, outdated military into conflict against the mightiest army ever assembled. One man's decision might mean the end of their youthful hopes.

A few days after the attack, Wilson states his views. "There is such a thing as a man being too proud to fight," he tells a crowd in Philadelphia. "There is such a thing as a nation being so right that it does not need to convince others by force that it is right."

So there won't be war, at least not immediately. But the pressure only mounts. One more incident, either premeditated or accidental, could force the country into the conflict. Nobody is ready for that— least of all not the grieving and inexperienced commander in chief.

To most Americans, the *Lusitania* crisis feels like a screw tightening. To Randolph Bourne, it's the opposite. Since he arrived at *The New Republic,* he had felt like "a very insignificant retainer on its staff," though he knows that he hasn't done anything to deserve a bigger role.[9] Without meaning to, he has drifted into the role of in-house education expert. It's an important subject, and his tutelage at the feet of John Dewey, the leading figure in progressive education, gives him a special grasp of the subject. But it's not the wide scope he had enjoyed while freelancing for *The Atlantic,* and it doesn't let him explore the big questions that he brought back from Europe: about what makes American culture unique, about how Josiah Royce's vision of "Beloved Community" might apply to our national life.

A magazine devoting more attention to the possibility of war has even less need for his services. A few weeks into the *Lusitania* crisis, Croly tells Lippmann to drop one of Croly's own stories from the next issue to make room for one of Bourne's—not because he particularly likes it, but because "we have got a lot of Bourne's stuff on hand . . . and unless we publish something of his pretty regularly we run behind on our account with him."[10]

Bourne is still only twenty-nine, but in the face of so much professional frustration, amid so many desires going unfulfilled, with his high hopes slipping away, he writes a long and melancholy letter to his friend Alyse Gregory that amounts to a surrender from the experimental life:

> I shall give up clamoring to be "in" things and "do" things, and accept my fate as a lonely spectator, reserved from action for contemplation. It used really to worry me, to be filled with so much reforming spirit, and to be so detached from any machinery of change. I felt very useless and treacherous, and envied those who were in the heat of the fray. But after the desperate attempts I have made this last year, only to be shouldered out almost before I knew it, I am convinced that some deep destiny presides over it all, and that I have unsuspected power of incompatibility with the real world. It isn't altogether good for me, either, for it makes me narrow and selfish and peevish and not very human, and this always comes out in what I write, becoming worse and worse.[11]

Bourne decides to get away for a while: away from the magazine, and the city heat, and the threat of war, and Beulah Amidon, a pretty girl who had broken his heart. (She didn't know she was doing it—he never worked up the nerve to tell her how he felt.) In Dublin, New Hampshire, he shares a little cabin with a friend. Bourne is a gifted pianist, and his friend is a violinist, which is lucky for them, because they are terrible cooks. They play duets at another house for their dinner. He trades gossip with Amy Lowell, visits the grave of his beloved composer Edward MacDowell, and lies in the tall grass, listening to the foxes bark, letting his mind whirl.

Like John Reed, who found that in Portland he could finally see Greenwich Village clearly enough to write an epic poem about it, Bourne finds that some of his hazy notions are beginning to take definite form. He thinks about his generation, so trusting and so naïve. They had studied their environment more attentively, and with more sophisticated tools, than any generation before them, but the war still found them staggeringly unprepared. How could this be? Why did they make the mistake of taking progress for granted? The problem, Bourne thinks, is that they trusted words instead of investigating realities. They thought of "democracy" and "socialism" as uniform waves that were sweeping the globe, not realizing that different cultures in different countries made those words mean different things.[12]

Seeking, seeking through those summer days and nights, under stars that are "superb beyond anything I ever remember to have seen," Bourne speculates about new ideals that could replace the ones shaken by the war. France and Britain say they fight for "democracy"—but Bourne had seen firsthand the condition of their democracies, and they looked to him like exploitation. Their enemies, the Germans, are denounced as butchers of the high seas, who violently impose a chauvinistic ideal on the world—but Bourne had seen their clean, efficient cities, their whirring social machinery, and he knew that Americans had something to learn from them.[13]

Bourne thinks his way around the globe, but America stays in the forefront of his mind. He is an intellectual patriot. He believes that the pioneering country that produced Emerson, Whitman, and William James is uniquely capable of fashioning a new ideal—nothing less than a new vision of the good life—that surpasses the old categories, that can unite the world. In 1915, he still can't see the ideal clearly, but he knows that one choice would prevent it from appearing: a decision to fight.

"War is a carnival of the instincts," he believes. "It is the apotheosis of small-boyism . . . a caricature of emotional thrills, a cunning fabric of instincts of destruction, sensuality, will to power and will to sacrifice."

Bourne wants the United States to resist these dangerous pleasures and stick to the harder, slower, and altogether worthier course of building up the country's education, industry, and politics. "America could have no nobler ideal than to show in its institutions the supreme reality of the pacifist state."[14]

That last line is a quote from "The Reality of Peace," an unsigned editorial that runs in the October 30, 1915, issue of the magazine. It is Bourne's third significant contribution since he attempted to leave the field. He retreated from the experimental life only to think and write his way back into the middle of it.

A few days after Bourne's editorial appears, President Wilson takes another consequential walk. He steps to the lectern in the banquet hall of the Biltmore Hotel. Eight hundred prominent New Yorkers pack the room, expecting the most important speech of his presidency, about America's foreign policy in a threatening world.[15]

In spite of German attacks and provocations, Wilson reaffirms his desire for peace. He acknowledges that America has not always fulfilled its mission of goodwill in the past—that it has taken aggressive actions, self-interested actions—but "they were the fruit of our thoughtless youth as a nation, and we have put them aside." He makes a solemn vow that America will never take another foot of territory by conquest, or subjugate another people.

He concludes this glowing statement of America's pacific purposes by calling for an enormous expansion of the country's military might.

He wants to train four hundred thousand citizen soldiers. He wants an energetic (if vague) expansion of the navy. He also demands "a reckoning" for certain residents of the country who show their loyalty to foreign powers, having forgotten that "their chief and only allegiance was to the great Government under which they live."

The crowd, which has applauded warmly for his military proposals, goes wild at his swerve into nativism. Many audience members snatch the American flags from their centerpieces and leap to their feet to wave them. For two minutes Wilson lets them scream.

Herbert Croly and the other editors of *The New Republic* want the United States to have the things that Bourne would prefer to a bigger army and navy—the educational advances, the industrial reform. They are not warmongers, are they? But after Wilson's speech, they decide that they *also* want the bigger army and navy.

The magazine rapidly becomes a leading voice for preparedness. And it never publishes another story about the war by Randolph Bourne.

Chapter 12

I t's romantic to think of the idealist as a solitary champion of right, the bold soul who keeps fighting in spite of all obstacles. It's less romantic, but more realistic, to picture the idealist as one who worries about the office rent, or frets about the payroll. Where is the glory in the electric bill, the glamour in keeping the pencils sharp?

These are some of the special burdens borne by Alice Paul and Max Eastman. When the president begins his preparedness push in late 1915, they are not just young radicals but young leaders: She is thirty; he is thirty-two.

They share more than a fervent belief in women's equality and affection for Max's sister, Crystal. Both of them are on the shy side; both might look right at home in a lecture hall, for they have genuine academic credentials: Paul earned a Ph.D. from Penn just before leading her suffrage parade; Eastman completed all the requirements for the same degree at Columbia, but didn't collect it. (He would have needed to submit a printed copy of his thesis, which would have cost $40—as he put it, "$39.70 more than the best Ph.D. ever granted is intrinsically worth.")[1]

They could always return to the academy. They could write and teach and take the summers off. Instead, with the threat of war growing, they go on navigating the paradoxes of leading a radical cause. They abandoned campus life because of a personal commitment to an individual vision, but leadership means being responsive to everybody else's vision, too. They take their responsibilities seriously, and want to lead effectively—and sometimes that means they need to quit.

Paul claims victory in her western campaign against the Democrats, but the Democrats do not act vanquished. In 1915, the suffrage amendment makes it to the floor of the House, where it is soundly defeated.

Once again it's time to try something new.

She begins to think that in order to push those intransigent men as hard as they need to be pushed, the tiny Congressional Union needs to apply pressure in their home states—all forty-eight of them. That will require an astonishing amount of new money. Since Paul is the group's most effective fundraiser, she offers to quit and focus her energy on that.

Her advisers do not like this idea. Dora Lewis, the one with whom she has the closest relationship, suspects that Alice feels overwhelmed, and that if she felt stronger, she would persist. The two of them spend a night together, as they often do. The question of Alice Paul's private life is as fascinating as it is impenetrable. (Later in life, she would do a remarkably thorough job of scrubbing the intimate details out of her papers. It's not even entirely clear how she divided her affections between men and women.)[2] Her most important relationship, then and always, is with the fight for women's rights.

Whatever Dora Lewis says or does, it persuades Paul to take back her resignation. She goes on running the Congressional Union. It means that she continues to be the primary target of the organization's growing list of enemies.

When Paul's new state offices begin to open, the NAWSA leaders, feeling threatened, attack her for "autocratic leadership and a philosophic irresponsibility to the suffrage movement."[3]

When she continues to insist, even amid Wilson's preparedness campaign, that suffrage is the most important issue in the country, she gets lectured by the editorial board of *The New York Times:* "It is no time for theatricals in Washington."[4]

And when she appears before the House Judiciary Committee, trying to steer the amendment back to the floor, the Democrats treat the hearing as a shooting gallery, relishing the chance to attack the impudent young woman who had campaigned against them.

"The women who have the vote in the West are not worrying about what women are doing in the East," says a Democrat from Kansas. "You will have to get more states before you try this nationally."

"We think that this repeated advice to go back to the states proves beyond all cavil that we are on the right track," she replies, standing her ground.

"Have your services been bespoken by the Republican committee of Kansas for the next campaign?" he demands.

"We are greatly gratified by this tribute to our value."[5]

Paul believes deeply in her cause and is willing to go on leading it, but she is no masochist: The abuse takes a toll.

Eastman tries to quit, too—though it's not entirely his idea.

"You're a dictator and you've got to be overthrown," Floyd Dell tells him when he arrives at the office one day. "You're going to be overthrown in the name of Art with a capital A."

There are factions within the staff of *The Masses,* as there are within any republic. On one side stand some committed socialists, mainly writers, who tolerate the apolitical parts of the magazine, mainly the pictures; on the other side stand the artists who draw those pictures, who just want to publish their images without a lot of words.

Eastman knows that a staff full of rebels is bound to rebel. It's only natural that a hothead young artist such as Stuart Davis would make a fuss. This "strike," as they're calling it, doesn't sound very interesting.

"It is," says Dell, "because they've got Sloan on their side."[6]

That *is* interesting.

John Sloan is one of the original stalwarts of *The Masses*. More than just the art editor, he is a pillar of the whole operation. When Max promised, in his first editor's note, to "tune our reading matter up to the key of our pictures as fast as we can," he meant Sloan if he meant anybody.[7]

If Sloan is involved, it's not a strike anymore—it's a coup.

At the next meeting, Sloan speaks first, reading from a prepared text.

"*The Masses* is no longer the resultant of the ideas and art of a number of personalities," he says. "We propose to get back to the idea of producing a magazine which will be of more interest to the contributors than to anyone else."

He wants to eliminate all traces of an editorial policy, socialist or otherwise. No more raucous monthly meetings. Writers will choose the stories, artists will choose the pictures, and a makeup committee will stitch them together. There will be no more editors—not even to raise money. Volunteers could take care of that.

This all strikes Eastman as insane, absurd, impractical. But he doesn't say that. Instead, he reads from his own prepared text.

"With every year since *The Masses* started, I have grown more skeptical of the principle of cooperative editing, and at the present time I am completely disillusioned. I do not believe in it any longer, and I do not want to take part in it any longer."

Since nobody seems to agree about anything anymore, it's a pretense to speak of cooperation. "The strain of the situation would be too difficult for me, even if I believed in the principle." So he offers to resign.

This is not going the way that Sloan and the other dissidents had expected. They ignore Eastman's resignation and vote to fire him.

The tally is 5–5, which settles nothing. They're short of a quorum. It means they have to get together and do this all again in a few days.[8]

To the outside observer, it looks like Eastman is about to get the freedom he has wanted. E. W. Scripps, the press magnate who has been supporting the magazine in spite of his distaste for its politics, likes Eastman but thinks he's ill-suited for the job. He has a nervous system that "should not and cannot safely be submitted to the strains inevitably attendant on such a business as the publication of *The Masses.*"[9]

Scripps fails to understand something about Eastman's connection to *The Masses.* It's the same thing people miss about Paul and the Congressional Union: The organization is so much a reflection of its leader that it makes no sense to speak of them separately. The fight between the committed socialists and the apolitical artists on the magazine's staff is the outward manifestation of the split in Eastman's soul, between the agitator and the poet. He cannot reconcile the two in his own life, because in choosing one he will be false to the other. All he can do is try to maintain a kind of equilibrium—in his life and in his magazine.

Alice Paul gets a second chance to make her burden lighter.

In December 1915, NAWSA holds its annual convention. On its sidelines, Paul and four other members of the Congressional Union have a closed-door meeting with five delegates from NAWSA. It's billed as an "efficiency" meeting. Really it's a summit.

In spite of the bad blood, there are good reasons to combine forces. The month before, suffrage measures had been voted down in four big eastern states—a major setback for NAWSA, which had led those fights. (President Wilson had voted "yes" in the New Jersey referendum, but said he was only doing it as a private citizen, which didn't change his view on federal suffrage. Paul is unimpressed.) Also the convention is going to install new leaders for the organization: Anna Howard Shaw, the longtime president, is stepping aside.

Alice Paul hadn't wanted to leave NAWSA in the first place; maybe something is possible. But any reconciliation is complicated by the fact that the woman sitting across from her is the one who initiated her exile.

At fifty-six, Carrie Chapman Catt has spent half her life trying to secure votes for women. She has lit the lamps and swept the floors. She has written and argued and raised funds and traveled. She nursed a husband, then buried him. In December 1915, she leads NAWSA's New York State affiliate, and she doesn't do it timidly. After the suffragists lost in New York the month before, she upbraided them at their state convention: "You women of New York must put the bric-a-brac out of your lives and your homes. It must be 'suffrage first' with you now. You are making history, and little things must not interfere."[10]

Catt and Paul have a lot in common, which is one reason they dislike each other. The Congressional Union is "exceedingly distasteful," Catt once told Jane Addams, accusing Alice Paul of "stupendous stupidity." Still, Catt knows what Paul has achieved. "The Congressional Union has pushed the Federal Amendment to the front, no matter what anybody says about it," she tells a fellow suffragist—though only privately.[11]

Catt also knows she isn't the first suffragist to watch a strong-willed upstart at work. "There never was a young woman yet who had just been converted, who did not know that if she had had the management of the work from the beginning, the cause would have been carried long ago," Susan B. Anthony said twenty years earlier, when a brisk junior suffragist took steps to hurry the movement along—the upstart being Carrie Chapman Catt.[12]

On this morning in 1915, at the New Willard Hotel, Catt lays out the NAWSA election policy for the benefit of Paul and her militant sisters. The organization does not support or oppose political parties, regardless of their positions on suffrage. It regards each candidate individually. NAWSA cannot accept an affiliate group that defies such a policy.

Could the Congressional Union abide by it?

There would be clear advantages for Alice Paul. The money. The organizational reach. The dispersal of abuse.

But she just reiterates what she told her tormentors on the Judiciary Committee: The Congressional Union *has* no election policy. Its actions depend entirely on what the Democrats do.

This is too coy for Catt, too tricky. It's the same kind of cleverness that had made her declare that she was "razzle-dazzled" by Paul's independence back in 1913.

"All I wish to say is, I will fight you to the last ditch," says Catt. Then she walks out.[13]

Eastman is in the chair when the staff of *The Masses* reconvenes to decide his fate—and maybe the magazine's. It's a Thursday afternoon in early 1916.

When Sloan's impractical plan for a leaderless magazine is put to a vote, the final tally is 8 in favor and 10 against. It seems that the storm has passed. And since Eastman no longer feels like resigning, they can all go back to work.

Except that now Dell is rising to his feet—and Max doesn't know why.

Dell moves that John Sloan and the four dissident artists be expunged from the list of contributing editors—a proposal even more hostile than Sloan's coup.

A bigger shock comes when Dell's motion is seconded by the best-loved member of the staff: the jolly, genial Art Young.

While Young isn't on the editorial side of magazine, he has no patience for mere aesthetes, the artists with no project more politically committed than a desire "to run pictures of ash cans and girls hitching up their skirts in Horatio Street."[14]

"To me this magazine exists for socialism," says Young. "That's why I give my drawings to it, and anybody who doesn't believe in a socialist policy, so far as I go, can get the hell out!"[15]

Dell's motion loses, but the sight of Young losing his cool shocks everybody out of their belligerent moods. In typically topsy-turvy fashion, they decide that instead of expelling the rebels, they'll promote them. John Sloan is named vice president.[16]

The meeting breaks up on a note of puzzled détente.

There's an irony to the challenges that Paul and Eastman face—another paradox of leading a radical organization.

Paul's 1914 campaign had been based on a promise of solidarity. Western women would vote against Democrats to stand with their disenfranchised sisters in the east. But her own movement has reached the limits of solidarity. She and Catt cannot find common ground, and now the potential ally is going to be a formidable foe. A few hours after the failed summit, Paul and her lieutenants learn that Catt has been elected the new president of NAWSA.

Eastman likes to trumpet the democratic character of *The Masses*. Yet the standoff between the writers and artists revealed the limits of collaboration among people who don't share exactly the same ideals—and even people who do. Later that night, Sloan sends Eastman a letter of resignation, depriving the magazine of one of its best minds.

A reporter asks Sloan what it means.

"It just proves that real democracy doesn't work—yet," he says.

These questions are more complicated than they appeared at Columbia and Penn.

Chapter 13

Week by week the war draws closer.

On November 8, 1915, a German torpedo destroys the Italian passenger ship *Ancona,* killing nine Americans.

On December 30, another torpedo sinks the British passenger ship *Persia,* killing two more Americans.

Neither boat gets a warning first.

President Wilson learns of the *Persia*'s destruction while on his honeymoon with Edith Bolling Galt, the forty-three-year-old widow who has become his second wife. He rushes back to the capital. But at the White House, he can only wait for reports, confer with the secretary of state, and pray. The dangers are, as he puts it, "infinite and constant."[1]

One hundred million Americans are reckoning now with the imminent threat of war—a conflict larger and more destructive than anything in their experience. Some super-patriots are spoiling for a fight, but those who have seen this conflict up-close fear and despise it. They don't need to imagine it; they don't even need to remember it. It has followed them home.

That winter, John Reed writes by day and has horrifying dreams at night.[2] He is finishing a book about what he had seen on the war's eastern front. He didn't want to go, but the western front was closed to him. (When he reached the trenches in France at last, it was on the German side, and when a lieutenant offered to let him shoot a rifle toward the French, he accepted, and when an account of that night ran in a New York newspaper, he was abused, denounced, shunned.)

In the East, he had hoped, maybe he would see Constantinople fall to the Allies, or at least get to ride on horseback through the mountain passes where Genghis Khan invaded Europe.[3]

He got nothing so romantic. Thus the nightmares.

In Serbia, "the Country of Death," where more people died from typhus than from combat, Reed had walked through the barracks-turned-hospitals: delirious shouting men soon to die, flesh rotting from gangrene. The sight and smell had turned Reed's stomach, and he had a strong stomach.

In Galicia, where Reed was trying to reach the Russian front line, an officer demanded his papers. Reed had gained access to the war zone after an American commissioner in Budapest had given him a list of Jewish Americans whose condition he was supposedly investigating. (Reed didn't think the list of names was long enough, so he added some—including "Walter Lippmann.") The Russian officer refused to believe that people with Jewish-sounding names could be American citizens, so he locked Reed and the artist Boardman Robinson, who was traveling with him, in their hotel room. For more than a week, they were trapped under the sloping tin roof—the stench of the open toilet down the hall hovering in the hot summer air, all contact with the outside world severed, three sword-wielding Cossacks at the door. They just missed being executed.

But Gucevo was the most horrific by far. The high plain in the Balkan mountains had been the site of a vicious battle, recently ended, in which Austrian and Serbian troops had butchered each other from trenches that were only a few dozen paces apart. In considerable pain—his kidney was torturing him—Reed had walked up to irregular piles of

earth between the trenches only to discover that the weird protuber-
ances were the broken ends of human bones, skulls with clumps of hair
peeling off, tatters of uniforms. Looking up, he saw that the piles continued all the way to the edge of the plain, where bands of half-wild
dogs slunk out of the woods, tearing at something he couldn't see, and
didn't want to. The dead lay so thick on the plain that there was no way
to avoid them. Reed stepped on bodies, heard the crunch of bones, felt
a boot sink sometimes into a shallow pit, where gray maggots swarmed.[4]

Back in New York, writing this all down, Reed's radicalism burns
ever hotter. The eastern front had shown him more clearly the staggering human toll of this capitalist swindle. He can't stand to hear people
talk about honor. In this war, honor is an absurdity—an obscenity—a
dead man's word. It's just exploitation on a grand scale, yet another way
that a nation can be "bound hand and foot to ambitious politicians."[5]

Reed is ready to oppose anybody who leads America nearer to that
abyss. Even an old friend.

While Reed types and fumes in Greenwich Village, Walter Lippmann
spends more and more time in Washington. *The New Republic* is "really
beginning to count" there, he is pleased to find. He has been treated to
confidential meetings with Colonel House. After years of mild contempt, he has begun to warm to the belief that President Wilson is
"really a very considerable man."[6]

Seeing government up close helps sharpen some of the views he'd
expressed in *Drift and Mastery:* his impatience with disorganization,
waste, and lack of ambition. That winter, he writes one of his longest
essays for the magazine, tracing his vision of "Integrated America," a
stronger and more effective national union, to be achieved through the
enlightened use of federal power. He invokes the spirit of Alexander
Hamilton, the greatest nationalizer in the country's history, as a model
for what he seeks. Hamilton's closest living analogue, he argues, is Theodore Roosevelt. Lippmann endorses TR's vision of "a more highly organized nation in which the great mass of the population lives a national

rather than a local life." To achieve it, Lippmann favors nationalizing the railroads, creating "a system of health, accident, maternity, old age, and unemployment insurance," and, in time, nationalizing the educational system. His enthusiasm doesn't extend to every program that Roosevelt has favored lately, especially universal training for military service: Lippmann still doesn't want a war. But that is a distinction that you might miss if you are distracted by, say, traumatic nightmares of a war zone, or mounting rage against every kind of militarist, or scorn for an ambitious friend going over to the enemy.

Reed responds to Lippmann's essay with a savage letter. He attacks him for betraying his principles—supporting a monster, in the pages of a magazine funded with Wall Street money, under the guise of advocating a so-called radical program. At least, it's a fair surmise of what Reed wrote. Lippmann, usually so conscientious about his tens of thousands of letters, didn't keep this one.

Lippmann, surprised and angry, returns fire. He claims to be "a little sorry" that Jack has decided to cast him out.

> I do not suppose that I was entitled to expect any kind of patient fairness from you even though I have tried to be pretty patient and fair with you for a good many years. I continued to believe in you even though many times I have felt that you had acted like a fool or a cad. I would have supposed that the least you would have done after you had come to your weighty conclusion about me was to talk to me about it instead of writing me an hysterical letter.

Lippmann declines to respond to his friend's specific charges, or list all the ways that Reed is mistaken about what he actually thinks and feels. "But I cannot help saying that you are hardly the person to set yourself up as judge of other people's radicalism."

> You may be able to create a reputation for yourself along that line with some people, but I have known you too long and I know too

much about you. I watched you at college when a few of us were taking our chances. I saw you trying to climb into clubs and hang onto a social position by your eyelids, and to tell you the truth I have never taken your radicalism the least bit seriously. You are no more dangerous to the capitalist class in this country than a romantic guerrilla fighter. You will prick them at one minute and hurt them at one point perhaps once in a while; but for any persistent attack—for anything which really matters, any changing fundamental conditions—it is not your line. You have developed an attitude which is amusing and dramatic. But do not get the idea that you are one of these great strong men who the vested interests of this country fear.

It sounds like "Legendary John Reed," but with all the wit drained away. And Lippmann's not through.

"I will just make one little prophecy, which may sound to you like a boast," he concludes. "I got into this fight long before you ever knew it existed and you will find that I am in it long after you quit."[7]

Jack is delighted. He knows that, as a classmate of theirs once pointed out, Lippmann's reaction to pain is almost always to turn coldly impersonal.[8] To make Walter lash out this way is a real, if petty, victory.

He shows the letter around. Then he hangs it on his wall: a spoil of war.[9]

A fight about ideals seems to burn the hottest, and to hurt the most, when it's with a friend. For while an ideal is, in one sense, just a mental construct—a name for a particular kind of change you would like to see in the big wide world—it remains a deeply personal thing. An ideal is a product of our life experiences, our hopes for our futures, the intimacies we develop among those who value the same things we do. Uproot a deeply held belief, and you're likely to take some of the trellis with it.

Lippmann, unsurprisingly, calms down before Reed does.

"You and I haven't any business quarreling," he tells Jack six days later. "You wrote hastily and hurt me. I answered hastily and hurt you. But it's all damn foolishness. Let's have lunch together some day this week."[10]

Reed replies back the next day: "I agree with you. Forgive my hurting you."

He says that he's about to leave town for a ten-day vacation, but he will write to make a lunch date when he gets back.[11]

There's no way to tell if they ever met for that lunch. If they didn't do it right away, they probably didn't do it at all.

Two weeks after Reed's return, the ferryboat *Sussex*—a crosstown bus on the waves—explodes. Some passengers die when the German torpedo strikes; others, panicking, drown after they leap into the English Channel.[12]

SUBMARINE TERRORISM blares the front page of a Washington newspaper.[13]

In a speech a few weeks earlier, President Wilson had said, "The world is on fire and there is tinder everywhere." Now he is the one holding a lit match. If he decides that the cool impartiality that he has preached since 1914 is no longer attainable, he will break relations with Germany. And that will lead to the unthinkable.[14]

Reed and Lippmann's friendship, like Paul's suffrage movement, and the staff of Eastman's magazine, and Bourne's relationship with his superiors, is already cracking: What will happen if the United States goes to war?

There is no turning back for any of them. Everybody has to grow up.

III. BIG AMERICA, OR THE GREAT CONSUMMATION

(1916–17)

What really exists is not things made but things in the making.

—WILLIAM JAMES

Chapter 14

A happier scene from an easier time: April 8, 1912, the Onondaga Hotel, Syracuse.

An overflow crowd packs the annual banquet of the city's chamber of commerce. More than three hundred businessmen sit at tables on the ballroom floor; one hundred women watch from the balcony. The place is decked in black and orange; the orchestra plays Princeton fight songs. Both are tributes to the guest of honor, who had recently been president of that college, and who hopes very soon to be president of the United States.

Governor Woodrow Wilson of New Jersey is not yet his party's nominee, so even though he is a rising star, he is a small-time operation. He'd needed to borrow a suit that night because the only one he had brought on his speaking tour had been stolen from his hotel room in Chicago. He was inconvenienced but not downcast. "I feel a sort of exhilaration in having been permitted to come into politics at this particular time," he'd said.[1]

The governor shares the stage with a lanky young orator and academic named Max Eastman. Eastman notices that Wilson is having trouble connecting with the small-town businessmen. "He would help the conversation along with quotations from Edmund Burke or Lord Acton that paralyzed it altogether."[2] So he sits next to Wilson at the head table. To pass the time through the long hours of *consommé excelsior* and *salade mignonette* and *cailles royale suzette,* Wilson asks Eastman to instruct him about the subject nearest his heart: woman suffrage.

The conversation leaves Eastman impressed. Wilson's alert attentiveness makes him feel good about himself, and the governor's knack for saying only things that Eastman wants to hear makes him feel good about Wilson.[3]

At last the moment for speeches arrives. Before Eastman can begin, he is taken aside by J. R. Clancy. As chairman of the entertainment committee, Clancy is charged with making sure that the banquet, the biggest in the history of the chamber of commerce, is also the best. That's why he'd hired Eastman for the night, to give a comic speech to offset Governor Wilson's more sober one. The man is leaving nothing to chance.

"Look here," says Clancy. "You're not a propagandist, you're a humorist. I want you to forget all about your principles, and just make 'em laugh, will you?"

Clancy backs up his request with cash: He offers an extra dollar for every minute that Max can keep the governor laughing.

As Eastman steps to the lectern, pondering this surprising offer, he notices Clancy take a watch out of his pocket and set it on the table. So he decides to tell the crowd about the deal.

"The reason I tell you is because I think if it doesn't entertain you to hear me talk, perhaps it will entertain you to watch Mr. Clancy lose money."

He earns his first extra dollar right there.

Eastman's theme that night is "humor as the result of disappointed expectations." Whenever he makes Wilson chuckle, he throws a significant glance at Clancy, which sets off one room-wide laugh after another.

He takes home an extra forty dollars that night, plus a blurb from

Wilson that's worth a lot more to him (and his lecture agent) than that: "the most brilliant combination of thought and humor I have ever listened to."[4]

Wilson has a good night, too. He is still a long shot to win the Democratic nomination, but he has burnished his reputation as a fresh voice on the national stage. "We are on the eve of a new age of creative politics," he says a few days later.[5]

J. R. Clancy has the best night of all: The grateful citizens of Syracuse elect him to Congress in the fall.

The next time Eastman and Wilson meet, the world has changed, and so have they. On May 7, 1916, the editor of the country's most obstreperous radical magazine—a pitched enemy of chambers of commerce—walks into the office of the president of the United States.

They shake hands. Wilson, exquisite politician that he is, recalls with a smile their delightful evening in Syracuse.

Only Eastman isn't feeling delighted. He has come to Washington to protest Wilson's plan for an enormous expansion of the country's armed forces. His sister, Crystal, leads the delegation that day. Her American Union Against Militarism is small but it punches above its weight. Social reformers such as Lillian Wald, Rabbi Stephen Wise, and Amos Pinchot are prominent enough citizens that even a busy president will make time to hear what they have to say.

Max is there only because a labor leader who was supposed to round out the delegation has fallen ill. It makes him feel an obligation to speak on behalf of workers. He interprets this to mean chastising the president for the company he has been keeping.

"If it could have happened, by some extraordinary accident, that instead of addressing the Daughters of the American Revolution or the women's section of the Navy League"—which Wilson had done on a recent trip to New York—"you had come to address such a representative body as the 60,000 striking garment workers in New York City, I am sure you would have met a response very different from this military excitement which seems to have seized our ruling and leisure classes since the European war, and the profits of the European war, began."[6]

Eastman knows it's a rude thing to say to Wilson's face. He can tell that Wilson thinks so, too. But the president isn't going to let himself get rattled by Eastman the way he had by William Monroe Trotter and Alice Paul.

He asks his guests to consider preparedness as a practical matter, not a philosophical one.

"This is a year of madness," he tells them. "It is a year of excitement, more profound than the world has ever known before. All the world is seeing red. No standard we have ever had obtains any longer. In the circumstances, it is America's duty to keep her head, and yet have a very hard head; to know the facts of the world and to act on those facts with restraint, with reasonableness, without any kind of misleading excitement, and yet with energy, and all that I am maintaining is this: that we must take such steps as are necessary for our own safety as against the imposition of the standards of the rest of the world upon ourselves."

It is the suavity that had impressed Eastman in Syracuse, but even more polished. Though they are arguing opposite sides of a question, Wilson always refers to the AUAM as if he is a member of it. The radicals see what he's up to, but somehow don't mind: They admire how beautifully they are being handled.

The president has heard them out, which is all they can ask. He could, without any hint of insult, open the door and bid them good day. Instead, he leads the meeting onto a path that neither of the Eastman siblings had foreseen.

Wilson returns to the practical matter of how to match military strength to national objectives. He sounds like he's thinking to himself out loud—though of course he has thought all this out before.

"Now, let us suppose that we have formed a family of nations, and that family of nations says, 'The world is not going to have any more wars of this sort without at least first going through certain processes to show whether there is anything in its case or not.' If you say, 'We shall not have any war,' you have got to have the force to make that 'shall' bite. And the rest of the world, if America takes part in this thing, will have the right to expect from her that she contributes her element of force to the general understanding. Surely that is not a militaristic idea. That is a very practical idea."

A family of nations! In all his speeches, through the many months of German attacks and American protests, he has never offered such a radical vision for the postwar world. Only his very closest advisers know about it. Eastman is flattered to recall that it is precisely the kind of move toward international federation that he has wanted the president to take. A year and a half earlier, he had written in *The Masses* that such a move would make Wilson's administration "a momentous event in planetary history—a thing not for historians, indeed, but for biologists, to tell of, because the elimination of war will profoundly alter the character of evolution."

Eastman never thought Wilson would do such a thing, so he had ended the column with a taunt: "Will he do this, or will he rest satisfied with that ludicrous incantation, the national petition to God? Is he capable of a man's prayer, a great act of resolution?"[7]

Now, face-to-face with Wilson, reeling from the expansiveness of the president's global vision, he has the opposite impulse. He wants to warn him about the difficulties he'll face.[8]

Three weeks later, the whole country gets to hear what Max Eastman has heard. At another banquet—much larger than the one in Syracuse, with a much fancier crowd—President Wilson shares his internationalist dream with the legal and political elite of New York City, the members of the League to Enforce Peace.

"The world is even now upon the eve of a great consummation," he tells them, "when some common force will be brought into existence which shall safeguard right as the first and most fundamental interest of all peoples and all governments, when coercion shall be summoned not to the service of political ambition or selfish hostility, but to the service of a common order, a common justice, and a common peace."

In other words, the most destructive of all wars might be the *last* of all wars. And the peace might be kept by a radically new international entity, with the full participation of the United States.

The press recognizes the enormousness of what Wilson is proposing. In *The New Republic,* a goggle-eyed Walter Lippmann declares that the speech "may well mark a decisive point in the history of the modern world. No utterance since the war began compares with it in overwhelming significance to the future of mankind."[9] For almost two years, Lippmann has been saying that the war meant the end of American isolation. Now the president is spelling out an active, positive vision of what comes next.

Lippmann, whom nobody ever accused of being overly excitable, thinks that Wilson's speech could mark the first move toward peace.

Americans can afford that kind of optimism thanks to a second surprising development that month. Wilson's threat to break diplomatic relations over Germany's murderous U-boat attacks has led to "the *Sussex* pledge": a German promise to impose strict new rules on its submarine commanders. It means that after a year of mounting tension, the threat of going to war unexpectedly recedes. In a decade with so many appalling surprises, here is a cheerful one.

The young radicals profit by it more than most. They will make the opportunity count. Back in the sunshiny days of 1912 and 1913, they were just starting out, taking big chances, feeling their way. Now they are more seasoned, more expert. And to the extent that ideals reflect each person's experiences, the trials of the past two years ought to give them a richer sense of what they want the world to be.

That summer and fall, they'll offer new expressions of those ideals—a quick and dazzling profusion of them. Some are a direct result of the burdens having lifted; others just have the good fortune to arrive when the country is not immersed in the war that had seemed to be fast approaching.

In these lucky circumstances, it might be possible to create something that will last. It might be that the future is nearer than they thought.

Chapter 15

ll day long, the parade streams north on Michigan Avenue. Every inch of sidewalk along Grant Park is occupied; the stoops and the windows are jammed. A spectator with enough time and fortitude to watch the whole thing would spend eleven hours on the reviewing stand. That's how long it takes 130,000 people, walking shoulder to shoulder, in lines stretching from curb to curb, to march by.

It's not just "the greatest parade ever held in Chicago," as its organizers boast, nor is it merely a show of support for preparedness: It's a *demonstration* of preparedness. All of the varieties of American citizen who march that day—lawyers, nurses, golfers (waving American flags at the ends of their clubs)—do so according to the whistled cues of an army captain.[1] Nobody breaks ranks.

Yet if you were to look down on the parade from a great height, you might notice its current being split in two, like a river divided by a rock. Only this rock isn't fixed: It is pushing its way upstream.

The rock is Alice Paul. Knowing a public relations coup when she sees it, she has made a quick decision to lead fifty suffragists from her

Congressional Union straight up Michigan Avenue, directly into the path of the parade.

It is the least audacious thing she will do all week.

Paul has come to Chicago because the Republicans and Progressives have come to Chicago. Both of the parties are having their national conventions here, a concentration of political power and media attention that she refuses to let slip. It is exactly the stage she needs to unveil her riskiest and most sweeping gambit yet, one that *The New York Call* deems "the biggest and most portentous mass movement of women in American history."[2]

Paul has spotted a unique opportunity in that summer of 1916—"this most precious summer," she calls it.[3] To seize it, she proposes a new plan that makes the nine-state western campaign of 1914 look like a pencil sketch. She creates the Woman's Party. It is not a suffrage organization, she explains, it is a *political party:* one that is of, by, and for women.

As usual with Paul, the plan is a mix of hardheaded strategy and rousing exhortation. President Wilson will need 266 of the country's 531 electoral votes to win reelection in November. He can't reach that number solely from the party's base in the South, even though that region would sooner elect the kaiser than go Republican; nor will he get it from the East, which has no use for a Democrat. That leaves the West, where 91 electoral votes are in the hands of the suffrage states. The four million women in those states could settle the president's fate if (and here is the rousing-exhortation part) they are jolted into recognizing their common interests, and organized to work on one another's behalf.[4]

"Some women will tell you that sex solidarity, the same sort of solidarity that has made labor in this country a power to be reckoned with, is impossible to women," Paul says in her first Chicago speech. "But I believe that when we say to the enfranchised women of this state and of the other free states of the West, 'Will you cast your vote this one time for the women of this country?' there is no doubt whatever as to what the women of the free states will say."[5]

Because the Woman's Party consists entirely of voting women in the western states, Paul limits herself to an ex officio rule. Anne Martin, from Nevada, is elected chairwoman. On the evening of June 6, 1916, at Chicago's Blackstone Theater, Martin steps forward from the tiered banks of suffrage leaders who are arrayed across the stage, and begins an epochal night in American political history.[6]

Martin tells the audience of more than a thousand women that they are about to hear from representatives of the other political parties. "We wish to make it clear that [the delegates from other parties] are not going to speak to us on the subject of what women can do for the political parties, but what the political parties will do for the women voters, in return for the women voters' support."

In other words: After seventy years of begging men for their rights, it is women's turn to be begged.

A representative of the tiny Prohibition Party walks onstage, proverbial hat in hand, to say, "We are your enthusiastic suitors."

Allan Benson, the Socialist Party's candidate for president, doesn't have very attractive things to say about why women should vote for his party (he is not a good politician; come November, he will forget to register and be unable to vote for himself),[7] but he declares that the socialists will vote for suffrage even if women don't vote for socialists.

C. S. Osborn, a former governor of Michigan, speaks candidly—maybe too candidly—for the Republicans. "I wish to confess that I am almost frightened to death here," he says, "and if you could only get the Republican Party as badly frightened as I am, you would get anything from them."

But the evening's main attraction is Dudley Field Malone, a prominent Democratic appointee and friend of the president. He describes some of the party's positions on issues besides suffrage, and suggests that women ought to support the Democrats on the basis of those, even if the president counsels patience. As for suffrage itself: "All the reasons that are given as to why women should not vote are so absurd that they shall have no discussion from me."

If this is an attempt to woo his listeners, it fails. "Tell that to the president!" they shout. It has a particularly lively effect on Harriot Stanton Blatch, the formidable daughter of the very formidable Elizabeth Cady Stanton.

"Mr. Malone tells us to be patient and polite," she tells the women before and behind her. "Good heavens, we have been patient and polite! We have got nothing by being polite. It was not until we began to respect ourselves (cheers)—it was not until we felt in our very souls that democracy for women was as great as democracy for men (applause)— that things began to move! Polite! Why, we have gone with perfect politeness to the president of the United States, again and again; and what have we received?"[8]

The Woman's Party has not made a friend of Dudley Field Malone or his boss, the president. But neither of those things is Alice Paul's objective. Congress is still in session that summer. If she can make the prospect of four million women voting as a single concerted bloc in a dozen swing states a terrifying enough prospect, the Democrats might push the amendment through Congress before the harvest comes in. The *idea* of the Woman's Party might obviate the need to deploy that party.

She hopes so. In June, five months before the election, she and her colleagues are already overwhelmed. "I do not see how we can possibly finish the work before us," she admits.

The Chicago office is understaffed; Washington sends dire updates about the bank account. Paul's immediate solution is, as ever, to work harder, to work constantly. When the housekeeper had gotten sick earlier that year, Paul had taken over her job, too.[9]

At a Woman's Party event in Chicago that summer, a speaker invites Alice Paul to come onstage to be saluted for her leadership—"her clear vision, her genius." The crowd gives her three cheers. But Paul doesn't step forward. She isn't even in the theater. Since she is sleeping only every other night that summer, most likely she is at her desk, working.[10]

If you want the Democrats to do something, Alice Paul knows, the surest way is to make the Republicans do it first.[11] Her aim in Chicago is

to make the Republican platform committee endorse the federal suffrage amendment. This would be a milestone: Neither major party has
endorsed votes for women before.

Paul is not alone in pressing the Republicans. Carrie Chapman Catt
has arrived in Chicago, too, backed by the full might of her very, very
large organization. On the eve of the Republican convention, ten thousand women march in a NAWSA parade to the Chicago Coliseum.
Catt wants to make a show of female resilience. The day is so cold and
wet and blustery that the city's *firemen* had canceled their parade. It
also shows NAWSA's ample resources. Elephants are involved.

Warm and dry in their meeting room, the Republicans do indeed
add a historic endorsement of suffrage to their platform. But Paul isn't
satisfied: The plank favors suffrage as a state-by-state matter, not a federal one. It is irritating. The Republicans get to congratulate themselves
for breaking new ground even as they push suffragists back to the complicated, expensive, time-wasting approach of the last generation.

Undaunted, Paul carries the fight to St. Louis, where the Democrats
will convene. So does Catt, backed once again by her legions of
NAWSA members. As the convention gets under way, NAWSA arranges for suffragists to line both sides of the street from the delegates'
hotel all the way to the meeting site a mile away. It is an enormous, silent, powerful plea for women's recognition.

Unlike in Chicago, here the agitation seems to be working. Josephus
Daniels, the secretary of the navy, writes a platform plank that endorses
woman's suffrage—as a *federal* measure. He shares it with Paul, who is
delighted and gives her approval. So does Catt.[12]

Yet authority flows in a peculiar way around the Democratic Party
that summer. *The New York Call* runs an editorial cartoon that depicts
"Prominent Figures at St. Louis Convention": the permanent chairman, the temporary chairman, the chairman of the credentials committee, the chairman of the resolutions committee, the chief of police, the
sergeant at arms, a delegate, and the nominee. All of them are illustrations of Woodrow Wilson.[13]

The president drafts a party platform at the White House and sends it to St. Louis in the personal care of Newton Baker. The secretary of war guards the document so carefully that he sleeps with it under his pillow on the train.[14]

Once that document reaches the committee room of the Planters House hotel, Democratic officials try to reconcile it with the work they have been doing. It takes them all night.

Outside, in the hallway, a group of suffragists keep a quiet vigil. Two groups, to be exact: a pair of women from NAWSA and three from the Woman's Party. In the course of the long night, as reporters mill around, committee members gawk at them, and loud, angry voices seep out of the parlor, the women from the two groups never interact at all.[15]

The sun comes up, the meeting ends, the full convention meets, and the platform is approved. It endorses suffrage only at the state level—exactly as the president had wanted.

Paul and Catt are furious about the president's intransigence, though neither can let that anger dictate her actions. At least not any actions that Wilson can see.

Publicly Catt keeps trying to ingratiate herself with Wilson, making NAWSA seem a powerful source of support. Privately—and literally within minutes of the end of the Democratic convention—she makes a series of swift decisions that allow NAWSA to start applying more pressure at the federal level. It begins to function more like Paul's organization. She even shifts the base of operations from New York to Washington—Paul's backyard.[16]

Paul hasn't completely abandoned hope that the prospect of women's concentrated power will bring the president around. Another chance arrives a few weeks after the convention, when the president grants an audience to four suffragists.

"I am sixty years old, Mr. President," says Harriot Stanton Blatch. "I have worked all my life for suffrage; and I am determined that I will never again stand up on the street corners of a great city appealing to every Tom, Dick, and Harry for the right of self-government."

All four of the suffragists warn the president that many, many thousands of voting women feel as they do. By refusing to support a federal suffrage amendment, he might force them to vote against him, which could mean the end of his presidency.

"If they did that," Wilson says, "they would not be as intelligent as I believe they are."[17]

Two weeks later, Alice Paul puts the Woman's Party into the field.

Chapter 16

I n the evening, when the honeysuckle opens, Randolph Bourne begins to play. He has the luxury of a majestic instrument that summer: a Chickering baby grand.[1] Because it's so muggy in Caldwell, New Jersey, all the windows in the house stay open. Bright melodies, subtle harmonies, intricate phrasings flow down his arms and fingers, through the keys to the hammers and strings, then across the dark lawn and through the trees.

He plays Brahms and Schumann and Chopin. He plays MacDowell and Bach and Ravel.[2]

He doesn't have the stamina for the long and thunderous pieces, but within the limits of his ability, with a good piano in front of him, he is a marvel. His mother thought his musicianship, so unlike any member of his family's, must have been God's compensation for his physical defects. A Columbia classmate, putting it more crudely, gaped at "how beautifully this strange misshapen gnome could make a piano sing and talk."[3]

Most nights he plays for the three women who share the summer house with him: his friend Frances Anderson, an editorial assistant at *The New Republic;* Agnes de Lima, who had been Frances's roommate at Vassar, an activist with an infectious laugh and what a friend calls "Spanish vivacity";[4] and Esther Cornell, Agnes's friend, a young actress preparing for a Broadway play in the fall.

"An unusually charming house," Bourne calls their bungalow.[5] It's a long commute from Manhattan, but that's fine by him. He has begun to think of New York the same way he thinks of Bloomfield: as a place where he has too many thwartings to remember. Beyond his mounting frustration with *The New Republic,* he has just gone through an ugly breakup with his first real girlfriend—a particular trauma for him, since how can a five-foot-tall hunchback with a lopsided face feel confident of finding any girlfriend, let alone two of them?

Meanwhile, Randolph Bourne, champion of youth, has turned thirty.

His friends are settling into adult life that summer. They are starting families, making homes. "I flit around from one to the other, a homeless, helpless waif, eternally passing out into the cold from their warm and confident firesides," he laments. "And I seem to face a long future of such waifness."[6]

By 1916, Bourne should know better than to predict what "a long future" might bring. One lesson of that decade of war and peace, of progress and reaction, of motorcars and telephones and ragtime, is that the long future can't be known; it shouldn't even be guessed. Even while it's happening that summer, amid his recitals of Beethoven and Brahms, he doesn't realize that he is fulfilling his youthful dream: "to be a prophet, if only a minor one."[7]

Bourne had come home in 1914 wanting to study America as closely as he had studied Europe: using fresh eyes to see his country anew.

He noticed that New York reflected many of the cultures he had left on the Continent. To nativists, these ethnic communities were a cause for alarm, a sign that the American "melting pot" wasn't melting new arrivals quickly enough. The threat of war gave a political expression to that fear, as when Wilson questioned the loyalty of immigrants in his first big preparedness speech.

Bourne thought Wilson and the more virulent nativists had the matter backward. At a time when half the world was butchering the other half, the various ethnicities coexisted in America in what he called "almost dramatic harmlessness."[8] The progressive schools of Gary, Indiana, where he spent so much time, peaceably welcomed children from thirty nationalities. "They merge," he observed, "but they do not fuse."

The more Bourne ponders this phenomenon, the more he views it as an advertisement for the American character. "In a world which has dreamed of internationalism, we find that we have all unawares been building up the first international nation . . . the continent where for the first time in history has been achieved that miracle of hope, the peaceful living side by side, with character substantially preserved, of the most heterogeneous peoples under the sun."

Like Horace Kallen, a disciple of William James who has written an influential essay on this subject, he sees that the "melting pot" isn't just bad sociology—it is a misguided, pernicious ideal. The people who speak highly of it don't want to let different traditions flow promiscuously together to make something new (which is what a true melting pot would do); they want to make new arrivals conform to a preexisting mold: the English American.

Bourne knows this process well, and knows this mold intimately, because it had shaped him. Growing up in Bloomfield—an Anglo-Saxon among Anglo-Saxons—he had been stifled by traditions, locked in by customs that dated all the way back to the colonists. "English snobberies, English religion, English literary styles, English literary reverences and canons, English ethics, English superiorities, have been the cultural food that we have drunk in from our mothers' breasts," Bourne believed. Only at cosmopolitan Columbia did he encounter the genuine American voice, the "pioneer spirit" of Emerson, Whitman, and William James. His new friends from different ethnicities gave him the chance to "breathe a larger air." They were more than neighbors and classmates: They were his liberators.

From his observations and his own experience, bolstered by his studies and his training—such as his teacher Franz Boas's belief that there are no intrinsically superior or inferior cultures—Bourne made an intellectual leap. The narrow mistake of the nativists is to insist on pouring new arrivals into the English American mold. The bigger mistake is to use *any* mold at all in this dynamic, diversifying country—in this society that couldn't ever be made, but could only be in the making.

"The failure of the melting-pot, far from closing the great American democratic experiment, means that it has only just begun."

Bourne wrote this all down in spring 1916 and sent a draft to Ellery Sedgwick, his first champion, at *The Atlantic Monthly*. Sedgwick had provided a boost of confidence when he'd started out and needed it most. He needed another now.

Sedgwick told Bourne he hated it.

He was appalled by Bourne's suggestion that "the last immigrant should have as great an effect upon the determination of our history as the first band of Englishmen who ever stepped on our coast. . . . What have we to learn of the institution of democracy from the Huns, the Poles, the Slavs? . . . For you to speak as though the New Englander of so-called pure descent and the Czech were equally characteristic of America seems to me utterly mistaken."

Sedgwick was not the ideal audience for this essay. He was a Boston Brahmin super-WASP, which makes his fulminating response read like self-parody. Still, he was editor enough to recognize that it was "perhaps the ablest and certainly one of the most interesting" essays that his protégé had written. So, to his everlasting credit, he published it.[9]

At a climactic moment of the essay, Bourne articulates a lofty vision of the national character: "America is coming to be, not a nationality but a trans-nationality, a weaving back and forth, with the other lands, of many threads of all sizes and colors." Sedgwick might not have liked the essay, but he liked that line—or at least a piece of it—and decided to showcase it.

So it is under the title "Trans-national America" that the great work of Bourne's writing life appears. It spans twelve pages in the July 1916 issue of *The Atlantic Monthly,* the one that reaches newsstands around the time that Bourne unpacks his clothes, his books, and his sheet music in Caldwell, and begins to play.

Bourne likes performing for his friends. It makes him happy to serenade his housemates—to let his long, graceful fingers do the talking for a while. That summer he plays for one housemate in particular.

Esther Cornell has copper-gold hair, a mellow intelligence, and a long train of admirers. Those suitors, the handsome sons of good families, aren't in Caldwell—but Bourne is.

He finds himself playing a lot of Chopin.[10]

Randolph and Esther take long walks together. Their legs are never going to scissor in unison, but they begin falling into step. Randolph can't get enough of Esther's "glowing inquiring look"; she "means light and air" to him.[11]

More than once that summer, Agnes returns to the house on Cedar Road to find Randolph and Esther sitting together on the porch swing. It is a humiliating sight: beauty and the beast. Randolph tries to play the lothario, adopting what he'll later call a "Captain Kidd swagger." Esther doesn't reciprocate—but she also doesn't push him away.

The music, the scenery, and the lively conversation attract plenty of houseguests. Bourne loves to preside over a dinner table, sparking conversations, egging people on. A friend describes him in such situations as being "throned like a little pope."[12]

Walter Lippmann is one of the first friends to visit. He is accompanied by Alvin S. Johnson, an economist and *New Republic* contributor. Over dinner, Johnson shares his idea for a new kind of school—really, a new approach to education, which will take shape two years later as the New School for Social Research.

Bourne, the disciple of John Dewey, the leading authority on the Gary schools, has a lot to say on this particular subject. He asks questions; he makes suggestions.[13] It could not have been a quick dinner. That's especially true if Bourne's new *Atlantic Monthly* piece came up. Because part of that essay seems to have been directed at the friend sitting across the table.

In presenting his trans-national ideal, Bourne anticipated two objections. The first is that letting so many different groups and associations thrive might amount to "a policy of drift." In 1916, "drift" has a pejorative meaning primarily because of Lippmann's book *Drift and Mastery*. Bourne also assures his readers that people who favor an absorbent, trans-national country still want "an integrated and disciplined America." "Integrated America" is the title of a major essay that Lippmann had written for *The New Republic* a few months earlier—in fact, it's the one that kicked off his fight with John Reed.

Watching Bourne and Lippmann address the same subject is a chance to trace the differences in their radicalism. In Lippmann's "ideal of Americanism," two concepts are pitted against each other. He wants America to be "a union of people rather than a congeries of groups, provinces, and racial stocks." Bourne shares Lippmann's desire for a union of people, but the point of the trans-national ideal is that people form that union while still belonging to different groups and feeling affinity with separate racial stocks.

It sounds like Bourne is trading in paradoxes, but only because he needed one last piece of his intellectual edifice: the keystone that locks it all together. After a couple of years of mental exertion, he had cracked the puzzle of Josiah Royce's "Beloved Community."

To Royce, communities form when people place their loyalty in something larger than themselves. The "Beloved Community" is a kind of super-elevated union, where all the loyalties flow together and are infused with grace. Bourne warmed to this idea without understanding how it applied to the real world; he complained of "the rocks in my path" when he puzzled over it. But in America, the interplay of different ethnic groups—the process by which various nationalities feed into one another without losing themselves, peaceably giving rise to a single trans-nationality—showed him Royce's ideal in action.

Bourne draws on Royce's idea at the culmination of his essay. It is also, in three ringing sentences, the consummation of Bourne's thought:

> All our idealisms must be those of future social goals in which all can participate, the good life of personality lived in the environment of the Beloved Community. No mere doubtful triumphs of the past, which redound to the glory of only one of our transnationalities, can satisfy us. It must be a future America, on which all can unite, which pulls us irresistibly toward it, as we understand each other more warmly.

Lippmann can contemplate preparedness calmly because it doesn't doom his vision of an integrated America. Bourne doesn't have that luxury. To live up to its trans-national ideal, to help bring about the Beloved Community, the United States has to remain at peace. It can't be equally welcoming to people drawn from Russia and Germany if it's sending its sons to help Russians kill Germans, or vice versa. America must remain aloof from the European war, Bourne believes: "a star wandering between two constellations."

Nor would the end of the war mean that America could begin to embark on foreign military adventures. If trans-nationality is, as Bourne believed, a permanent condition of American life, then peace needs to be, too. That prospect fills him not with dread or suspicion but a vast hope: "It bespeaks poverty of imagination not to be thrilled at the incalculable potentialities of so novel a union of men."

A century after Bourne conceived of this ideal, it's *still* thrilling. And the fact that a thirty-year-old social critic, in a one-off essay, articulated a vision that still seems prophetic after a hundred years' time, confirms that Bourne was right to say that we live in "a world of horizons and audacities."[14]

Bourne likes to live in such a world. It's the only place where someone like him has a chance with Esther Cornell.

Chapter 17

"Everybody pretends to work. Nobody works."[1]

This concise report by Bobby Rogers, a friend and former classmate of Walter Lippmann and John Reed's, confirms every smirking assumption that Lippmann probably holds about Reed's life in the summer of 1916.

Rogers writes to Lippmann from Provincetown, the ramshackle fishing village at the tip of Cape Cod. Reed has traveled there to escape Greenwich Village for a season. But then so has most of Greenwich Village. The artists and the anarchists and the poets and the cranks are there. Everybody is there. In the summer of 1916, Provincetown is Greenwich Village by the sea.

Rogers omits something important in his letter to Lippmann: For Reed, not working that summer *is the point*. He has turned down offers for exotic reporting trips because the kidney ailment that struck him in the Balkans hasn't gone away. A doctor has prescribed quiet rest, in hopes that it will let him avoid a serious, dangerous, extremely painful operation. Alas for that kidney, Reed has as much capacity for quiet rest as a firecracker. By August, he will complain to a friend that he has overdone it yet again, and exhausted himself. He vows that he's really going to relax after that.[2] But then he doesn't.

Since the outbreak of war, Reed has led a life of action: chasing battles, seeking adventures. There is another side to Reed, though: the poet who wrote *A Day in Bohemia,* the showman who dreamed up the Paterson Strike Pageant. It's the side of him that his friends won't let him forget.

"I do wish you'd emit a lot of poetry, or a novel, or something," Rogers had told him a few months earlier. "Now you've had all the earth and the waters around the earth, not to mention New York, and I wish you'd begin to make a painting out of the snapshots."[3]

Jack is dreaming bigger than a painting that summer. He's thinking about *plays.*

In Provincetown, there is a rickety wharf that sticks out into the bay, and at the end of that wharf, there is a majestically rickety shack. It is built of weathered gray planks that look as if they have been scavenged from other rickety shacks. You would need a keen and transfiguring eye, or a very good sense of humor, to see this dilapidated structure as a performing arts venue, but the summering Villagers do just that.

They put a row of lanterns with tin reflectors on the floor, and call them footlights.

They set planks on sawhorses, and call it audience seating.

When the surf bursts through the cracks in the floor, they accept the spray as a picturesque touch.[4]

This unlikely playhouse is where Reed and his merrymaking comrades go a long way toward inventing serious theater in America.

The driving force of this work is one of the few radicals who matches Reed in physical stature and galvanic charisma. George Cram Cook— "Jig" to all who come within the range of his booming voice—is a man of many ill-assembled parts. Like Floyd Dell, his friend and protégé,

Cook has come from Davenport, Iowa, through Chicago, to Manhattan, and then to Cape Cod, accumulating disciples along the way.

"Give it all to me," he says at parties, seizing the punch bowl, "and I guarantee to intoxicate the rest of you."[5]

The previous summer, Cook; his wife, Susan Glaspell; and other residents of Provincetown had been feeling unhappy, stifled, lost. How could they, as creative types, play any role in a country that didn't seem to have room for their values—that seemed to be teetering on the edge of a calamitous war? "Without a truthful effort for a deeper culture, all our large social purposes are impossible," believed the journalist Hutchins Hapgood.

They weren't professional theater people. They might have done a little writing, but they didn't produce plays, or even bother *seeing* plays, feeling alienated from the commercial veneer of Broadway and living at a time when there were only a few viable alternatives: Maurice Browne's Little Theater in Chicago, the Washington Square Players in New York, and the Liberal Club Players, all of which they found wanting for one reason or another.

But Cook and Glaspell had seen the Paterson Strike Pageant, and had come away impressed by Reed's ability to give nonprofessionals a chance to tell their own stories. It helped to inspire them, and their vacationing friends, to perform plays of their own devising in one of their living rooms. The plots were drawn directly from life: one was a send-up of psychoanalysis, the other a satirical depiction of what was very plainly the collapse of Jack's relationship with Mabel. "It was a delightful change from the preoccupation of the War and the poison of 1915," according to Hapgood.[6]

That winter, Cook and Glaspell enlisted collaborators, especially Reed. They were determined to exploit the barely traced possibilities of that tantalizing fish shack, the one with the big back door that opens onto the sea.

They begin to do so on the night of July 14, 1916, when the company presents its first evening of one-act plays. The lineup includes *Freedom,* a comedy written by Reed. Not surprisingly for the man who has spent so much time in jails, it is about prisoners: A handful of men who discover an escape route but can't decide if they should use it. It's a funny, lightly drawn way to explore the same question that Bourne and Lippmann had tackled in their books, and that made Eastman writhe: *What do you do with your freedom when you get it?*

"Life was all of a piece," Susan Glaspell would write, looking back fondly on that summer, "work not separated from play, and we did together what none of us could have done alone."[7]

Jig Cook keeps one eye on the stage, making sure the plays are turning out to his satisfaction, but he's just as focused on the men and women rehearsing them. Cook has long dreamed of a company of artists that would be "the Beloved Community of Life-Givers . . . a whole community, working together, developing unsuspected talents."[8]

A ragtag little theater company on a fishing wharf on the edge of the continent is a small, fleeting way for Americans to begin to realize the vision that Randolph Bourne espoused—a vision that has come to Cook independently. But then what other way *could* it begin?

Doing summer theater with friends doesn't need a justification: A cast party on the grass is its own reward. But Cook and Reed and Glaspell and the rest are doing more than amusing themselves at the end of that wharf.

The success of the first program makes them eager to produce more. But where will they find enough plays? Most of the little companies at that time draw on a mix of European playwrights (Shaw, Galsworthy, Ibsen), and long-established classics. In Provincetown, they refuse to do the same. They want to produce original work by playwrights who are right there in the theater with them, ideally as fellow members of the company. By insisting on that ideal, they crystallize one of the era's great themes: the value and the necessity of free expression.[9]

You can see it in the arts, of course, where young critics have been attacking the idea that a canon should be fixed and universal—that culture is, as Matthew Arnold wrote, "the best that has been thought and said." Randolph Bourne, for one, wants to liberate each listener and reader and audience member to cultivate his or her own taste, making standards dynamic and pragmatic, and not a series of laws handed down by your grandparents' textbooks.

But you can also see it in the suffrage movement, in the rejection of the argument that it is a man's duty, or pleasure, or something, to cast his vote on behalf of what he thinks will be best for the women in his life. Women decline this chivalry. They demand the ballot because it will be, among many other things, a way for them to express their own desires on their own behalf.

And you can see it in the socialists' desire for industrial democracy. Empowering workers would end the economic exploitation that leads to rich and poor, which is reason enough for them to want it. But it would also acknowledge that workers are as capable of discerning their needs in the shop or on the factory floor as they are in the ballot box.

For a theater troupe, this notion that new plays should be an organic part of a company's life sounds good in theory. But the theater is a place where things that sound good in theory often make for a long night (and a short run). The reason why that summer in Provincetown is hailed as the origin of serious theater in America is that their long-shot experiment works immediately. One of the first seeds they plant turns out to be the magic beanstalk.

One day, Susan Glaspell runs into an acquaintance, an anarchist drifter named Terry Carlin. She asks him if he has any plays.

Carlin says he doesn't, but that his friend has a trunk full of them.

Glaspell suggests that his friend bring one of them to their meeting that night.

The friend, who is Eugene O'Neill, obliges. That is how the man hailed at his death as the greatest American playwright who ever lived has his first play produced.

Bound East for Cardiff, a haunting play about a sailor dying at sea, is performed on the rickety pier, surf spraying around the audience's feet, for the first time on July 28, 1916. Reed is in that cast, which would make him a footnote to history if he did nothing else with his life.

Reed falls for O'Neill about as completely as the company falls for his writing. Their personalities don't exactly align: O'Neill is moody and saturnine where Reed is jovial and bighearted (for example, on a trip to Central America, O'Neill had called the locals "human maggots" and worse; Reed would have picked a fight on their behalf).[10] But what they share runs deep. Both are downwardly mobile sons of prosperous fathers, both are Harvard boys who would sooner tramp through a godforsaken seaport than preen in Cambridge. And they both love the same woman.

The previous fall, after his difficult trip to eastern Europe, Reed had returned to Portland to visit his mother. There he found—or, more precisely, was found by—Louise Bryant. Small, pretty, quick-witted, and very unhappy in her marriage to a dentist, she yearned for just the kind of life that Reed was leading. She is the first woman Reed loves without reservation.

In Provincetown, Louise and Jack both write plays for the company. Both snap naked pictures on the dunes. Both clatter away at their typewriters, for Bryant is a working writer, too. And though Louise seems as happy with Jack as he is with her, she can't stay away from O'Neill. They begin an affair.

Of the two of them, O'Neill seems more torn about the affair than Bryant does. She tells him that Reed's kidney trouble has been forcing them to live chastely, as brother and sister. O'Neill believes her, or pretends to. He likes his new friend Jack, but he is overcome with desire for Louise. "When that girl touches me with the tip of her little finger, it's like a flame," he tells Carlin.[11]

In Provincetown they have indeed formed a Beloved Community, though some are more beloved than others.

The sun sets earlier, and summer is waning, and the men and women of the company face a dilemma. Has it been a summer lark, a hobby they'll pick up again next year? Or is it the seed of something that could survive in New York?

They don't have any money, Glaspell reminds her husband. They don't have a theater. They don't even have plays.[12]

"Jack Reed thinks we can make it go," Cook replies, as if that's all that needs to be said.[13]

In early September, the participants meet to hash it out. If they're going to take their work back to New York, they will need the trappings of a proper company. A four-person committee is delegated to go off, draft a constitution, and present it for ratification the following night. Cook and Reed are obvious choices for the first two seats on that committee. The actor Frederick Burt is the third, because it's worth having one actual theatrical professional involved in forming a theater company.

The fourth is Max Eastman.

He hasn't thrown himself into the project that summer as whole-heartedly as Reed, or his wife, Ida Rauh, who flashes a real and formi-dable talent when she gets onstage. But he has done his bit. He has appeared in a play. And he has been part of the social milieu, which is nearly as important.

Years later, when researchers seek to learn more about the origins of the Provincetown Players (which is what the company calls itself), Eastman will be modest about his role. He will say that during that twenty-four hours of constitution writing, his sole contribution had been to read the draft that Jack showed him and say, "I think that's swell!"[14] But when the company reassembles on the night of September 5, and Jack reads the draft constitution to the group, Max must feel a powerful sense of déjà vu.

The company's primary objective, Reed says, is to "encourage the writing of American plays of real artistic, literary, and dramatic—as op-posed to Broadway—merit." It sounds just like the manifesto that Reed and Eastman wrote for *The Masses*, about publishing a magazine that will print what is too naked or true for a moneymaking press.

Reed says that decisions about which plays to produce would be made collectively by the members, who will exercise "essential demo-cratic control" over artistic choices. And this sounds like *The Masses*, too, with its raucous collective mode of publication.

Reed says that an author of a play will have the freedom to stage it "without hindrance according to his own ideas," which draws a huge cheer from the crowd. And Eastman might feel a little pang, because Reed has expressed the exact view that sparked the artists' rebellion against him earlier that year.

The same radicals, pursuing the same dreams, facing the same problems: *The Masses* and the Provincetown Players are, at heart, twin children of the zeitgeist. Both explicitly reject the limiting, falsifying effects of commercial production. Both see a true and honest reckoning with the facts of American life as a step toward liberation. Both proceed not with doggedness, but with a light heart. There is, in both, a lively spirit of play.

Edna Kenton, one of the stalwarts of the group, will later call the company "a democratic experiment begun in such childlike good faith."[15] Eastman might wince at that, too. He still hasn't recovered from what John Sloan and the other rebel artists had taught him about the way such experiments often end.

Still: When the future is put to a vote on the wharf that night, he raises his hand like all the rest.

The Provincetown Players descend on New York "with a fierce contempt for Broadway in our hearts, blaspheming the Tired Business Man," according to the announcement drafted by Reed. Jig Cook secures space at 133 Macdougal Street, around the corner from Washington Square Park. Reed writes a motto for the façade: "Here Pegasus was hitched."[16]

Reed is on the executive committee. So are Bryant and Dell. They meet with the rest of the regulars every week in Reed and Bryant's apartment. But Eastman can't keep playing with them. *The Masses* pulls him back in. It always pulls him back in. There is always too much to do, never enough time, never enough money.

That fall, he really thinks the end has come. With prices going up, he sees no way to scrape together the money to keep publishing—and though part of him wants to be free of the obligation, the rest of him looks for a solution. He turns the back cover into a plea for help:

> If You Were Editing a Magazine_____
> that was
> three leaps ahead of its printing bill
> two leaps ahead of its paper bill and
> one leap ahead of its enemies who want to suppress it
> You'd admit that it was a joyful life though hectic.[17]

It brings in enough to keep the presses running, for a little while, at least. But his personal obstructions remain. That fall, he is walking on Thirty-fourth Street when he sees, coming his way, under a little Japanese umbrella, the most beautiful woman in the world. He turns on his heel, catches up to her, walks alongside her, but doesn't say a word—can't work up the nerve to say a word.

A few weeks later, amid thunderous recriminations, he and Ida have one last fight, and make their split bitterly, irrevocably final.

Eastman's fellow radicals—at the magazine, at the theater—can see him struggling. They know how important *The Masses* is, and know the toll it takes on him to keep it alive. Few perceive it more clearly than Susan Glaspell, whose plays in those years are just as good as O'Neill's. She writes a one-act about the editor of a radical magazine trying to decide, in the face of all sorts of frustrations, whether it's worth it to press on. *The People,* the fictional magazine in her play, is clearly patterned on *The Masses.* But it's just as clearly inspired by the Provincetown Players, which faces the same anxieties about raising money, finding writers, keeping a staff going.

When Glaspell's play has its world premiere in that first season on Macdougal Street, the role based on Max Eastman, the editor of the magazine, is played by Jig Cook, the leader of the theater. For one night, the overlap between the political radicals and the cultural radicals—their hopes and their struggles—is perfect.

Reed appreciates what Eastman is doing, too. One day, he calls Max and asks if he could dedicate a book of poems to him.

Max, flustered and abashed, stammers out a yes.

Jack calls his tribute "A Dedication (To Max Eastman)." It's just as honest, just as clear a reflection of their values, as anything staged by their theater company or published in their magazine. It reads, in part:

There was a man who, loving quiet beauty best,
Yet could not rest
For the harsh moaning of unhappy mankind,
Fettered and blind—
Too driven to know beauty and too hungry-tired
To be inspired.
From his high-windy-peaceful hill, he stumbled down
Into the town,
With a child's eyes, clear bitterness, and silver scorn
Of the outworn
And cruel mastery of life by senile death;
And with his breath
Fanned up the noble fires that smoulder in the breast
Of the oppressed.
What guerdon, to forswear for dust and smoke and this
The high-souled bliss
Of poets in walled gardens, finely growing old.
Serene and cold?
A vision of new splendor in the human scheme—
A god-like dream—
And a new lilt of happy trumpets in the strange
Clangor of Change!

Max, astonished, thinks it is one of Jack's best poems. And he feels sure that he doesn't deserve it.[18]

Chapter 18

The achievements of American culture and politics and thought that summer aren't coordinated—there is no plan. But they all tend in the same direction, and they all have the same effect: the vitalization of American democracy.

The creation of the Woman's Party brings about some of what the suffrage movement had long struggled to achieve. In fighting to become full citizens, women are becoming more fully citizens. It gives them new authority, new stature, a new way to exercise agency within the political system. Alice Paul proves that they can play the game with as much savvy as the men do, despite having a fraction of their power.

For the Provincetown Players—and for its magazine sibling, *The Masses*—new plays and new stories and new poems and new cartoons, freed from commercial pressure, given the widest latitude this side of the censor, are all ways to tell the truth. If you take a pragmatic view of democracy—that it is the best form of government because the collected wisdom of the entire community gives us our best chance of finding the good life—then every one of those expressions is another little step toward progress. Each one is another chance to understand people more fully. Each one increases the odds that America will get it right.

For Bourne, the trans-national ideal, the fruit of years of mental struggle, opens up a new prospect for American life. He is not merely saying that different ethnic groups should be allowed to coexist: He is saying that the friendly interplay of those groups will create something greater than the sum of its parts. The point isn't that every tree deserves a share of sunlight; it's that one day the branches will link and form a canopy, and a thriving new environment will be formed—he calls it the Beloved Community.

There is no coordination and there is no plan, but there is one vision that unites all these pursuits: the radical democracy of Walt Whitman. He saw more clearly than any other American that democracy is more than a procedure for setting tax rates and counting votes. He grasped its beautiful essential paradox. Democracy sets each man and woman free to live independently, but it also does the opposite, giving rise to "adhesiveness or love, that fuses, ties, and aggregates, making the races comrades, and fraternizing all." All the breakthroughs of that summer reflect this dual action. They liberate the individual in the interest of strengthening the community, even as they treat communal action as the surest route to individual fulfillment. Democracy is the star they're all trying to reach, and democracy is the rocket that gets them there.

Americans celebrate liberty, but we're shaky on fraternity. We love our individual freedom, but tend to forget the collective action that secured it, and is required to sustain it. The founders, who needed all their ingenuity to make thirteen fractious colonies fight together to drive out the British, suspected we would do this, which is why they worked so hard to create a sense of union. The young radicals are less explicit than their revolutionary predecessors were, but their achievements that summer teach the same lesson. It is, in fact, the essential truth of the American experience, from 1776 to their time to ours: *Nobody gets free alone.*

There are many interesting implications of this democratic summer. We could say more. But an actual exercise of democracy is looming: It's time to pick a president.

The 1912 race had been taxing for Woodrow Wilson: a newcomer, with a suspiciously bookish background, trying to sell himself to a country that hadn't elected a Democratic president in a generation. To win, he had to defeat a sitting president and that president's predecessor, who happened to be the most popular man in America.

The 1916 race will be harder.

Last time, Roosevelt's third-party candidacy had siphoned four million votes out of the Republican column. Now that the Progressive Party has disintegrated, those votes are up for grabs, and the election might hinge on whether progressives choose Wilson or the Republican nominee, Charles Evans Hughes. Wilson knows that he must find ways to woo these reform-minded voters. These voters who care about reining in big business. Voters who want to stay out of war. Persuadable voters. Voters who edit magazines.

"So, you've come to look me over," the president says, inviting Walter Lippmann into his office.

Lippmann had requested the interview, so he has brought a sheaf of questions. Wilson doesn't let him use them.

"Let me show you the inside of my mind," he says, embarking on a long, erudite, and very seductive tour of the pressing issues of the day.[1]

Lippmann is flattered to be courted by the president—is he made of steel?—but he is still not sure. He suspects Wilson of harboring the "village view of life" that he finds so demoralizing. But he suspects it less and less after Wilson's "family of nations" address and the dazzling array of progressive legislation that passes in the fall: a restriction on child labor; the Adamson Act, which sets an eight-hour workday on railroads; and the Revenue Act of 1916, which pays for preparedness by making the income tax more progressive, implementing the first-ever estate tax, and levying an excess-profits tax on munitions manufacturers. Accompanied by Bourne, he travels to Shadow Lawn, the summer White House, and hears Wilson's formal acceptance of his party's nomination—a rousing speech that declares the end of protectionism, provincialism, and the narrow-bounded era of "Little Americanism."

"We are Americans for Big America," the president proclaims.[2]

"I have come around completely to Wilson," Lippmann tells a friend.[3]

In October, Lippmann goes public with his support for the former object of his ire. The president has grown "from a laissez-faire Democrat into a constructive nationalist," he writes. Before Wilson, the Democrats were reactionary and parochial; now they are "the only party which at this moment is national in scope, liberal in purpose, and effective in action."[4] In other words, the only party that could realize Lippmann's desire for an integrated America.

He doesn't stop there. He persuades Herbert Croly, who thought even less of Wilson than Lippmann had, to support the president. Then he goes further still: He hits the campaign trail.

Amos Pinchot, one of the country's leading progressives, organizes a group of high-profile independents to make speeches for the president. The "Wilson Volunteers" fan out to address crowds all over New York State. Lippmann does his part, climbing on the back of a truck to make pro-Wilson speeches at factories, foundries, and other places where votes might be won.[5]

They know they're unlikely to swing the reliably Republican state to Wilson, but their prominence means the mere existence of the group will draw a lot of attention, especially among the progressives that Wilson needs to woo.

The announcement of the group's formation gets picked up in major newspapers. It makes its case for Wilson by quoting Lippmann's endorsement.[6]

In Chicago, Alice Paul struggles to delete votes from Wilson's column faster than Lippmann and other surrogates can add them. The Woman's Party campaign is unfolding "like a snowball rolling down a hill," boasts *The Suffragist*.[7]

That is not entirely true. In the crucial weeks of October, a lack of staff and money persists. She uses every trick she has learned in the past four years to stretch her resources across twelve large states, and to stretch her own energies across too many jobs to count. "I am in despair," she tells a confidante.[8]

One gray, grim day, a desire to have the biggest show of strength possible leads her to pick up a sign and stand on a Chicago sidewalk.

When Wilson's car pulls up at the Auditorium, the site of his campaign rally, Paul and a hundred other suffragists are waiting for him. They hold up signs that say "Wilson is against women" and "Wilson prevented the passage of the suffrage amendment" and "President Wilson—how long do you advise us to wait?"

(This last one is a reference to his address to the NAWSA convention in Atlantic City a few weeks earlier, at which he had expressed a great many handsome sentiments about suffrage without committing himself to doing anything at all. Catt found it encouraging; Paul didn't care.)

When the president steps out of his car, a huge crowd of partisans cheer. He waves and steps into the Auditorium.

No sooner does the door close behind him than those happy partisans wheel on Paul and the other protesters. With cries of "Shame!" and "Disgrace!" and "Get the banners!" they attack.

The suffragists are struck, knocked down, trampled. They limp back to headquarters.

Paul is not displeased. She will wring good press out of it.

Mainly she is pinning her hopes on women in the West, which means pinning them on Inez Milholland Boissevain. Paul had prevailed on her to be the face of the Woman's Party, carrying a plea from women of the eastern states to the women of the western states. Inez draws big crowds because she is one of the most beautiful women in the country, and because she is a vibrant, forceful speaker.

"If women don't respect themselves, no one else will," she tells an overflow crowd in Boise. "Don't dare to say that you are free until all women are free."[9]

Paul intends to exploit Inez to the fullest. There is nothing reprehensible about it: Paul needs to exploit every single resource she has. Hasn't she been exploiting herself most of all?

She crafts an itinerary that calls for Inez to make fifty speeches in thirty days, on a trip covering twelve thousand miles.

Suffragists who have less grueling assignments have begun to break down because of the stress, the difficult conditions. Anxious telegrams start reaching Paul from California.

Inez has hit her limit. She has been giving speeches to crowds of hundreds or more than a thousand people—without amplification—battling heat, cold, humidity, altitude. There's no time to eat and no way to sleep and too many painkillers.[10] It's her throat, her teeth, the way her heart keeps skittering.

On the morning of October 23, doctors examine her in Santa Barbara and are alarmed by what they find. They present her with a couple of stern options.

Inez doesn't decide; she asks Alice Paul what to do.

Should she cancel the tour so she can return for an operation on her tonsils? Or should she rest there and hope to recover?

Paul doesn't like this one bit. She agrees to limit the amount of time that Inez needs to spend onstage, but she needs her to keep showing up. She wires back: CALAMITY FOR YOU ABANDON TOUR.[11]

Inez tries her best to do what Paul wants. That night, she takes the stage at Blanchard Hall in Los Angeles, a thousand people watching.[12]

"President Wilson, how long must this go on?" she demands. "Let me repeat: We are not putting our faith in any man or in any party but in the women voters of the West."[13]

Then she collapses at center stage.[14]

As Inez is carried offstage, Beulah Amidon, the young Columbia grad who had broken Randolph Bourne's heart the year before, vamps until she recovers.

Inez remains seated for the rest of the speech, looking pale and drawn, the crowd cheering her.

Afterward, in a Los Angeles hospital, she is too weak to lift her head from the pillow. Paul scrambles to find speakers for the next few days, anticipating that Inez will get back on her feet. *She needs her to get back on her feet.*

For the grand finale of the tour, Paul plans to subvert Wilson's campaign message, "He kept us out of war." The closing message of the Woman's Party will be "He kept us out of suffrage!"[15] She still expects Inez to deliver it.

It is going to be very close. Wilson and Hughes are emptying every cupboard in search of votes.

There is one more place to look.

The 1912 election wasn't a three-way race—it was a *four*-way race. The socialist candidate, Eugene Debs, polled 6 percent. Six percent is nine hundred thousand votes. That could decide a close race, assuming all those voters don't stick with the socialist line, which seems like a fair assumption. There is no way that nine hundred thousand Americans will be voting for the feckless Allan Benson.

That is where Max Eastman comes in.

In *The Masses,* he writes that Democrats and Republicans both represent the forces of capitalism, but there is a crucial difference between them—one that emerged on the day he visited Wilson at the White House and heard the preview of his "family of nations" idea: "It is militarism against democratic good sense. Brassy nationalism against the beginnings of international sympathy and union."[16]

He writes a letter for the Woodrow Wilson Independent League, which shares it widely.

"I would rather see Woodrow Wilson elected than Charles Hughes because Wilson aggressively believes not only in keeping out of war, but in organizing the nations of the world to prevent war," he writes. "His official endorsement of propaganda for international federation in the interest of peace is the most important step that any President of the United States has taken towards civilizing the world since Lincoln."[17]

Eastman's fellow socialists attack him for endorsing a Democrat, flooding him with what he mocks as "letters of excommunication from keepers of the sacred dogmas."[18] Eastman fires back at his critics—including at least one contributor to *The Masses*, who attacked him in his own magazine—by saying the Socialist Party needs to shed "this sectarian dogmatism, this doctrinaire, *index expurgatorius* mode of thinking."

"Let us try to use our brains freely, love progress more than a party, allow ourselves the natural emotions of our species, and see if we can get ready to play a human part in the actual complex flow of events," he writes.[19]

The socialists have one more surprise coming. Socialist Party leaders contact John Reed asking him to sign a letter of support for Benson.

Reed refuses.

"I am going to vote for Wilson," he says, "because the only real principles he has (few enough) are on our side, and he can be reached, and influenced. And no one else can. I'm not a believer in anything lasting coming out of purely political action; but I don't want this country to become a hell for the next four years."

Reed adds that he has never voted for a president before.[20]

It's not clear if it will be enough.

When the polls open on November 7, 1916, the bookies call Wilson a slight underdog. He wins the southern states, sometimes with more than 90 percent of the vote. The big states of the Northeast go overwhelmingly for Hughes.

As night falls, thousands of New Yorkers gather in Times Square to learn who has prevailed. (Max and Jack aren't among them—they're at the theater on Macdougal Street, acting.)[21] Colored lights have been installed on the roof of the *New York Times* building to signal the victor.

Red means that Hughes has won; white indicates Wilson.[22]

The president and his family are at Shadow Lawn, playing Twenty Questions, when the phone rings. It is ten o'clock. Somebody is calling from New York.

The light has come on, and it is red.[23]

Wilson absorbs the news, hangs up the phone. He thinks about conceding, but decides to drink a glass of milk and go to bed.

"I might stay longer," he tells his family, "but you are all so blue."[24]

By sunrise, the outcome does not seem so certain. One state after another declares a victor without putting either candidate over the top. Eventually only California remains. Some of its ballots arrive slowly, over mountains, through snow, on horse-drawn carts. These votes will decide the presidency.

But how will California decide, and what will it mean? If Hughes wins, Paul will claim that the state's female voters deserve the credit.

For Eastman, a Wilson victory would mean something new and promising in American life: the coming to power of a "state capitalistic social reform party." It's not as revolutionary as he would like, but it still represents a genuine counterweight to plutocracy.[25] He is excited about its possibilities even though—split-minded, second-guessing, self-hijacking Max—he voted for Benson!

But in California, the final vote might rest on something having very little to do with ideals. Back in August, Hughes had come to Long Beach on a campaign swing. He happened to stay at the same hotel as Hiram Johnson, the governor. Johnson was a prominent progressive—Roosevelt's running mate in 1912—exactly the kind of figure that Hughes needed in his corner. So Johnson expected a courtesy call. Only, Hughes didn't make a call. He left Long Beach without realizing that Johnson was even there. The papers reported it as a snub. It hurt his chances, though nobody could be sure how much. Could it really determine the whole election?

Wednesday comes and goes, and there's still no winner. On Thursday the tension ratchets higher. Lippmann hovers at Democratic National Headquarters, one anxious Wilson partisan among many. It is past eleven o'clock that night when news comes zipping across the continent.

Out of nearly a million votes cast in California, the margin is 3,773 votes—less than four-tenths of 1 percent, about one vote per election precinct. It is an infinitesimal difference, but enough to reelect Wilson.

The Democrats at headquarters scream and cheer. They jump up and down, they jump on desks, they give speeches that nobody hears. (Many haven't slept in two days.) Lippmann joins the celebration—and why shouldn't he, having done his bit for victory?

Somehow, from somewhere, a marching band appears. As it blares, a committeeman from Pennsylvania kisses Lippmann in his delirium.[26]

Chapter 19

For the young radicals, a coda follows the climax of Wilson's reelection. Confident that peace and progress are going to continue, they start to build on the extraordinary advances of 1916.

Two weeks after the election, John Reed lies in a Baltimore hospital, having accepted the inevitable. He overexerted himself in the theater when he was supposed to rest. Now his ailing kidney needs to come out.

Louise Bryant waits with him. She has come down from New York to keep Jack's spirits up while the doctors prepare to operate.

So has Walter Lippmann. Since their tentative reconciliation earlier in the year, their friendship seems to have rekindled. Maybe it was the experience of sharing the same side in the presidential race, and having that side win. Or maybe it's the fact that a nephrectomy is, in 1916, a potentially deadly procedure—the kind of danger that puts things in their right perspective.

Jack spends a full month recovering, or trying to. The letters he sends to Louise, who has returned to New York, only hint at his overwhelming pain. He develops an infection that requires a fresh incision; the doctors jam a seven-inch-long, half-inch-thick rubber hose into his wound so it drains. When the pain allows him to work, he nibbles at a play. In and out of his fevers, he dreams about the future that's almost here.

All his life, he has fantasized about seeing the Far East. Now he makes plans to do it. He wants to see Korea, India, Japan. He wants to sail up the Yangtze to Tibet.[1]

Reed intends to make the trip as a roving foreign correspondent for *Metropolitan*, where his writing talent and his charm have let him back into the editor's good graces. The magazine begins to run ads for his forthcoming coverage of China: "He will hold up the mirror to this mysterious and romantic country, and we shall see its teeming millions and the big forces at work there."[2]

His wife will go with him. A few days before coming to Baltimore, Jack and Louise had gotten married, without making any great fuss or letting more than a few people know. He loves her, loves being married to her, even wants to have children with her. But her recent letters from New York refer to some illness, some ill-defined trouble with her "insides." Lying there in Baltimore, he hates the thought that she is sick.

With the benefit of all the circumstantial information, it seems that Bryant could have been suffering the complications from an abortion. But Reed, ailing in Baltimore, doesn't have that information. Nor does he know that on the day she returned to their apartment in New York, Eugene O'Neill had moved in.

Jack looks forward to getting well. Louise will get well, too. And then they'll resign their places on the executive committee of the Provincetown Players, which they'll regret, but the adventure of a lifetime is calling them both.[3] Soon they'll be on the other side of the world, far away from the war, and their sickbeds, and Eugene O'Neill.

Lippmann takes a trip of his own after leaving Baltimore—one that's just as dramatic, in its way, as the one Reed is planning.

On December 12, 1916, he goes to the White House for a state dinner. Considering the modest size of the affair—only eighty attendees, including cabinet officials, family members, essential donors to the campaign—the mere fact of his invitation reflects how he is coming up in the world.

His vision of "Integrated America" is looking up, too. After the election, the editors of *The New Republic* say that Wilson "has really been creating a new party." He has steered Democrats away from their reliance on states' rights, making them a party of progressive reform. In fact, the Democrats maintain control of the closely divided House only with the support of the chamber's handful of Progressive and Socialist members. Wilson will be leading a coalition of the left. "Every circumstance connected with the election combines to give the work of reorganization increasing authority and momentum," the editors write. In other words, he has new and more powerful tools "to pull the American nation together."[4]

It would be a lively subject of conversation at the dinner, except that just before the president's guests arrive, news from Europe intrudes. Washington learns that Berlin is making an offer of peace.

Lippmann takes one official by the elbow, lets another whisper in his ear. He watches history ripple through the room—maybe the most powerful room in the world. Nobody seems inclined to accept the German offer. In fact, it might be a trap.

"We've got to stop it before we're pulled in," the president tells Lippmann.[5]

We?

Lippmann is young, but he has proven himself. Not just with his campaign speeches, but also the way he had marshaled so much support for Louis Brandeis when the president nominated him to the Supreme Court.

The most powerful men in the country like him. And he likes them. Wilson's reelection means they will spend the next four years together. There is no telling what they might do.

"I am good friends with my father," says Prince Hal after he quits the tavern and joins the king, "and may do anything."

Randolph Bourne is surprised to find Madison so agitated. He has been invited to give a speech on education at the University of Wisconsin, only to learn that a scandal is splitting the even-tempered campus in two.

The scandal is Max Eastman. On the January day that Bourne arrives, Eastman had been scheduled to address a student group on "The Hope of Democracy"—that is, socialism. University officials, citing a rarely enforced rule against propaganda on campus, deny him the use of any lecture hall.[6] Outraged students and assorted local socialists think, correctly, that Eastman is being censored because of his politics. Ultimately Max gives his speech off campus, reaping far more attention than he would have received otherwise.

The commotion allows the two visiting New Yorkers, Eastman and Bourne, to spend a few days together.

"I like him," Bourne says. "His tempo seems even slower than mine."

What seems odd—what seems extraordinarily unlikely—is that Bourne and Eastman didn't realize that sooner. Bourne describes those few days in Madison as "my first chance to get acquainted with [Eastman], our Village lives never having crossed."[7]

They are both protégés of John Dewey. They live a few blocks apart in Greenwich Village—which is no bigger than an actual village. They have many friends in common. Whatever prevented it from happening sooner, their encounter in Madison belatedly reveals what Bourne calls "the firm bond of a common enemy."[8] More than one, actually. They oppose militarism, patriotism, capitalism—anything that interferes with a more equitable socialistic society, anything that would preclude the kind of pluralism they desire.

Also, they are both in love with actresses.

A few weeks before leaving New York, Eastman had presided over the annual Masses Ball, a big fundraising party. He had danced with a beautiful brunette named Florence Deshon. She had given him her phone number, and, in spite of his natural timidity, he had used it.

He fell in love quickly and so did she. Many of his neurotic hang-ups dissolved on their first night together. Only later did he realize that she was, incredibly, the very beautiful woman he had seen walking on Thirty-fourth Street.

"My life began in January 1917!" he wrote in his diary.[9]

Bourne's path to love was longer, lonelier, more difficult. "Having led the experimental life, and sifted and sorted, I feel that I know now exactly what I want," he had told a friend in November. "Love, fame, joy in work, would bring, perhaps, the resources for the freedom that I want to move about and yet have a center and a hearth." Of all his interwoven problems, he thought the key problem was love, and his lack of it "the one impediment to blossoming."[10]

The day after sending that letter, he had written to Esther Cornell, beautiful object of his summer desire. Once again he trusted music to say what he couldn't, and took her to the symphony. That afternoon, she told him how much she cared for him. It turned his life upside down.

He wrote to her a few days later, still reeling.

I don't know whether to enjoy the full implications of what you told me Sunday. It would be so easy for me to delude myself into thinking that you cared for me more constantly than you do, and really even imagined marrying me. When I come to my senses it seems grotesque of me to imagine your being willing.

All my life I have alternated delusions of greatness with the most cowering and abject feeling of worthlessness. I turn cold when I think that someday you might find me out and drive me into the latter state again.

Oh, what an adventure it would be to try to get the most out of life together![11]

Bourne consulted a doctor in 1916 because he feared he might still be carrying the germs that had ravaged his spine when he was younger. He didn't want to pass them on to a lover—or a child.[12]

The memorial for Inez Milholland Boissevain is held on Christmas Day 1916. The Congressional Union, exerting all its influence, has secured the use of the National Statuary Hall at the United States Capitol. The high vaulted chamber is filled with the flags and pennants of the suffrage cause—the one for which Inez gave her life, her eulogists will say.[13]

Alice Paul had thought that Inez would rally. She expected her to rally, *needed* her to rally. But once Inez entered the hospital in Los Angeles, she never left. She had anemia, much worse than anybody realized. Her husband rushed to her side, as did her parents. Then came the leave-takings, brave last words, and a flag-draped coffin heading east. She was thirty years old.

What did she die for? Paul says it was to secure a victory, but then she always says that.

The numbers do not tell a clear story. Women's votes are counted separately from men's only in Illinois, where Hughes does indeed do better than Wilson among women, and where he wins the state outright. But Wilson wins ten of the eleven other states where the Woman's Party had campaigned against him. Far from defeating him, women seem to have been the key to his triumph.

The meaning of the election, and of their friend's martyrdom (for Paul wastes no time in decreeing Inez a martyr, her face tragic and beautiful on the cover of *The Suffragist*), lies tautologically in what happens next. Have their labors and arguments and their sacrifices gotten through to the Democrats? As ever, only one Democrat really counts.

On January 9, 1917, President Wilson grants an audience to a delegation of three hundred suffragists who wish to present him with a memorial to their late friend. He expects sorrow, and there is sorrow. But there is also resentment, indignation, bitterness, and, as an editorial in *The Suffragist* puts it, "anger against the people in high places whose opposition to justice makes such a sacrifice necessary."[14]

Instead of one brief speech, Wilson hears several.[15] Instead of a tribute to a brave fallen woman, he gets a dressing-down. The theme of the suffragists' speeches is that his administration is to blame for Inez's death, and the deaths of other women that are sure to follow hers.

Wilson, reeling, reiterates his position as both a private citizen and a party leader. Then—a volcano rumbling—he lectures his guests about the role of political parties in America.

Exhausted, depleted, insulted, patronized, the suffragists walk back to headquarters. Alice Paul is waiting for them. For some time now she has been working on a plan with her closest advisers. She cedes the floor to Harriot Stanton Blatch, who now presents Paul's plan, in dramatic fashion, to the incensed women.

"We can't organize bigger and more influential deputations," she says. "We can't organize bigger processions. We can't, women, do anything more in that line. We have got to take a new departure. We have got to keep the question before him all the time. We have got to begin and begin immediately."[16]

The next morning, twelve women walk out of Congressional Union headquarters, position themselves outside the White House gates, and raise signs and banners inscribed with the words Inez had spoken just before her collapse: "Mr. President! How long must women wait for liberty?"

The women return to the White House the next day, and the day after that, and vow to keep returning until Congress approves the suffrage amendment. The "silent sentinels" incite a level of anger hard to imagine today. But then nobody had picketed the White House before, let alone a bunch of women who don't know their place.

"Iron-jawed angels," one man calls them.[17] He is an anti-suffrage Democrat, so he must have intended it as an insult. In fact, he could hardly have chosen a more complimentary way to describe women who are resolutely playing what they think might be the last card they have left.

———

After all the leaps forward in American life in the past few months, the biggest leap is still to come. The interlude that had begun with a speech by Woodrow Wilson, about his "family of nations," ends with one, too. The era is rising to its culmination.

At noon on January 22, 1917, the vice president informs the Senate that the president will arrive in exactly one hour to deliver an address. As if the short notice doesn't make the speech dramatic enough, Wilson is also breaking a precedent. The last president to address the Senate in person was George Washington.

Wilson tells his audience that a month earlier, he had sent a note to belligerents on both sides of the war, asking under what terms they would make peace. Those responses let him know that it is time to think about what will come after the war ends.

Evoking his "family of nations" speech, he says that the war must yield "some definite concert of power which will make it virtually impossible that any such catastrophe should ever overwhelm us again." He wishes to state the conditions under which the United States will take part in that concert.

Americans cannot accept an international order that is merely a new balance of power, he says. "There must be, not a balance of power, but a community of power; not organized rivalries, but an organized common peace." And that cannot be achieved if one side stands over the devastated remains of the other. The only peace worth having, he says, is a peace among equals—"a peace without victory."

The equality that serves as the basis for this peace, he says, must be "an equality of rights": Protection must be given to small states as well as large, weak as well as strong. This peace must be based on the principle of "a common participation in a common benefit." Within each state, he envisions democratic values prevailing. "No peace can last, or ought to last, which does not recognize and accept the principle that governments derive all their just powers from the consent of the governed," he says.

Wilson knows that for 120 years, the official philosophy of American foreign policy had been to avoid "entangling alliances." So he makes a deft reversal. He says that his proposal is an *antidote* to such an alliance, for it will create a concord among all the states. Far from breaking with American tradition, it is "a fulfillment, rather, of all that we have professed or striven for."

"These are American principles, American policies," he says. "We could stand for no others."

The effect of the speech is sensational. One reporter says that friends and opponents alike call it "one of the most startling declarations of policy ever enunciated in the history of the United States."[18] In New York, Herbert Croly rushes to the home of Colonel House, and calls it "the greatest event of his own life."[19]

(*The New Republic* had published an editorial by Lippmann a few weeks earlier under the headline "Peace Without Victory." Though Lippmann had used the term in a different way, it didn't stop Wilson, suave as ever, from thanking Croly for publishing something that "served to strengthen and clarify my own thought not a little.")

Lippmann tells Colonel House that the more he thinks about the speech, the more he likes it. Bourne thinks it "the most hopeful possible basis for the covenant of nations." Eastman offers the most fulsome defense of Wilson's vision: "I believe the histories of all the nations of the world will hold a venerated record of President Wilson's address." A peace like the one Wilson describes is, he believes, "the one hope of preserving that struggle for a new civilization which we call Socialism, or Syndicalism, or the Social Revolution, or the Labor Struggle, from the continual corruption of militarism, and the ravaging setback of patriotic war."[20]

What the president has done, with almost every point he has made, is to extend the radical spirit of that year to the field of world affairs. He places his faith in democracy as both an instrument of liberation and a step toward common action; he insists on universal equality; he presents American principles as open, tolerant, accepting. He even shows concern for whose voice is heard. At a time when much of the world's population lives in autocracies or European colonies, he says he wants to express the wish of "the silent mass of mankind everywhere who have as yet had no place or opportunity to speak their real hearts out concerning the death and ruin they see to have come already upon the persons and the homes they hold most dear."

Afterward one of Wilson's detractors will say, "The president thinks he is the president of the whole world." What's really thrilling about the "peace without victory" address is that, for the first time in history, that is precisely what he is.

"I have said what everybody has been longing for but has thought impossible," the president tells a senator on his way out of the chamber. "Now it appears to be possible."

It will appear so for exactly nine days.

On February 1, 1917, the German ambassador informs his American counterpart that the kaiser's navy will resume unrestricted submarine warfare, sinking any ship, anywhere, at any time, without warning.

The decision isn't meant as a rebuke of Wilson's speech. In fact, Germany's military leaders had settled this policy weeks earlier, the same day that Wilson faced the suffragists. They are gambling that they can starve Britain into submission before the United States can retaliate.

The president has delivered a ringing statement of some of the best American values. He is pointing the way toward a future in which America will never face the kind of war that is ravaging Europe, and all the barbarity that war provokes. It is a way to guide the world without partaking in its suffering. It is a chance to realize the young radicals' most ardent dreams.

It sounds so thrilling and forward-looking—an ideal to cap all the other ideals—but he is dreaming of a future that is already gone.

IV. THE REAL AND THE IDEAL

(1917–18)

There is life; and there, a step away, is death. There is the only kind of beauty there ever was. There is the old human struggle and its fruits together. There is the text and the sermon, the real and the ideal in one.

—WILLIAM JAMES

Chapter 20

Starting out young and hopeful. Mustering your courage, leaping into the stream.

Confident of success, taking the measure of things as they are, picturing things as they should be. Conceiving of the concrete steps you (and only you, equipped and situated as you are) might take, so that the real might veer closer to your ideal.

Feeling sure that progress—that deliverance—is a question of "when" and no longer of "if"; that freedom and equality are within reach, are coming in the future, and not the far-off millennial future, either.

Noting, with relief, that the chaos and violence of the world isn't spoiling your dream; that somehow, on the contrary, the nation is being spurred to even quicker progress, even more rapid realization of its promise.

Then one day discovering that you have been wrong about nearly everything, wrong all along.

Grappling now with the possibility that the future might be something to fear, not to desire, that the feeling of headlong motion has been propelling you, unsuspecting young citizen of a naïve young republic, into terrible danger.

Fretting now about how quickly time is flying. Dreading the thought of what tomorrow might bring.

Trying to stop before it's too late.

Who doesn't know this feeling? The world, even now, keeps finding fresh ways to disabuse its dreamers. But rarely does the experience seem as bewildering, or as sudden, as it does to the young radicals of 1917.

From the distance of a hundred years, it might seem that Germany's declaration of unrestricted submarine warfare led to an immediate American response. It didn't. A gap divides the two events—a chance for thinking and rethinking. Americans have a lot to learn in 1917, but they have already discovered that the mind can cover a lot of ground in a brief interval, even in the half heartbeat between the screech of tires and the smash of metal and glass.

The young radicals don't know it, but their interval is sixty-one days.

There are fifty-seven days to go when Randolph Bourne and Max Eastman put their newly forged friendship to work. As two leaders of the Committee for Democratic Control, they publish open letters in newspapers and magazines demanding a referendum on a declaration of war.[1] The letters are as exquisite as you'd hope, considering that two of the sharpest writers of their time are behind them.

Only Wall Street titans and their allies will profit by the war, they argue:

> The editors will not do the fighting; nor will our bellicose lawyers, bankers, stock brokers and other prominent citizens, who mess at Delmonico's, bivouac in club windows, and are at all times willing to give to their country's service the last full measure of conversation. No, the people themselves will do the fighting, and they will pay the bill. In death, in suffering, in sorrow,

and in taxes to the third and fourth generations, the people who fight will pay. And therefore, we say that the people themselves should speak before Congress is permitted to declare war.[2]

By the time these letters reach their readers, all the eloquence in the world can't call forth a referendum. Germany makes good on its threat and begins sinking American ships. On February 26, 1917, President Wilson responds by declaring a policy of "armed neutrality," which means equipping American vessels to defend themselves. He hopes it will avert open warfare.

Eastman isn't satisfied. A few days later, he joins another delegation of pacifists to see the president. Eastman expresses his "fervent support and admiration" for Wilson's peace without victory address, which he hails as the "Declaration of Interdependence." But he pleads with the president to back away from armed neutrality. Like Bourne, Eastman prefers the immediate creation of a league of neutral countries. It might form the basis of a true family of nations without exposing the country to the depredations of war.[3]

Wilson listens cordially; he is always cordial. In fact, Eastman marvels at how calm he seems, considering he holds "balanced in his hand the whole future history of his country."[4] But the president declines to act on Eastman's request and bids the delegation good day.

Eastman leaves the White House in disbelief. Doesn't Wilson see that his program of international federation, of democracy on a global scale, could be the fulfillment of American promise—a millennial wish made real? "We are throwing away the gift of hope we were bringing to the nations, for nothing," Eastman tells a crowd later.[5]

There are thirty-three days to go.

With twenty-nine days left, Alice Paul overrules some of her closest advisers and steps up her picketing campaign. Nearly a thousand women brave a frigid, slanting rain, marching around the White House fence, banners held high. To mark Wilson's inauguration day, they want to deliver a petition asking him to endorse the federal suffrage amendment—the only way they feel they can win their liberty.

Late in the day, a car forces the procession to divide: It's the president himself, coming home with the First Lady. The Wilsons look neither right nor left, ignoring the banners, ignoring the silent pleas, disappearing through the gates.

The suffragists trudge home to Cameron House soaked, cold, and furious. Also more determined than ever to bring Wilson around.

The threat of war raises huge and difficult questions for the movement and its leaders. Paul, true to her Quaker heritage, is a pacifist. Carrie Chapman Catt inclines that way, too. They both decide to give up pacifism to do what seems best for suffrage. Catt declares that NAWSA will support the president if he decides to fight—a stand that wins plenty of official praise but also gets her expelled from her leadership role in the Woman's Peace Party. Paul, interested in nothing but suffrage, chooses the logical but politically fraught course, and keeps the Woman's Party neutral on war and peace.

It's a matter of principle, but also a practical necessity. Paul can't afford to have the Woman's Party divide its focus. "The minds of pacifists and militarists alike seem to be so entirely upon the war that we can hardly get them to give any thought to the suffrage amendment," she complains to an ally.[6]

She's having trouble making payroll. She persists. Her mother writes to say, "I hope thee will call it off."[7] She persists. In spite of the scorn of NAWSA, the defection of allies, the sullen opposition of the people who walk past them on Pennsylvania Avenue, and the total freeze-out by the only man who can help, her picketers keep taking their positions every morning, when there are only twenty-four days left, and twenty-three, and twenty-two. . . .

With twenty-one days to go, Walter Lippmann steps off a train at Union Station, hoping for some face time with the president. He

THE REAL AND THE IDEAL 163

doesn't think much of Eastman and Bourne's "league of neutrals," and lord knows he doesn't believe in putting anything as weighty as a declaration of war to a popular vote. He trusts in democratic choices when they are filtered through the channels of representative government, just as he thinks that ideals are achievable if they are lashed to realistic vision and, if possible, sweeping federal power.

That is one of the themes of the memo that he hopes to deliver. It's a proposal that he and Herbert Croly have drafted, on their own initiative, for Wilson. They hope to avoid war, but if it comes, they think Wilson should make a ringing statement to achieve several goals: revive the idea of a league of peace; capture liberal opinion in Allied countries; warn jingoists at home that even in wartime, liberal policies would prevail; and, above all, frame the war in idealistic terms.

"Forgive me if I have intruded," Lippmann tells the president in the note that requests the meeting. "More than anything else it is a deep personal affection for you which prompts me."[8]

Wilson declines to see Lippmann—a rare disappointment for the young man that one newspaper had recently described as the administration's "fair-haired boy." But a few days later, when a cold keeps the president in bed, Croly and Lippmann's memo is one of the documents he considers most carefully.[9]

Wilson's cold is ill-timed; the pressure of events keeps rising. The intercepted Zimmerman telegram reveals that the German government—insanely, ludicrously—has tried to entice Mexico to attack the United States.

On March 20, 1917, Wilson assembles his cabinet. He asks every person at the table to declare for peace or war. They answer alike: war.

Wilson himself says nothing. His cabinet officers leave the room not knowing whether he agrees with them. They're still not sure the next day, when he calls Congress into a special session. It will open eleven days hence.

———

With a precious few days left, John Reed publishes a heartfelt plea to President Wilson, the country's other leaders, and all his fellow citizens: *Don't do this.*

"I have been with the armies of all the belligerents except one, and I have seen men die, and go mad, and lie in hospitals suffering hell; but there is a worse thing than that," he writes. "War means an ugly mob-madness, crucifying the truth-tellers, choking the artists, side-tracking reforms, revolutions, and the working of social forces."[10]

The adventure that he and Louise Bryant were planning to make to China, India, and Japan is canceled. *Metropolitan* tells him that the possibility of war makes it impossible. Now he is stuck in New York, doomed to play Cassandra: sure of what's coming, unable to make anybody listen.

What Reed doesn't know—what nobody knows—is that President Wilson doesn't need any educating about the threats and costs of war. In those last agonizing days of his deliberation, with pacifists pleading in his office and liberals flinging memos his way, with militarists shouting at him from the front pages and suffragists at the gates, he tells a reporter, in private, what lies ahead.

"Once lead this people into war and they'll forget there ever was such a thing as tolerance," he says. "To fight you must be brutal and ruthless, and the spirit of ruthless brutality will enter into the very fiber of our national life, infecting Congress, the courts, the policeman on the beat, the man in the street. . . . If there is any alternative, for God's sake, let's take it!"[11]

That is the essential question; he has framed it precisely: *Is* there an alternative to war—for him, for the country, for *any* country, no matter what ideals it might profess, in a violent, shrinking world?

He gives his answer in the House of Representatives, before an audience that includes congressmen, senators, Supreme Court justices, cabinet officials, diplomats, and anxious members of his own family, looking down on him from above.

It is eight P.M. on Monday, April 2, 1917, the evening of the sixty-first day.

Standing there on the dais, speaking more quietly than usual, Wilson sounds every bit the scholar in chief.

"We must put excited feeling away," he says.

Germany has violated international law. It has sunk American ships and ended American lives. Every measure short of war has been tried. None have stopped the bloodshed—not even armed neutrality.

"With a profound sense of the solemn and even tragical character of the step I am taking and of the grave responsibilities which it involves, but in unhesitating obedience to what I deem my constitutional duty, I advise that the Congress declare the recent course of the imperial German government to be in fact nothing less than war against the government and the people of the United States."

So the choice is war—but a high-minded, well-bred sort of war. He still hopes for "peace without victory." And thanks to Russia, which has risen up against the czar, Wilson can frame the war more idealistically still. On one side of the Hindenburg Line are the monarchies: Germany and Austria-Hungary. On the other are the democracies: France, Britain, Russia, the United States. What might have been a specific response to specific German violations of international law blossoms into something more sweeping and much more fraught.

"The world must be made safe for democracy," he declares.

By framing his argument on such idealistic grounds, Wilson makes this a war of ideas. Winning such a war requires more than troops, guns, ships. Within days of his address to Congress, he creates the Committee on Public Information, the federal government's first large-scale propaganda bureau. Its objective, according to George Creel, the progressive journalist who runs the agency, is "no mere surface unity, but a passionate belief in the justice of America's cause that should weld the people of the United States into one white-hot mass instinct with fraternity, devotion, courage, and deathless determination."[12]

The young radicals are about to face a whole new set of consequences from their decisions to pursue their ideals in the tumult of
public life. They had made those choices against a backdrop of peace
and relative stability. A world of abundant promise now seems a world
of unknowable danger.

The question is no longer *Will you work to see your ideals realized?*
The new reality asks *How far will you go? How much risk can you handle? How much pain can you endure?*

"We were children reared in a kindergarten," according to Max
Eastman, "and now the real thing was coming."[13]

Chapter 21

"Dear Walter," writes a plaintive Randolph Bourne. "Can I see you for a few minutes in the near future to get your advice on a matter which concerns me very closely? I can meet you anywhere that is convenient to you."[1]

What's the matter with Bourne? His letter doesn't say. Since he doesn't have an intimate friendship with the Olympian young Lippmann (almost nobody does in 1917), it's unlikely that he's asking advice about a romantic difficulty: namely, that his beloved Esther Cornell is about to drift out of his life. But with a world skittering off its axis, that still leaves plenty of possibilities.

If Lippmann's track record is any guide, he probably gives Bourne the help he needs: There's a reason why friends have sought his assistance since his schoolboy days. But a few weeks after Bourne writes that letter, the foundations of their relationship begin to quake. Going to war forces the American people to reckon with huge new questions about the country's identity and its place in the world. Fresh alliances form; old friendships collapse.

For idealists such as Bourne and Lippmann, one particularly divisive issue arises almost immediately. The trouble begins—where else?—in an editorial in *The New Republic*.

A few days after Congress declares war, the magazine's editors write that the United States has joined the conflict in spite of "the manifest indifference or reluctance of the majority of its population." That is a startling claim: It's the exact reason why Bourne and Eastman had argued for a referendum on declaring war. But instead of regarding this anti-majoritarian act as a failure of democracy, the editors see it as a cause for champagne.

The minority that railroaded the peaceable American people into war wasn't the bankers or the munitions manufacturers, the editors argue: It was the *intellectuals*. The term is a recent addition to the American lexicon. It was coined by the French thinkers who defended Dreyfus, and popularized in 1908 by William James.[2] When the editors of *The New Republic* use it, they mean lawyers, clergymen, magazine writers, and college professors, up to and including the college professor in the White House.

"The American nation is entering this war under the influence of a moral verdict reached after the utmost deliberation by the more thoughtful members of the community," they declare.[3]

Bourne can't believe what he is reading. He considers war to be "the most noxious complex of all the evils that afflict men." Anybody who leads the country into one should feel shame, not pride. The men doing the boasting in this case are his colleagues, and a few of them are his friends, but he doesn't care. He responds by writing the most incandescently furious essay of his life.

A war made deliberately by the intellectuals! A calm moral verdict, arrived at after a penetrating study of inexorable facts! Sluggish masses, too remote from the world-conflict to be stirred, too lacking in intellect to perceive their danger! ... An intellectual class, gently guiding a nation through sheer force of ideas into what the other nations entered only through predatory craft or popular hysteria or militarist madness!

This doesn't run in *The New Republic,* needless to say. It appears in a new monthly magazine, *The Seven Arts.* The editor, James Oppenheim, is repelled by Bourne's appearance—"that child's body, that humped back"—but dazzled by his work. He gives him fourteen pages of the June issue, and Bourne fills them with every argument he can muster to reject the notion that a war can advance ideals.[4]

The New Republic's editors claim that they are leaders: Bourne asks whom they are leading. The conservatives, the jingoists, and the plutocrats—"the least democratic forces in American life"—are the people who had craved war. "Only in a world where irony was dead could an intellectual class enter war at the head of such illiberal cohorts in the avowed cause of world-liberalism."

The pro-war intellectuals congratulate themselves on their coolness, their rationality, but Bourne argues that they chose war because of their emotions. *Hamlet* gets something backward, he suggests: Intellect doesn't prevent people from acting; it spurs them to act more quickly. To keep thinking, to defer action, to remain in suspense, is the course that requires fortitude.

What really motivates the pro-war intellectuals, Bourne argues, is a small and petty desire: to hear their voices echo in the halls of power. He finds this naïve beyond belief. "The realist thinks he at least can control events by linking himself to the forces that are moving. Perhaps he can," writes Bourne. "But if it is a question of controlling war, it is difficult to see how the child on the back of a mad elephant is to be any more effective in stopping the beast than is the child who tries to stop him from the ground."

Bourne's essay causes a sensation among pacifists. Jane Addams sends her compliments and asks if she can reprint it.[5] Crystal Eastman distributes it in pamphlet form to thousands of members of the American Union Against Militarism. John Reed keeps his copy for years.

"May time reward you for that essay in the *Seven Arts*," Max East-man tells Bourne. "It is one of the finest exploits of intellectual energy and idealism I've ever seen."[6]

Lippmann's reply would be fascinating to read, but he never makes one. Or, rather, he never *writes* one. By the time Bourne's essay runs, he has gone to work for the War Department.

Wartime Washington is nothing like socialist Schenectady, Lippmann is glad to find. He had quit his previous government job in a fog of disillusion, frustrated with the slowness of change, the lack of vision. But in the War Department, he has real power, real responsibility—a chance to make a difference when making a difference is vital. A few months earlier, in an essay criticizing shabby utopian thinking, he had mocked certain unnamed writers for *The Masses*, the kind "who are fond of saying: that pile of stones would look better if it were on top of that mountain, and having indicated this desirable conclusion, go home to dinner."[7] In Washington, he moves the stones.

Lippmann had needed every bit of his finesse to get there. In one of his memos to the president, he had advised against building a volunteer army, because the recruitment drive would stir up the jingoistic passions that the country needed to keep in check. Wilson had agreed with this view, and ordered a draft of the country's able-bodied young men. That's good for Lippmann, because it shows he's in step with the president, but bad for Lippmann, because he is himself an able-bodied young man.

To escape from this predicament, he had written to his friend Newton Baker, the secretary of war. He had only reached out, he assured Baker, because friends urged him to do so.

"You can well understand that that is not a pleasant thing to do, and yet, after searching my soul as candidly as I know how, I am convinced that I can serve my bit much more effectively than as a private in the new armies." There's a personal side to the request, too: "My father is dying, and my mother is absolutely alone in the world."[8]

In fact, Jacob Lippmann would live another ten years. He seems to have a powerful capacity for self-preservation—one that he shares with his son. Because Newton Baker responds to Lippmann's letter by hiring him, thereby removing him from draft eligibility.

Lippmann's work is difficult and vital. He handles the labor negotiations to build new facilities for the military. Those facilities need to sprout like mushrooms if America is to have any chance against the larger, more experienced, better equipped, terrifyingly up-to-date German military machine. (When Wilson sends the country to war, the United States has the world's seventeenth-largest army.)[9] Lippmann's reputation helps. A young radical has a better chance of connecting with an irascible labor leader like Samuel Gompers than, say, a bureaucrat freshly arrived from Wall Street would.

Baker is delighted with his new hire. He tells colleagues to treat Lippmann as his "alter ego." Lippmann is delighted, too. Before moving to Washington, he had quietly married Faye Albertson, a pretty blond dance teacher he had known when she was a girl. Because of a wartime housing crunch, they move into a group house near Dupont Circle. The townhouse serves as the intellectual epicenter of Washington, drawing young government officials and diplomats together: Louis Brandeis, Herbert Hoover, even Oliver Wendell Holmes, Jr. The revered and rather conservative Supreme Court justice nicknames the place "the House of Truth." He also comes to admire Lippmann, in spite of his liberal views.

"Monstrous clever lad," Holmes says.[10]

Some radicals are heartened to see the Wilson administration hire young men such as Lippmann and Felix Frankfurter, who had traded a post at Harvard Law School for a room at the House of Truth. Crystal Eastman calls it "a guarantee of good faith" on President Wilson's part—a sign that, in spite of his bellicose speeches, he really does intend to fight the war for enlightened purposes.[11]

Randolph Bourne is not consoled. On the contrary. The flow of idealistic young liberals to Washington gives him further reason to lash out against the war. He keeps up his attack month after month in *The*

Seven Arts. By helping to wage a foolish war, he writes, these proficient young men are succumbing to "the allure of the technical." They are "immensely ready for the executive ordering of events, pitifully unprepared for the intellectual interpretation or the idealistic focusing of ends."

It is fanciful, he thinks, to believe that the government has any deep commitment to the ideals it claims to be fighting to preserve. Bourne cites evidence that comes straight from the president's mouth: "The day has come to conquer or submit," Wilson declares that summer. Isn't this the kind of brutal outcome that Wilson said he wanted to avoid—isn't it a flat refutation of "peace without victory"?[12] Bourne thinks the intelligent young helpers of the cause have been made to look like fools.

"For once," he writes, "the babes and sucklings seem to have been wiser than the children of light."[13]

Yet for the second time in half a year, Lippmann's actions offer a retort to Bourne's words. Even as Bourne is arguing that idealists have no ability to shape the outcome of the war, Lippmann gets a new chance to do just that.

Colonel House summons Lippmann to a private meeting and gives him a special and secret charge. President Wilson has realized how unprepared American diplomats are for the peace conference that will follow the war. There is a century of isolation and indifference to counteract, and not much time to do it. The administration needs to harness the scattered, partial knowledge of American scholars and amalgamate it, to make sure that the war yields the most democratic outcome possible.

To lead the team, House has chosen Sidney Mezes. The president of City College of New York doesn't thrill a lot of people, but he has the sterling credential of being House's brother-in-law.[14] Many operational duties will need to be handled by a committed, discrete, and more or less omnicompetent secretary. Out of all the candidates available—all the bright boys at the House of Truth, and everyplace else—House had proposed Lippmann.

"The objection to Lippman [*sic*] is that he is a Jew," House told the president, "but unlike other Jews he is a silent one."[15]

Wilson is a horrendous racist, but he is no anti-Semite. He passed over House's comment in silence, and approved.

"Nothing has ever pleased me more or come as a greater surprise," Lippmann tells House. "The work you outlined is exactly that which I have dreamed of since the very beginning of the war, but dreamed of as something beyond reach. I'd literally rather be connected with you in this work in no matter what capacity than do anything else there is to do in the world."[16]

A year earlier, Lippmann had called for an "integrated America," in which progress would be achieved through forthright federal actions, such as nationalizing the railroads. As a leader of the Inquiry, he does the thing he'd advocated, but with a twist: He is nationalizing America's brains.

As Lippmann rises ever higher through the Wilson administration, Bourne gets a chance to make a parallel ascent in the antiwar camp. The People's Council, a radical new pacifist organization, proposes him for several leadership roles, including one alongside Max Eastman on the Committee on Timely Literature.[17] Here is the kind of opportunity that Bourne has craved since leaving college, when he told friends how much he envied their activism.

Except that the war has given Bourne a new point of view. He recognizes the moral gulf between the pacifists who spend their days opposing the war and the wayward idealists who help the government to wage it, but as a practical matter, both sides are hopelessly enmeshed in it. If radicals throw all their energy into resisting the war, they will be unprepared for the reconstruction that must follow.

The man who once boiled his philosophy of life down to a single word—"Dare!"—begins to preach a new gospel: "Apathy." It doesn't entail staying in bed all day, or ceasing to care about the world. Apathy, in this context, means "a heightened energy and enthusiasm for the education, the art, the interpretation that make for life in the midst of the world of death."[18] It means focusing on the work that it's possible to do in wartime, to be ready when peace returns.

By leaguing himself with neither Lippmann and the proficient liberals nor Eastman and the fervent pacifists, Bourne sets himself on a lonely course. It is painful to lose the companionable feeling of working jointly for an ideal, a feeling that Bourne has always needed more than most, but he is too much of a realist to go along with the illusions of the crowd.

Having disenthralled himself this way, Bourne still has to suffer the most painful shock of all.

A few weeks after Bourne attacks *The New Republic,* the magazine publishes a pronouncement on the war by John Dewey, the leading American philosopher since the death of William James. Dewey is Bourne's mentor—his "chosen rabbi," as a writer for *The Nation* puts it.[19] But Dewey doesn't rise to his protégé's defense or back up his argument: He belittles it.

Young pacifists are the victims of "moral innocency and inexpertness," he writes. Their vaunted sense of conscience is just "self-conceit." And the worst offenders of all are the "apathetic."

Three more installments follow this essay, each making a fresh attack on the "futile gesturing" and "stupidity" of the pacifists. All four essays flow from a single pragmatic calculation, the same one that had sent Walter Lippmann to Washington: Going to war offers possibilities for social progress that far outweigh the risks of what could go wrong.[20]

Bourne is stricken. Two years earlier, he had hailed Dewey as "a prophet in the clothes of a professor of logic." What has become of his prophecy? He has a queasy feeling of "suddenly being left in the lurch, of suddenly finding that a philosophy upon which I had relied to carry us through no longer works."

So he takes up his pen.

In "Twilight of Idols," his fifth essay in five months for *The Seven*

Arts, he maintains a cool, controlled tone. He needs it. Because his target this time is not just Wilson's decision to fight, or Lippmann's decision to join the administration, or Dewey's endorsement of both those choices, but the kind of instrumental thinking that all three of them share—and that Bourne once shared, too.

In peacetime, Bourne writes, Dewey's instrumentalism allows people to proceed through life experimentally, choosing freely among courses of action, trying to live out their ideals. It is "a philosophy of hope, of clear-sighted comprehension of materials and means." In wartime, though, no such freedom is possible. Military necessity demands concerted action, unity of thought. Every choice is coerced in the direction of supporting the war. But, as Bourne has been arguing, no choice that supports a war will realize any ideal worth the name.

The naïveté that Bourne felt in 1914, with Europe going up in flames around him, is nothing compared to the self-reckoning he is forced to make now.

To those of us who have taken Dewey's philosophy almost as our American religion, it never occurred that values could be subordinated to technique. We were instrumentalists, but we had our private utopias so clearly before our minds that the means fell always into its place as contributory. And Dewey, of course, always meant his philosophy, when taken as a philosophy of life, to start with values. But there was always that unhappy ambiguity in his doctrine as to just how values were created, and it became easier and easier to assume that just any growth was justified and almost any activity valuable as long as it achieved ends.

Bourne takes no pleasure from casting off his mentor this way, or declaring that the country has come to "a sudden, short stop at the end of an intellectual era." It brings no profit to *The Seven Arts,* either. After five months of publishing Bourne's attacks on the war, the proprietor decides she can no longer tolerate the scorn of her friends, all of whom are trying to do their duty and support the president. She withdraws her subsidy, and the fractious staff can't go on without it. The October issue, which includes "Twilight of Idols," is the magazine's last.

James Oppenheim doesn't hold the death of *The Seven Arts* against Bourne. Other contributors are less forgiving. An up-and-coming poet named Robert Frost sends Oppenheim a bitter limerick:

> In the Dawn of Creation that morning
> I remember I gave you fair warning:
> The Arts are but Six!
> You add Politics
> And the Seven will all die a-Bourneing.[21]

When Bourne decided to oppose the war, he knew it would mean being exiled to what he called "the outer darkness." This is darker than he had foreseen.

"The magazines I write for die violent deaths, and all my thoughts seem unprintable," Bourne laments to a friend. "What then is a literary man to do if he has to make his living by his pen?"

In his bewilderment and his mounting despair, there's one thing that Bourne doesn't do: attack Walter Lippmann. In private, Bourne can be scathing. "Walter's 'Stakes of Diplomacy' is a handy manual for the enlightened imperialist exploiter," he wrote to a mutual friend early in the year.[22] In public, he stays silent.

Does Bourne feel too loyal to Lippmann to call him out? Is he intimidated by the vituperative younger man, who is at least Bourne's equal at flaying an adversary? Whatever the explanation, he spares Lippmann the ad hominem abuse he heaps on Dewey, among others.

Instead, in the middle of his run of hostile essays, Bourne once again asks Lippmann for help.

This time, the request isn't for Bourne himself, it's for a friend: Edward Murray, the musician with whom he had spent the summer of

1915 in New Hampshire. Murray is desperate to declare himself a conscientious objector, but he doesn't know what to do.

"If you could [assist Murray], I should be more convinced of the
sincerity of the Government in conducting a democratic war, and in
your assumption of the power of liberal forces to control it," Bourne
writes. "You once said to me, when I complained about something at
the *New Republic*, 'We are very busy men.' I fancy you reacting in the
same way to my letter. Yet it is exactly effort like this which I am bringing to your attention which would justify your presence in Washington,
indeed, almost to be the essence of that justification."[23]

Lippmann writes back quickly, having asked around, to suggest that
Bourne's friend make a direct approach to the secretary of war.

"You are quite wrong in your guess as to how I react to your letter,"
he adds. "I don't believe a day has passed since I have been in Washington in which I haven't had this thing on my mind."[24]

This note of mutual misunderstanding marks the end of the known
correspondence between Walter Lippmann and Randolph Bourne, the
two sharpest writers and thinkers of their generation—two brilliant
idealists, two inspired expressers of American promise, who didn't always agree with each other, but who were nevertheless colleagues, and
even, for a little while, during a brief, hopeful, and fleeting period of the
country's adolescence, friends.

Chapter 22

Max Eastman and John Reed blast away in *The Masses*, byline after byline, page after page. Entire stretches of the magazine during that first summer of war consist of nothing but their alternating attacks on the logic and justice of the American effort. Their styles are as complementary as their personalities. Eastman will offer a long, thoughtful critique of patriotism—"Men are willing to be dead, if they can only be dead in a pile"[1]—then, a few pages later, Reed will lampoon the Social Register types who patriotically cut back from seven-course meals to five, fretting all the while that they're not spending enough to help the economy.

"What shall we do? Possibly we made a mistake," writes Jack. "While thinking it over, let's order up a bottle of champagne."[2]

For once, Eastman and Reed are in step with the Socialist party line. The party's leaders call an emergency convention in St. Louis, where they pass a resolution against American involvement in the war. Because no other prominent group in American life does so, the party's composition begins to change: Pacifists and other irreconcilables flow in; pro-war moderates flow out. The split reaches all the way to *The Masses*. William English Walling, an essential longtime contributor, accuses Eastman and Reed of taking "exactly the same view of the duty of Americans at this juncture as the Kaiser," and resigns.[3] Other writers join him. The contributors who stand by Max and Jack amuse themselves at their former colleagues' expense. Art Young draws one of them peeking under his bed, making sure the kaiser isn't going to get him.[4]

Their fun won't last. Congress, flush with martial spirit, passes the Espionage Act, most of which has nothing to do with espionage. It outlaws making false statements that hamper the war effort or that promote "insubordination, disloyalty, mutiny, or refusal of duty." It is a censorship law, the strictest limit on what American citizens can say and write since the Sedition Act of 1798. One provision of the Espionage Act in particular is about to confound radicals: Any periodical that publishes objectionable material can be barred from the mail. Even worse, the responsibility for determining what violates the law is entrusted to the last man in America who ought to wield it.

Postmaster General Albert S. Burleson is a former congressman from Texas, the proud son of a Confederate army officer, the instigator of some of the Wilson administration's most flagrant segregation, a bully, and a fool.[5]

Why do so many hardworking men end up poor? a reporter asks him around this time.

"It's the shape of his brain," says Burleson. "God Almighty did that, and you can't change it."[6]

It takes him only a few weeks to come after *The Masses*.

In early July, the post office informs the editors that certain elements of the August issue violate the Espionage Act. Consequently it will not be mailed. The letter doesn't specify which stories or pictures violate the act, merely finding fault with the "general tone."

Unlike other targets of Burleson's wrath (and there are many targets; within five months of the act's passage, he bans every major socialist publication from the mail at least once), Eastman has a way to fight back.[7] He can draw on his friendly relationship with Burleson's boss, the president, dating back to their merry dinner in Syracuse in 1912.

Eastman, Reed, and prominent progressive Amos Pinchot write Wilson a sociable letter—they even refer to themselves as "friends of yours"—about the problem they all share: the overzealous Texan who runs the post office. They don't complain about the unfairness of the Espionage Act. In fact, they say that they have been careful not to violate it. "What we wish to ask you is, whether you think that free criticism, right or wrong, of the policy of the government ought to be denied at this time the right of public expression."[8]

Without quite saying so, they are asking him to make a public defense of free speech. One vintage Wilsonian address about the value of civil liberties would make this problem go away—not just for them, but for all of the pacifists.

The president writes back with gratifying speed, having read their letter "with a great deal of interest and sympathy." He declines to make a public statement, he tells them, because "it would undoubtedly be taken advantage of by those with whom neither you nor I have been in sympathy at all." But their attempt to depict themselves as his friends seems to have worked. Wilson assures them that he will take up their complaint with the postmaster general. And he does.

Wilson forwards their letter to Burleson. "These are very sincere men and I should like to please them," he writes.[9]

Burleson waits until the next cabinet meeting to give Wilson his answer.

"If you don't want the Espionage Act enforced, I can resign," he says. "Congress has passed the law and has said that I am to enforce it. We are going into war, and these men are discouraging enlistments."

People who talk this way to Wilson, the man who bears the smoldering volcano, tend to suffer for it. Think of William Monroe Trotter protesting segregation; think of the suffragists who presented their memorial for Inez Milholland. But this time Wilson just laughs.

"Well," he says, "go ahead and do your duty."[10]

Eastman doesn't learn how feeble an effort the president has made on his behalf. All he knows is that Burleson goes on refusing to release thousands of copies of his magazine, which need to get mailed soon to have any value at all.

Pressed for time and lacking other options, Eastman takes his chances in court. It is as trailblazing an experiment as any radical action of that decade. For in the summer of 1917, America had virtually no tradition of civil liberties jurisprudence: no "clear and present danger" test, no ringing paeans to "the marketplace of ideas."[11] In their letter to Wilson, the *Masses* supplicants had cited an "Anglo-Saxon tradition of intellectual freedom," because a specifically *American* tradition didn't exist.

To Eastman's delight—and his surprise—the legal gambit works. Learned Hand, a federal district judge, places strict limits on enforcement of the Espionage Act. He rules that an expression should be banned only if it incites illegal *acts,* not merely because it states unpopular *views.*[12]

The radicals are victorious—for "about six minutes," in Eastman's estimation.[13]

On the same day that Hand announces his decision, Burleson's subordinates track a conservative appellate judge to his country house and get him to issue a stay. The judge can't think of a precedent for what is, effectively, an injunction of an injunction. But he gives it anyway. It means that the August issue of *The Masses* will remain locked up until the court date—*in October.*[14]

Furious and defiant, the writers and artists whip the September issue into shape. It is not designed to appease, mocking Burleson in word and image. Before it is finished, an ominous, official-looking letter arrives at the *Masses* office. It invites the editors to demonstrate why their second-class mailing privileges shouldn't be revoked altogether.

Those privileges, the post office wishes to remind them, are reserved for magazines that are mailed *regularly.* But the lack of an August issue means that *The Masses* has become "*irregular* in publication."[15]

Nowhere does the letter acknowledge that the postmaster general is the cause of that gap.

The magazine that has made so many good jokes over the last five years now finds itself the butt of a terrible one. Without those mailing privileges, *The Masses* is finished.

"I spent the whole winter trying to think up the worst possible consequences of our going to war, and advertise them in the public press, but I never succeeded in thinking up anything half so bad as this," Eastman tells a New York crowd that summer.

The attack on *The Masses* is only one part of what he's describing. A month after the passage of the Espionage Act, he marvels that the American government has suppressed the socialist press more quickly and completely than the Germans did.

"You can't even collect your thoughts without getting arrested for unlawful assemblage," he continues. "They give you ninety days for quoting the Declaration of Independence, six months for quoting the Bible, and pretty soon somebody is going to get a life sentence for quoting Woodrow Wilson in the wrong connection."[16]

He gives his speech at one of the first events held by the newly formed Civil Liberties Bureau. This offshoot of the American Union Against Militarism seeks to promote a couple of ideas that are novel to Americans in 1917: that there is an intrinsic value to free speech for everybody, not just the better sort of citizen; that Americans whose speech is suppressed deserve adequate legal aid. The need for this work grows so vast that the organization's leaders, Roger Baldwin and Crystal Eastman, make it a fully independent organization. It will soon be called the American Civil Liberties Union.[17]

Yet refusing to mail magazines may be the mildest form of repression that summer. When the president declares that unanimity is necessary for victory, officers of his government take him literally. Any form of organized opposition and even many private dissents come to be regarded as dangerous disloyalty. In Chicago, federal agents raid the headquarters of the Socialist Party. Big Bill Haywood and more than a hundred members of the IWW are rounded up in a mass arrest. In

New York, socialist meetings and anti-conscription rallies are disrupted. In Boston, soldiers break up a peace parade.[18]

"We always used to say that certain things would happen in this country if militarism came," writes Reed. "Militarism has come. They are happening."[19]

The most grievous harm that summer isn't perpetrated by the government—it's what American citizens inflict on one another. While the Department of Justice is staffing up its Bureau of Investigation (what will become the FBI), Attorney General Thomas Gregory asks every loyal American to be a "voluntary detective," reporting any suspicious activity. His office is swamped by thousands of reports *every day*.[20]

People who are so eager to spy on their neighbors aren't likely to stop there.

In San Jose, a brewery worker is tarred, feathered, and chained to a cannon in a public park for making pro-German remarks. In Collinsville, Illinois, a citizen is dragged from his home by a mob of five hundred people, accused of being a German spy, wrapped in an American flag, and murdered.

Sometimes the violence doesn't have much to do with Germany, and is merely a cover for old-fashioned industrial warfare against workers. In Bisbee, Arizona, twelve hundred striking miners and their allies are herded onto cattle cars, shunted out to the desert, and left there without food or water.

The worst violence befalls black Americans. As northern workers enlist in the army, black families stream up from the South to take their places. In East St. Louis, a volatile mixture of factory owners, white union members, and black newcomers explodes in race riots that leave more than a dozen people dead. Eastman rightly connects this violence to America's shameful tradition of lynching. He notes in *The Masses* that a black man has been lynched every four days since 1885. His only mistake is to call the East St. Louis riots the "culmination" of that legacy.[21]

The most striking fact about all this ethnic, economic, and racial violence is how little is perpetrated by rabble-rousers or outlaws of long standing. Much of the organized repression—including the "slacker raids," used to round up or at least intimidate thousands of young men—is instigated by organizations such as the American Protective League, the National Security League, and the American Defense Society. Their members are primarily businessmen, lawyers, community leaders—upstanding citizens of one kind or another.[22] Strange how little it takes to turn a clerk or a banker into a vigilante.

The Masses, which keeps a running account of these horrors, reprints a quote from *The Wall Street Journal:* "We are now at war, and militant pacifists are earnestly reminded that there is no shortage of hemp or lamp-posts."[23]

Radical organizations persist anyway. The People's Council arranges speaking tours in the Midwest. But who will give the speeches? It requires more than idealistic commitment and oratorical flair to stand up for radical ideals in 1917: It takes raw physical courage.

This does not sound like a job for Max Eastman. In his thirty-four years, Max has shown little interest in throwing a punch, and even less in taking one. It's one reason why he likes Reed so much—Jack's swaggering belligerence complements Max's poetical desire to loaf and invite his ease. Summer 1917 is a particularly dangerous time for Eastman. His feud with the post office gets him named an "Enemy Within" by the *New-York Tribune.*[24]

Still, Eastman is troubled by a gap between his words and his actions. For five years, he has been spouting bright red statements of revolution in *The Masses.* He thinks of Plato, the subject of his longago studies at Columbia, who was invited to trade the security of Athens for the tumult of Syracuse, where he would help the licentious young ruler become a philosopher-king.[25]

"I feared to see myself nothing but words," Plato wrote, explaining why he chose to go.

In the summer of 1917, Eastman makes the same choice. He does so knowing how things turned out for Plato. The world's greatest philosopher got detained by his erstwhile pupil in Syracuse, which improved not a bit because of his teaching.

In August, in the midst of his fight with the post office, Eastman bids farewell to his beloved Florence Deshon and boards a train. It takes him from New York to Detroit, then to Chicago, then to points west.

"I'm as nervous as a rabbit's nose all night," he tells Florence.[26]

Some of the crowds that he addresses are receptive, some sullen, and the whole thing comes to seem absurd. It's fiendishly hot; the train rattles; he can't sleep. He fantasizes about telling the tour organizers that he's dying, or that he has enlisted in the army. On top of everything else, Florence stops answering his letters.[27]

"This is the most difficult thing I ever did in my life, and I do want your help," he writes. "You don't know how lonely it is to be alone and all the press and the power and the prestige against you."[28]

In this downcast heartsick state, he arrives in Fargo.

From the moment he steps off the train, things seem wrong—ominously wrong. All of the meeting halls are closed to him. The proprietor of his hotel tells him that if he tries to give a speech under his roof, he'll shoot Eastman himself. Max improvises, and makes a plan to speak outdoors, at a prominent intersection in the heart of town. Then the local militia announces a drill next to his meeting site—with loaded rifles.

The prudent course is to do nothing. Stay silent. Move on. But Eastman, the meek child of two ministers, wildly overcompensates. He decides to make a stand.

That night, hundreds of people jam the Fargo Civic Center and hundreds more cluster outside. Some want to hear his message; others want to make trouble; more than a few want to see how badly things will go. The answer is *very, very badly*.

Five minutes into his speech, the door bursts open and a half dozen soldiers stream into the room—"low in the brow, big in the torso." Eastman tries to wrong-foot them by inviting them to sit onstage. He even backs up a few sentences in his speech so they can follow his argu-

ment. The Russians have offered civilized peace terms—no annexations, no indemnities—but the president hasn't responded. Wilson is
even refusing to answer a letter from the pope, who is trying to broker
a peace based on those terms. Eastman demands that Wilson state his
intentions clearly, and prove once and for all that he is really waging a
war for democracy.

The soldiers shout him down.

In a touching show of faith in democracy, Eastman proposes a vote
on whether he should keep going. All but eleven people in the audience
raise their hands. The commotion grows anyway.

"Are we going to war for a cause that has been officially announced?"
yells Eastman.

"Yes!" the patriots yell back.

It's not the answer Max wants.

He's frustrated, baffled. Why do the vast majority of his listeners—
those who raised their hands—remain silent, leaving only the disrup-
tive minority to speak? *Why won't they fight?* Only later does he realize
that these quiet Midwesterners had done him a favor: They know that
at the first sign of real resistance, he could be shot.

The door bangs open. More soldiers pour in.

"Company B to the front!" somebody shouts.

The troops rush the stage. In a flash, fifteen men surround Eastman.

"All the ladies will please leave the building!" one of them says.

Eastman holds his ground, his escalating terror held in check by his
desire not to let everybody see how terrified he is.

The soldiers begin a booming rendition of "The Dear Old Flag."

It's too loud for Eastman to be heard. He leaves the stage, huddles
with his hosts. One of them says that if he were Eastman, he would
start giving a speech about something else.

Eastman refuses. He would literally rather die than roll over that
way.

Soldiers now sing on every side of him. Max feels calm, despite his
growing certainty that he is about to be beaten, maybe lynched. He'd
hardly be the first. He thinks of Florence.

Just then, real life veers toward the theater: a flash of Provincetown in North Dakota. A diminutive woman emerges from the crowd. She says that she has traveled a long way to meet Eastman, and to tell him how much she loves *The Masses*. This is, almost precisely, what happens to his alter ego in Susan Glaspell's play *The People*.

Eastman's guardian angel stands near him, hoping it might prevent or at least slow down whatever the soldiers plan to do to him. Max thinks maybe she's saved his life.

The soldiers are singing "The Star-Spangled Banner" now, and when two men refuse to stand, they are jerked patriotically to their feet. This is Max's cue to go.

He walks through the jeering crowd and steps through the doorway—*"with extreme leisure,"* he insists to Florence later. Another crowd mills outside, but once he steps into it, he disappears. None of them know what he looks like.

A couple of friendly locals spot him and whisk him to a house where he'll be safe. Somebody calls to warn him not to go back to his hotel. It's surrounded by soldiers, some of whom want to throw him a "necktie party" when he arrives. But Max shouldn't stay where he is, either. Soldiers are headed there, too.

Eastman's hosts give him a hat and coat to disguise himself and a loaded revolver for when the disguise fails. He ducks outside, through a neighbor's yard, and behind a bush, where he waits until a car roars up. He lies on the floor of the backseat, clutching the gun.

He feels sick. He feels cold. He makes it past the posse and out of town. They cross the state line and keep driving. He thinks he loves that gun more than any other object in his whole life.

Max is desperate to get back to New York and to Florence. He tells her so in a terror-addled, nonsensical letter: "So again—to prove that I am a man—but I am not, I am a baby and I yearn for your breast. O my beautiful and beloved I want to lie down in your arms. That is all I want."

Except he doesn't go home, not yet. Eastman is scheduled to give one more speech in defense of his ideals. He gathers up his tattered courage and gives it.[29]

The same night that Eastman gets railroaded out of Fargo for advocating "no annexations, no indemnities," the Wilson administration makes public the president's reply to the pope: He advocates "no annexations, no indemnities." It might be funny if the stakes weren't so high.

Wilson's surprisingly liberal-minded view of peace terms, one in line with what the People's Council had wanted, emboldens Eastman to approach him one more time.

He presents two issues.

The first is his brush with death in Fargo, which he describes at length. "Is there not grave danger to our civil liberties in these hundreds of thousands of armed men, if in the name of patriotism they are allowed with impunity to degenerate into gangs of marauders?"

The second is the government's suppression of *The Masses*. He calls it a direct threat to Wilson's own policies.

"You know that the powers which would like to kill the propaganda of socialism are mighty, and you also know that this propaganda will surely play a great part in the further democratizing of the world," he writes.

In other words, he is hoping that a common belief in democracy could be grounds for keeping alive the socialist-liberal coalition that was so helpful to the president's reelection.[30]

Wilson writes back with his usual prompt warmth, thanking Eastman for the kind words. Yet the rest of the president's letter is bizarrely, unaccountably breezy. He says nothing about Eastman's ordeal in Fargo. On censorship, he strikes a tone of lofty generality:

I think that a time of war must be regarded as wholly exceptional and that it is legitimate to regard things which would in ordinary circumstances be innocent as very dangerous to the public welfare, but the line is manifestly exceedingly hard to draw and I cannot say that I have any confidence that I know how to draw it. I can only say that a line must be drawn and that we are trying, it may be clumsily but genuinely, to draw it without fear or favor or prejudice.[31]

Eastman shares the letter with the newspapers. It appears on front pages around the country, where it is billed as the "first utterance from the President on the subject of free speech during war time."[32]

That fall, other voices rise in Eastman's defense. Walter Lippmann pauses in his weighty wartime labors to write to Wilson. He tells the president that he has less concern for *The Masses,* which he uncharitably describes as "an obscure and discredited little sheet," than for Wilson's standing with liberals. Censorship, he argues, "is breaking down the liberal support of the war and is tending to divide the country's articulate opinion into fanatical jingoism and fanatical pacifism."[33]

Even this appeal doesn't change Wilson's mind.

The end comes a few weeks later. The appeals court throws out Learned Hand's ruling that had favored *The Masses.* The magazine is now barred from the mail. And thanks to the newly passed Trading with the Enemy Act, a publication barred from the mail can't be distributed any other way.[34] The Wilson administration has killed *The Masses.*

"We live in a world of the kind we believe in," Eastman writes in one of his final editor's notes.[35] The death of *The Masses* shows that the world he is talking about is gone. A society forming up ranks for war has no room for a magazine that exists to taunt authority and defy conventions, or a bunch of rebellious artists and writers who are happy to live, as Falstaff does, "out of all order, out of all compass." As Floyd Dell would write: "It stood for fun, truth, beauty, realism, freedom, peace, feminism, revolution."[36] No wonder the government hated it.

Once in a very long while, a research librarian makes a mistake, and instead of giving you the reproductions that library policy insists you use (low quality, black and white, printed long after the fact), you are handed the actual original magazines: spare, bright, vivid, beautiful. A century after its demise, *The Masses* is as vibrant as anything being published today: an artifact of a young republic scrambling to get itself expressed, and to enjoy it.

If Eastman had merely been silenced, it would be insult enough. But in another echo of Falstaff, who is forsaken by a ruler whose affection he had overestimated, he faces the prospect of jail.

On November 19, 1917, Eastman, Reed, and a handful of their *Masses* colleagues are indicted for violating the Espionage Act.[37] By that time, Reed is in Petrograd, where he has gone to report on Russia's lurch toward another revolution. The other editors send him a telegram, breaking the awkward news that when he comes home, he might be facing twenty years in prison and a fine of $10,000.

Max can't bear the thought of being separated from Florence for even one year, let alone spending twenty of them behind bars. That's not even his biggest problem: "Some of us have 20 years, but none of us has $10,000."[38]

Chapter 23

A dark paradox has taken hold. To make the world safe for democracy, Americans are undermining their own democracy: free speech curtailed, freedom of assembly infringed, vigilantes turned loose—everywhere and all at once.

At the same moment that Wilson presides over a weakening of American democracy, he trumpets its vibrancy to the rest of the world. He has no choice. The collapse of the czar's regime has made Russia an unsteady partner in the Allied cause. If the leaders of the new Provisional Government decide that Britain, France, and the United States are fighting for nothing loftier than the spoils of empire, they might quit the war. That would allow Germany to swing an entire army from the eastern front to the deadlocked West. The Allies could lose before American soldiers join the fight.

Wilson sends former secretary of state Elihu Root to Russia to vouch for America's proud legacy of "universal, direct, equal, and secret suffrage."[1] He even invites Russian diplomats to visit him in Washington, to continue the courtship in person. With so much at stake, he wants to ensure that nothing goes wrong.

Something goes wrong.

On June 20, 1917, as the Russian diplomats' car draws near the White House gates—a huge crowd watching—two women unfurl this banner:

> TO THE ENVOYS OF RUSSIA
>
> President Wilson and Envoy Root are deceiving Russia. They say, "We are a democracy. Help us win a world war so that democracies may survive."
>
> We, the Women of America, tell you that America is not a democracy. Twenty million American Women are denied the right to vote. President Wilson is the chief opponent of their national enfranchisement.
>
> Help us make this nation really free. Tell our government that it must liberate its people before it can claim free Russia as an ally.[2]

By making America's commitment to democratic ideals an instrument of war, President Wilson has handed Alice Paul and her fellow suffragists a powerful new weapon. They are going to expose Wilson's hypocrisy—and the nation's. They are going to show that the ideal of American democracy does not match the reality of widespread disenfranchisement. And they are going to keep repeating the charge until Wilson declares his support for the federal suffrage amendment.

Paul knows they will pay a price for embarrassing the president, but she is willing to pay it. At least, she thinks she is. Like Max Eastman, she is about to learn a painful lesson about the new hostility of wartime America.

The day after the Russian diplomats' visit, as on virtually every day for the past five months, the suffragists take their positions around the White House gates. Some hold the purple, white, and gold pennants of the movement; others hold a banner repeating the message about Russia.

A crowd forms: uneasy, seething. From Paul's perspective at headquarters, half a block away, it must look like moths swarming on silk.

A woman in the crowd—the mother of a son in the armed forces—stalks back and forth in front of the pickets.[3] She announces that she will spit on the banners if the men will come with her.

With one will, they attack.

"Traitors!" and "Shame!" and "Sedition!" they cry, falling on the suffragists, ripping their banners to pieces, knocking the women down.

One suffragist climbs up the White House fence, trying to keep her pennant above the mob's reach, but the woman scratches and claws at her, wrests the pennant away, and throws it to the crowd. They roar and rip it to shreds.

The police take a desultory attitude toward the riot, which now involves several thousand people. Eventually they bestir themselves, and the fighting stops.

The riot is widely reported in the national press, just as Paul had wished. The suffragists of the National Woman's Party are almost universally called "militants" now, even though, strictly speaking, they did nothing militant. In England, the Pankhursts had thrown bricks and started fires; at the White House, the women merely stood holding signs. They *suffered* violence—they didn't perpetrate it.

President Wilson says nothing about the riot that unfolds literally under his windows. It's another gift that he unwittingly gives the suffragists. Washington is run by federal appointees, which means the suffragists can hold Wilson responsible for anything and everything that happens to them.

And so a second, darker paradox takes hold. In order to win the security and dignity that would come from enfranchisement, suffragists must expose themselves to danger and shame. The more grievously they suffer on the sidewalks outside the White House, the more pressure they apply to the man inside. It is a question of who will crack first: Alice Paul or Woodrow Wilson.

Day after day in the weeks that follow, pickets raise their banners, crowds menace them, and cops make arrests—sometimes peaceably, sometimes violently, but almost always of the women holding the signs, not their attackers. The district attorney, after much urgent flipping through statute books, finds a charge that might stick: "obstructing traffic." He uses it even though the women (who stand in small groups on sidewalks) do not, strictly speaking, obstruct traffic.

When the pickets are brought before a judge, they refuse to cooperate. When they are fined, they refuse to pay. Paul had not expected it to come to this, but it has: American women—largely middle-class and upper-middle-class women, dozens of them—are going to prison for demanding their freedom.

Radicals cheer the suffragists' courage. MAGNIFICENT. PERFECT FROM EVERY POSSIBLE POINT OF VIEW. ENDLESS ADMIRATION, wires Max Eastman.[4] Randolph Bourne sends a supportive word to Joy Young, a friend from the interlocking worlds of socialism and pacifism, who forced the cops to drag her into a police automobile: "Must have been a wonderful row, and has kept you all on the front page."[5]

John Reed pays his tribute in person. At a welcome-home breakfast on the morning of the first prisoners' release, just before he leaves for Russia, he congratulates his "fellow convicts" and encourages them to keep fighting. He quotes Walt Whitman: "I will write a song for the president full of menacing signs / And, back of it all, millions of discontented eyes."[6]

Eastman, Bourne, and Reed are, as usual, in the minority. Most Americans view the pickets with fury or horror. Congressmen, even some who are sympathetic to suffrage, complain about this insult to the president in wartime. Nobody is more exasperated than Carrie Chapman Catt. She is in the midst of a painstaking campaign to win a New York State referendum to enfranchise women. It is the linchpin of her "winning plan," which focuses on state-level victories that drive up pressure at the federal level. The whole mighty edifice is undermined by Alice Paul's antics.

Catt writes to Paul directly, asking her to stop picketing "for the sake of the political freedom of women, and our hope of success in this country in the near future."[7] Less diplomatically, NAWSA's magazine runs an editorial suggesting that men are manipulating the pickets "as grown-ups encourage a froward child." The magazine invites the American people to ignore the wayward women. The editorial is reprinted in the official bulletin of the Committee on Public Information, which suggests that the Wilson administration feels the same way.[8]

Paul ignores every demand to quit. She remains so obstinate that two officials from NAWSA's New York affiliate finally travel to Washington, intent on confronting her face-to-face.[9]

They reach Cameron House on July 11, 1917, but they do not get to see her.

She has collapsed. She has been taken to a sanitarium. The papers are calling it a nervous breakdown.[10]

Alice Paul didn't grow up a crusader; she wasn't a martinet. She had been an athlete in her school days, and a good one. Always on the small side, she won and kept winning because of stamina and a blunt refusal to lose. But her imprisonment in England, with its barbaric force-feeding, had sapped some physical resources that never returned. She is thirty-two in the summer of 1917, but she looks older, largely because she treats her physical and mental capacities as a reserve fund to be tapped anytime the suffrage cause runs short. The night before one major demonstration at the White House, when Cameron House had filled up with picketers, she slept on the fire escape, waking to find snow on her sleeping bag.[11]

The picketing campaign had added military generalship to an already crushing list of responsibilities: raising money, propping up morale, keeping the public focused amid the distraction of war. Soon after the demonstrations turned violent, the owners of Cameron House told her to move out.[12] No wonder people thought she was having a nervous breakdown.

In fact, the doctor discovers a different ailment. When fourteen members of the executive committee gather around her sickbed, she tells them that she has been diagnosed with Bright's disease. It's the same kidney condition that had killed President Wilson's wife a few years earlier.

The doctor has told Alice that she has a year to live.

Reeling from the news, the suffragists do what she asks, and patch together plans to keep the organization going. Lucy Burns, Paul's associate since the suffrage parade four years earlier, will lead in her absence. The committee votes unanimously to take care of Paul during her illness. Somehow they will find a way.[13]

The pickets, newly energized, return to their posts the next day, which happens to be Bastille Day. But now they face reprisals beyond anything they have suffered so far. The women arrested that day are sentenced to extraordinarily long sentences: sixty days, in some cases. And it's not any old jail this time; it's Occoquan, a work camp located an hour away in Virginia. The men who run the prison attempt to break the wills of these well-to-do white ladies by forcing them to share facilities with black prostitutes. It doesn't work—the women do not share the guards' racism—but it shows that the authorities are willing to use psychological warfare in addition to physical force.

Dudley Field Malone, a longtime friend and ally of the president, tries to make Wilson see the injustice of these long sentences—and, more generally, of denying women the vote. (He is having an affair with Doris Stevens, one of the Occoquan-bound picketers.) Malone's message is echoed by J.A.H. Hopkins, an even closer and longer-standing friend of Wilson's, whose wife is bound for the workhouse, too. After ignoring the hundreds of women who have spent half a year trying to persuade him, Wilson decides to listen to these men. He pardons all the pickets.

A reporter travels to Paul's bedside to get her reaction, finding her "wan and big-eyed." She says she is obliged to the president, but the Woman's Party has no intention of changing course.

"The pickets have brought the issue before the eyes of the world and put Wilson in the final corner," she says. "Now he has got to the point of practically declaring for the federal amendment, and we have placed him where he will be obliged to do something to prove that."[14]

The suffragists will be picketing again on Monday.

The most important aspect of this interview is its location: Baltimore. Dora Lewis had insisted that she get a second opinion at Johns Hopkins—the same place where Reed had his ailing kidney removed eight months earlier. The doctors there tell her she's not dying; she was just so exhausted, mentally and physically, that it *looked like* she was.

A month after her initial collapse, and much sooner than her doctors would like, Paul returns to Washington, eager to resume command. Every day now, the picketing draws closer to being a three-way battle among suffragists, rioters, and police. The women do all they can to help it along.

In mid-August, the suffragists deploy their most incendiary banner yet:

Kaiser Wilson

Have you forgotten how you sympathized with the poor Germans because they were not self-governed?

Twenty million American women are not self-governed.

Take the beam out of your own eye.

Naval reservists in crisp white uniforms see the signs, grab the signs, and destroy the signs. Normally the cops put an end to such manhandling, but on this day, they hang back.

The men realize they can abuse the women with impunity. So they do.

As suffragists return to headquarters to replace the banners that have been destroyed, the men pursue them to Cameron House itself. When Lucy Burns emerges with a new banner, three men spring at her on the very doorstep, tearing the banner away.

There is now a mob, several thousand strong, blocking Madison Place in front of Cameron House. Anybody who emerges from the building is attacked. Alice Paul, who doesn't often take part in picketing, gets knocked down by a man trying to seize her suffrage sash. She refuses to let go, so he drags her twenty feet across the sidewalk. She is less than a month removed from her hospital bed.

The suffragists refuse to surrender. They hang banners from the upper windows of the building. The men grab a ladder from the theater next door, tip it against the façade of Cameron House, climb up, and destroy them. Down on the street, the mob is hurling rotten eggs and tomatoes. Then somebody fires a gun. The bullet pierces a second-floor window and buries itself in the ceiling.

At last, more than an hour after the riot began, police reserves push the crowd back. They make few arrests.

The suffrage fight keeps growing more destructive; nobody seems able to stop it. The president refuses to endorse the federal amendment; Paul refuses to stop protesting his refusal; Catt can't make Wilson move any faster or Paul any more slowly. The secretary of the navy orders sailors to stop attacking the women; they ignore him. On the night of the "Kaiser Wilson" riots, one of Paul's lieutenants goes to a hardware store and orders a .38-caliber revolver with fifty bullets, to be delivered to Cameron House.[15]

As the fighting in the streets gets hotter, so does Alice Paul's rhetoric. Despite all the dangers of suggesting that something is awry with American democracy in the summer of 1917, she does more than suggest it—she proclaims it.

"We have no true democracy in this country, though we are fighting for democracy abroad," she says. "Twenty million American citizens are denied a voice in their own government. We must let the public know that this intolerable situation exists because, toward women, President Wilson has adopted the attitude of an autocratic ruler. We have stood at the gates of the White House for six months in silent protest. We have gone to prison for asking for liberty at home. We have to make the situation definite and concrete."[16]

The logic is unimpeachable. A fresh escalation is necessary. It's the only way to increase the pressure on Wilson, which she feels sure will eventually cause him to move, as surely as steam drives a piston. But how can she do it? The ranks of picketers have thinned since the government started sentencing women to *six months* in Occoquan.

Like Bourne deciding to denounce his mentor, like Eastman bracing himself to take the stage in Fargo, Paul faces the essential question of the idealist in wartime: How far will I go?

She gives her answer on the brisk morning of October 20, 1917. Four pickets report for duty that day, bundled against the chill.

They are led by Alice Paul herself.

Her banner quotes Wilson: "The time has come to conquer or submit; for us there can be but one choice—we have made it."[17]

She expects to be arrested, and she is. She is prepared for a jail sentence and gets it, though she is surprised that it is longer than any others: *seven months.* She asks her mother not to worry, trying to assure her, "It will merely be a delightful rest."[18] Maybe she believes it.

The judge sends her to the district jail. It's not Occoquan, but it's gruesome all the same. Severe and forbidding on the outside, it's filthy and decrepit within. It's so cold that prisoners wrap themselves in newspapers to stay warm.[19] The cramped, crowded cells have open toilets that can be flushed only from the outside, by the guards. There are rats and bedbugs everywhere.

Paul's experience in English prisons now serves her well. On her first night, she sees that the closed windows are forcing everyone to breathe foul air. She grabs the rope and pulls the window open. Two male guards try to pull her away. She clings to the rope, then to the iron bars, and doesn't give up until they close her cell door behind her. And she's still not done. She and the other inmates throw every loose object they can reach at the windows until they crack the glass.[20]

In prison, as on the outside, Paul's convictions put an immense strain on her body. The food is vile beyond belief, consisting of worm-ridden pork, bug-ridden soup, and stale bread. A few days of trying and failing to eat it leaves her so weak she can't get out of bed.

The authorities hate her, but they can't let her die. They carry her to the prison hospital. Grudgingly they offer her eggs and milk.

And once again Paul has to choose.

A few weeks earlier, at Occoquan, Lucy Burns had surreptitiously circulated a petition that made a radical claim: that the suffragists were political prisoners and should be treated accordingly. They demanded an end to solitary confinement; access to paper, books, and their lawyers; and freedom from the menial work that inmates at Occoquan were expected to do. One suffragist calls the petition "the first organized group action ever made in America to establish the status of political prisoners." But it hadn't worked. The men who run the District of Columbia said they didn't know what the term "political prisoner" meant.[21]

Paul thinks about Burns's protest as she regards those much-needed eggs and that cold glass of milk. "The hunger strike is a desperate weapon," she had said a few months earlier, "which should only be used as a last resort in resistance of authority."[22]

This is her last resort. She uses it.

Paul pushes the food away. At the other end of the hospital, so does Rose Winslow, a suffragist and social worker from Brooklyn. The guards try to intimidate Paul, to confuse her; they threaten to take her someplace worse than the prison hospital. A day passes, then another. Still she won't eat.

"Now they demand a right which has never been recognized in this country," one exasperated reporter writes, "to be regarded when in prison as different from the other prisoners."[23]

Paul does indeed demand that right, but not just for the suffragists. "We are protecting the rights of political offenders everywhere in the nation," she says in one of the rare messages that she can slip out of jail.[24]

Like Eastman, a socialist who stumbled into being a free-speech crusader, Paul is forced by her suffrage beliefs to become a pioneer in the field of political incarceration. Eastman and Paul are, in effect, architects of a new infrastructure for radicalism, helping to build systems that make other radical protests possible.

The treatment of Paul and other suffragists is beginning to upset even people who don't believe in suffrage. President Wilson finally hears enough of these complaints to ask for an investigation of prison conditions. The district commissioners send an outside doctor to see Paul.

He asks about her cause: how she agitates for it, her feelings about President Wilson, why is she so fixated on him?

Paul realizes that the man is a psychiatrist. He is looking for a reason to commit her to an insane asylum.

The doctor declines to do that, but Paul soon lands in more distress anyway. She is placed in the care, if that's the word, of the prison physician, Dr. J. A. Gannon. "I believe I have never in my life before feared anything or any human being," Paul will say later. "But I confess I was afraid of Dr. Gannon."[25]

After seventy-eight hours of waiting for her to eat, Dr. Gannon orders her carried to the hospital's mental ward. The guards take off the door and replace it with iron bars, which means there is nothing to muffle the shrieks of the lunatics.[26] They scream for hours. Soon so does she.

There are several ways to force an unwilling woman to eat, especially if she weighs only ninety-five pounds, has recently been ill, and is weak from malnutrition. Restraints—either straps or the weight of guards or nurses—secure the arms, the legs, and the chest. Then a tube is forced into the mouth and down the throat to the stomach. If the prisoner refuses to unclench her teeth—which some do, until their strength fails—then the tube is pushed up one nostril, down the throat, and into the stomach. A nurse whips together a pint of eggs and milk, and it is poured into the retching body of the patient. Then the tube is removed, and sometimes there is blood, and often there is sobbing, but rarely is there death.

The authorities assure President Wilson that "no force or persuasion [is] necessary" to feed Alice Paul.

Every person who knows her knows that is a lie.[27]

Paul is taciturn about the experience, and the physical and mental toll that it takes. Rose Winslow, who is also force-fed, is more forthcoming: "One feels so forsaken when one lies prone and people shove a pipe down one's stomach." It couldn't have been any easier for Paul, based on what Winslow sees: "Miss Paul vomits much."[28]

Dr. Gannon doesn't allow her doctor to check on her. Instead he orders a prison nurse to "observe" her, which means that once an hour, all night long, a bright white light floods her room.[29] Alice Paul has asked for her political rights and now she is being tortured for it.

At Cameron House, the other suffragists are nearly frantic with worry and anger. In a show of solidarity, they decide to stage the biggest picket yet. Forty-one women—"our best and bravest," according to Lucy Burns—march forth in waves. They hail from all over the country, and range from teenagers to septuagenarians.[30]

They are arrested in bunches and brought to court. The judge, having lost his appetite for sending women to prison, surprises them by letting them go.

Two hours after leaving the courtroom, most of the women are back in front of the White House, picketing again.[31] This time the judge sends them to jail.

They arrive at Occoquan on the evening of November 14, 1917, angrier and more determined than before. They demand to see the superintendent himself. Like Paul, they insist on being treated as political prisoners. They don't realize what they are bringing on themselves.

The superintendent—a despot with "stiff white hair, blazing little eyes"—has heard more than enough of this talk.[32] He orders the guards (all male, wearing street clothes) to put the women in their cells. It is the beginning of what the suffragists will later call "the night of terror."

Some women are thrown headlong into metal beds; others are dropped spine-first onto benches. There are bruises and sprains; a couple of them, including Dora Lewis, lose consciousness. When Lucy Burns calls to an ailing woman to make sure she is all right, the guards handcuff her to the bars of her cell and leave her that way for the night.

The superintendent allows no one to see the prisoners. So it takes a while for the world to learn that he is threatening to beat them at the whipping post.[33]

When word of the melee at Occoquan leaks out, a lawyer for the suffragists gets a writ of habeas corpus. He knows that lives are at stake. By this point, almost all of the imprisoned suffragists are on a hunger strike. Like Alice Paul in her student-athlete days, they will win by refusing to lose.

Ten days later, the imprisonments end as capriciously as they began. Nobody knows how direct a role the president played in letting the suffragists go, or in putting them there in the first place.

The imprisoned suffragists are allowed to go home. Many need to be carried to get there.

"The victory of our hunger strike is complete," Paul declares.[34] Of course, after everything the women have suffered, what else *can* she say?

Cameron House becomes a field hospital. Some of the suffragists recover in days; many are never quite the same. One young staffer from *The Masses* spent her incarceration thinking about poverty and injustice, and how even outside prison, she wasn't really free: "Never would I recover from this wound, this ugly knowledge I had gained of what men were capable [of] in their treatment of each other."[35] This quickening in the social conscience of Dorothy Day, hero of the Catholic Worker movement, is an accidental result of making idealists suffer to realize their ideals.

But what if all that suffering was for nothing? While Paul and her fellow militants were locked in godforsaken jail cells, the men of New York voted to amend the state constitution, enfranchising women. It is an enormous leap forward—"the Gettysburg of the woman suffrage movement," according to Carrie Chapman Catt—but it happened largely because NAWSA spent years organizing at the state level, not because Alice Paul and the militants fought in Washington for the federal amendment.[36]

On November 9, 1917, the second day of Paul's force-feeding, Catt and a few other NAWSA leaders went to the White House to thank the president for supporting their New York campaign. Catt and Wilson had drawn closer together, in part because of their shared disdain for the militants. She spent an hour with the president, never once mentioning her fellow suffragist who was being tortured a few miles away.

"I see Alice Paul is in for 7 months," Catt wrote to another NAWSA leader after Paul's arrest. "Poor little misguided idiot. I suppose she will try the hunger fast. It is time for something new."[37]

It takes Alice Paul three weeks to regain her strength, rise from her sickbed, and continue her fight for women's rights. Wilson, Catt, and even some of her former advisers are against her, but her conviction that she is doing the right thing for the right reason is enough to sustain her. She might have a fruitful conversation with Randolph Bourne on this point, if only these singular radicals had a way to find each other. To see their visions of American democracy made real, they have shown that they are willing to suffer abuse—psychic, physical, or a combination of the two—more grievous than most of the doughboys will suffer for Woodrow Wilson's.

Chapter 24

A cold, damp wind stings John Reed's face. Days of drenching rain have created lakes of slippery mud. Weeks of strikes have led to idle crowds, shuttered factories. Years of war and privation—of food rations that are tight and getting tighter, of unheeded demands for bread and peace and land—have fostered a mood of angry dread. Even in the middle of the night, it hangs in the air. Reed, climbing down from his train, can scent it like a hound hunting foxes.[1] He is very glad to be in Petrograd.

He has come to Russia because Lincoln Steffens told him the new world was being born there. But at every stop along the way, Reed heard worse and worse news, conflicting and confusing. It seemed plausible that the city might fall to either the counterrevolutionary General Kornilov or to the Germans, or maybe both in succession. He is glad to learn that the Provisional Government remains in control—although that is confusing enough.

Reed is lucky to find an astute guide to enlighten him. Albert Rhys Williams, a friendly acquaintance from Greenwich Village who has been covering Russia for the *New York Post,* helps him to understand the jittery factions in Russian politics. They include the Provisional Government, led by Alexander Kerensky, which keeps a tenuous hold on power; the Cadets, bourgeois democrats who would like to see an end to even this moderate socialist government; and the party on the leftmost edge of the spectrum, the Bolsheviks, who favor a workers' revolt and an immediate end to the war. Their leader, Vladimir Lenin, is considered so dangerous that on his return from European exile, the German authorities had sent him across the country in a sealed train, in hopes of keeping the Marxist virus contained. Now he is thought to be hiding near Petrograd, waiting for the decisive moment.

Williams describes Lenin with such naked admiration that Reed teases him for it. Isn't Williams a Congregational minister and therefore a man of peace? Reed thinks he sounds like a "full-blown Bolshevik."

Don't be so jolly, Williams warns Reed. The Bolsheviks want a revolution and will start one if they get the chance. They mean business. And what are the two of them by comparison?

"A couple of dilettantes," Williams says, answering his own question. "Well, that's impossible here. Either you're on the side of Lenin and his party, or you become an apologist for the war."[2]

To learn more about the Bolsheviks, Reed goes to the source: the Smolny Institute. The genteel building on the banks of the Neva is a ludicrous place for revolutionaries to meet: It had been a finishing school for daughters of the Russian nobility.

Reed likes the bustle of the place, the sense of hectic purpose. He joins packed, noisy meetings upstairs, and downstairs he stands in enormous lines with workers and soldiers in the dining hall, where anybody can get cheap cabbage soup. But he finds the answers he seeks in the attic. There, on a rough chair at a bare table in the center of the room, sits Leon Trotsky. The thirty-seven-year-old revolutionary has a "pale, cruel face" that tapers to a pointed goatee—a face, according to Reed, that could be "positively Mephisthophelean in its expression of malicious irony."[3]

Trotsky listens to the young American's questions, then disregards them and lectures him on the nature and function of "soviets," the councils of workers, peasants, and soldiers that have risen as an alternative to bourgeois Western political democracy. The soviets are "the most perfect representatives of the people—perfect in their revolutionary experience, in their ideas and objects," he explains. "Based directly upon the army in the trenches, the workers in the factories, and the peasants in the fields, they are the backbone of the Revolution."

He imparts the lesson in a dazzling hour-long gallop through the theory of revolution—a theory that Trotsky believes is imminently turning into reality on the streets of Petrograd.

"It is the *lutte finale*," he says. Any socialist could quote that phrase from the "Internationale." Trotsky makes it sound like it's happening this hour, this minute.[4]

It is exactly what Reed needs to hear.

The American declaration of war had wrecked Reed. He'd begun to doubt that the workers would ever rise, or that true democracy—the kind that was political *and* industrial—was possible. The philosophical doubts fed, and were fed by, personal troubles.[5]

"I am 29 years old, and I know that this is the end of a part of my life, the end of youth," he had written in a long essay, likely never meant to be published. "Sometimes it seems to me the end of the world's youth, too; certainly the Great War has done something to us all."

After his depleting kidney surgery, he knew he was no longer the same old Jack—"some of that old superabundant vitality is gone, and with it the all-sufficient joy of mere living." He consoled himself that he had the love of his life, but then he lost her, too. While helping Eastman attack the government in *The Masses,* he had carried on an infidelity and confessed it to Louise. Despite her affair with Eugene O'Neill, she refused to forgive him and fled to Europe, getting accredited to cover the war.[6]

All summer, from across the ocean, Reed had tried to patch things up. He acknowledged "how far I have fallen from the ardent young poet who wrote about Mexico." He promised to do better. "Please god I intend to get back to poetry and sweetness, some way."[7]

She decided to give him a chance. So the damp wind that stung Reed's face stung hers, too. She mucked through the same muddy streets as him, looked up at the same heavy clouds, sniffed the same trouble in the air.

They have twin hopes in Petrograd. As professional journalists, they want to catch history as it happens. As husband and wife, they want to salvage their fractured marriage. The first will take a combination of skill, diligence, luck. The second requires Jack to shake off his gloom, to recover himself—and he knows it. "You thought you were getting a hero—and you only got a vicious little person who is fast losing any spark he may have had," he said.[8]

A few weeks after their arrival in Petrograd, Reed tells a friend in America what he and Bryant have seen. "It is possible that the proletariat will finally lose its temper and rise; it is possible that the generals will come with fire and sword; at any rate, blood will flow—in rivers," he writes. "It looks like a show-down soon—and the whole country will welcome it—any kind of a show-down."[9]

He will welcome it, too.

By early November—late October, according to the Russian calendar—the tension is making them crack. It's not just Trotsky and Kerensky, but the American journalists, too. They assail each other's revolutionary bona fides.

"Humanitarian! Sky pilot!" yells Reed.

"Harvard Red! Football cheerleader!" Williams yells back.

"You're both acting like small boys," says Bessie Beatty, who is covering Russia for the San Francisco *Bulletin*. "Call yourselves radicals? You're a couple of spoiled American brats. Why don't you learn discipline from the Russian-American Bolsheviks?"[10]

With worker demands getting more insistent, the threat of insurrection keeps growing. Who will make the first move? Smolny is frenzied: "a center of storm, delegates falling down asleep on the floor and rising again to take part in the debate." Kerensky draws his artillery into the Winter Palace, preparing to make a final stand.[11]

Then it all happens fast.

Kerensky orders government troops to shut down the Bolshevik newspapers. Trotsky orders his troops to break the government seals, then shut down *Kerensky's* papers. "We're off!" cries one of the comrades at Smolny, clapping Reed on the shoulder.[12]

On November 7, 1917, Reed and Bryant try to see Kerensky at the Winter Palace. They are told he has fled the city.

That night, at Smolny, a historic meeting occurs. The room is teeming, close. There is no heat "but the stifling heat of unwashed human bodies," Reed notes. Above them hangs a vile cloud of cigarette smoke. Now and then an official steps to the podium and asks the comrades not to smoke. Everybody, smokers and all, takes up the cry, then resumes smoking.[13]

Over the clamor, delegates hear a deep dull sound. They look to the windows, anxious. It comes again, unmistakable: cannon fire.[14] The artillery batteries of the Peter and Paul Fortress and the naval cruiser *Aurora,* both of which are in Bolshevik hands, have begun firing toward the Winter Palace.

The moderates think that the Bolsheviks are making a power grab. They begin to storm out of the hall. An official rings a bell, trying to stop them. But Trotsky rises and utters the famous cry: "They are just so much refuse which will be swept away into the garbage-heap of history!"

The room erupts. Workers and soldiers scream, the cannons pound away. "So, with the crash of artillery, in the dark, with hatred, and fear, and reckless daring, new Russia was being born," according to Reed.

Jack and Louise rush out of Smolny, hoping to witness the climax of the fight at the Winter Palace. They arrive just as the Red Guards—the proletarian militia, drawn from the city's factories—press their final assault. Reed and Bryant join them, stooping low, bunching together. They stream toward the barricades "like a black river," in Reed's words.

"Look out, comrades!" says a man in front of Reed. "Don't trust them. They will fire, surely!"

But the defenses are unmanned. The troops loyal to Kerensky have drifted away. The Red Guards heave up and over the barricade and pour into the palace. Jack and Louise go with them.

And just like that, it's over. The old order has fallen to the new. But what is the new?

Reed thinks he knows, but he can't believe it: "For the first time in history the working-class has seized the power of the state, for its own purposes—and means to keep it."[15]

At 8:40 the next night, the man who intends to wield that power emerges from hiding, striding across the stage at Smolny. Vladimir Ilyich Ulyanov, known by his pen name, Lenin, has trained for this moment for decades. His self-discipline is staggering. At various points in life, he has given up Latin, Beethoven, chess, and skating because they distracted him from realizing his ideals. Terror pleases him: Over the years, he has advocated the use of guns, bombs, paving stones, acid, boiling water, and marrying for money as instruments of insurrection.[16] He has pursued violent revolution with a zeal that scares other violent revolutionaries. And now he is a head of state.

Lenin grips the edge of the lectern; he lets the ovation roar. At last he makes the epochal declaration: "We shall now proceed to construct the Socialist order!"[17]

In brisk fashion he proposes to make a separate peace with Germany, to publish the Allies' secret treaties, to invite the exploited workers of Europe to stop fighting one another and turn their guns on their leaders, and to abolish the private ownership of land.[18]

Every measure passes almost unanimously. There is great weeping and cheering and singing of the "Internationale."

Reed is dazed, disbelieving. Five years earlier, Walter Lippmann had gotten excited by the merest inklings of socialist theory coalescing into practice in one city in upstate New York. Now the Bolsheviks, in winning their revolution, have brought socialism to much of a continent and more than a hundred million people.

"Whether it survive or perish," Reed writes, "whether it be altered unrecognizably by the pressure of circumstances, it will have shown that dreams can come true."[19]

John Reed's account of the October Revolution runs beneath an enormous front-page, full-width, double-deck headline in *The New York Call*. He extends to his fellow American socialists the first official greeting from leaders of the world's first proletarian republic.[20] Then he wonders what to do next.

He knows that the Bolshevik victory is tenuous. The bourgeois forces linger within Russia; the country is surrounded by enemies. For Reed, this uncertainty dredges up the last and deepest part of his crisis a few months earlier. His doubt that the workers would rise is linked to his doubt about what he can do to help them.

"All I know is that my happiness is built on the misery of other people, that I eat because others go hungry, that I am clothed when other people go almost naked through the frozen cities in winter, and that fact poisons me, disturbs my serenity, makes me write propaganda when I would rather play—though not so much as it once did."

Here, in Russia, in the middle of a new kind of nation, he might have a chance to help. To put down his reporter's notebook and join the Bolsheviks' fight. If he's cut out for it.

"Do you think we'll ever make the grade?" Reed asks Albert Rhys Williams. "Or are we tagged for life—the humanitarians, the dilettantes?"[21]

They soon get the chance to find out. Lenin and Trotsky think that European countries will rapidly follow Russia's example and rise up. At least they hope so. Otherwise, the bourgeois leaders of those countries will crush the revolution. To speed things along, Trotsky establishes a Bureau of International Revolutionary Propaganda. It attempts to foment revolution among the war-weary, exploited workers of Europe. It needs stylish writers and hard workers—people like Reed and Williams.

They begin their work amid the once-glorious trappings of the czar's foreign ministry. Hampered at every turn by bourgeois sabotage and what Reed calls "the inherent Russian penchant for tea and discussion," they still manage to publish three newspapers aimed at the eastern front. Millions of copies are dropped from airplanes, hand-carried across the front lines, and delivered by the "diplomatic couriers" who turn up in various European capitals with trunks full of the stuff.[22]

Reed's job is hard, but it revives him. Soon the gray autumn mud is wiped clean by snow. It's so cold in Petrograd, and fuel is so scarce, that Jack and Louise sleep in their overcoats. Food is even scarcer than fuel: They subsist on rabchick (a little bird), cabbage, revolutionary zeal, and their rekindled love for each other. When Williams, Beatty, and other friends come for soup, Reed heats the cans on an open fire on the bathroom floor.[23]

It's like Provincetown again, or the old days at 42 Washington Square: Life is all of a piece, work and play together. When the Foreign Ministry is threatened, Reed takes a turn standing guard duty with a rifle.[24] And when he hears that the intellectuals have gone on strike in Ukraine, he tells Williams that the two of them should take over.

Williams wonders what Reed will do in the job he has picked out for himself: commissar of art and entertainment.

"Oh, thousands of things," Jack says. "First of all, put joy into the people. Get up great pageants. Cover the city with flags and banners. And once or maybe twice a month have a gorgeous all-night festival with fireworks, orchestras, plays in all the squares, and everybody participating."[25]

Reed's sympathy with the new leaders of Russia is total, but his passport is American. The Wilson administration has no patience for radicals who threaten the country's security, even if they do it on the other side of the planet. Strange things begin happening to Reed. He thinks he has lost his wallet, until it turns up at the American embassy, of all the mystifying places. He doesn't know that an American agent had picked his pocket on a streetcar and brought it to the ambassador for inspection.[26]

The tug-of-war between Reed's political loyalties and his legal citizenship reaches a crisis in January 1918, when Lenin convenes the Third All-Russian Congress of Soviets. This is not a bourgeois parliamentary congress. (Lenin had dissolved the Constituent Assembly, where the Bolsheviks' power would have been weaker.) It is the first industrial parliament in history—"the crowning and extreme hope of the Socialist dream-theory," according to Max Eastman.

Edgar Sisson, the U.S. Committee on Public Information representative in Petrograd, knows that Reed will be tempted to do something conspicuous on such an occasion. He makes Reed promise not to make a speech.[27]

Reed promises. Then he makes a speech.

"The appearance of Comrade Reed is met by stormy applause," reports a journalist watching in the press gallery—the very spot where Reed had recently sat.[28]

He is introduced as a socialist who is under attack in America's bourgeois justice system for editing a revolutionary journal, now violently suppressed by the capitalists. His jail term may be lengthy. To Jack, this introduction is all that a boy could wish.

Reed tells the delegates that yes, he must leave Russia to face the capitalists' charges against him, but he goes knowing that the social revolution is not a dream—it is real. He will carry to America the message that Russia has a true people's government at last. All the previous regimes, he says, were "as futile a representative body as the Congress of the United States!"

Applause ringing in his ears, Reed is ready for whatever Sisson and the American government want to throw at him. But the denouement of his Russia adventure turns out to be the most madcap part.

Reed knows he will be interfered with at every turn on the way home. He asks Trotsky to name him a courier, the same treatment that Bryant had been accorded a few weeks earlier.

Trotsky goes Reed one better, naming him the Soviet consul in New York.

Jack is flattered—he is *delighted.* It is just the kind of grand and somewhat cracked gesture that fires his imagination.

"When I'm consul, I suppose I shall have to marry people," he tells Williams. "I hate the marriage ceremony. I shall simply say to them, 'Proletarians of the world, unite!'"[29]

Trotsky's reason for making the offer isn't clear. It could have been a joke, a send-up of capitalistic diplomatic protocol—though Trotsky is not exactly whimsical. More likely, it's a publicity ploy. Reed is facing a trial that will be covered heavily. Newspapers would certainly mention his association with the Soviets, giving the regime valuable exposure.

It's also possible that Trotsky's offer is on the level. Maybe he really does want Jack Reed to be the face of Soviet Russia in New York.

Only there's a price to be paid for all the times Reed thumbed his nose at his countrymen. The news of Reed's appointment sets all of his enemies scheming against him. One of them, or all of them, get it canceled. Perhaps someone showed Lenin a prospectus that Reed had drawn up for a periodical that would serve the interests of American corporations that wanted to do business with the new regime. Reed didn't care about the work, he just needed the money, and seemed to be subverting the thing even as he was helping to design it. (He had proposed that the masthead say "This paper is devoted to promoting the interests of American capital.")[30]

Chagrined by having his fun spoiled, Reed bids farewell to Lenin and Trotsky and his fellow hacks, and starts the long trip home. But the government isn't done tormenting him. The State Department maroons him in Scandinavia for two months, reducing him to selling freelance stories to pay his bills. By the time his boat reaches New York, he has fallen ill—food poisoning, maybe—but the authorities detain him onboard anyway: searching his possessions, interrogating him, confiscating the papers he needs for a book he'd like to write about the revolution.

They can slow him but they can't stop him. Eight hours after the boat docks, Reed is striding down the gangway. The towers of Midtown rise above him; Louise waits below.

A lot has changed in America since Reed left eight months earlier, especially among the young radicals, all of whom he knows. Eastman has been nearly lynched, his magazine has been shut down, and he is facing twenty years in jail. Paul has been on a hunger strike and withstood force-feeding to win her liberty. Bourne has denounced his mentor and seen the best outlet for his writing disappear. Only Lippmann has thrived, seeming to rise higher by the month. When Lenin took Russia out of the war, and Trotsky published the cynical secret treaties that the Allies had concluded with the czar, Wilson had tried to prop up the Allied effort by making a sweeping statement of American war aims; Lippmann had a hand in writing eight of his Fourteen Points.

All of the changes in their lives bring the young radicals to an endgame. In 1918 they will reckon with the consequences of the fights they started the year before.

Reed is coming to a reckoning, too. None of the other radicals has changed as profoundly as he has. When he left New York eight months earlier, he had been a baffled, wayward reporter. He comes home a revolutionary.[31]

Chapter 25

Alice Paul waits in the snow, shivering. For a year, suffragists have stood outside the White House, trying to send the president a message. Now, on January 9, 1918, she stares up at his windows, impatient to find out if he's heard them.

Behind those windows, President Wilson is meeting with a dozen congressmen. They have come to seek his advice. The suffrage amendment will reach the House floor the next day. How should they vote?

Wilson listens to each of their concerns in turn. Then, discarding his old view, which he had written into the 1916 party platform—that suffrage is a matter for the states—he urges them all to vote for the federal amendment. The war has changed the situation, he says. In light of all that women have done for the cause, it would be "an act of right and justice to the women of the country and of the world."

John Raker, chairman of the House suffrage committee, walks out of the White House to tell Paul and the others the news. One reporter likens their reaction to a flinging of bonnets in the air. They float back to headquarters, impervious to cold.

A few blocks away, Carrie Chapman Catt and some of her NAWSA associates are going through the motions of celebrating her birthday. (They've been lobbying congressmen all day—they're tired.) The news makes them scream and cheer and raise a glass to Wilson, "the best friend suffrage ever had."

The next afternoon, exactly forty years after Susan B. Anthony pushed for the amendment to be introduced, Paul, Catt, and the other leaders of the cause are crammed into different sections of the House gallery. The debate stretches for five hours: suffrage allies rising to echo Wilson's view; suffrage opponents trotting out the same arguments that women had been stomaching for generations. The bulk of the opposition comes, as ever, from southern Democrats, who see suffrage as a threat to good old-fashioned American womanhood and white supremacy.

At last the roll call begins. The first count is so close that they do it again. But the original numbers hold: The suffrage amendment secures its two-thirds majority with a single vote to spare. All twelve of the men who visited Wilson vote yes.

The suffragists stream out of the gallery, cheering and singing, voices echoing around the rotunda.

Alice Paul doesn't join them. She isn't there. It is the greatest triumph in the seventy years since Seneca Falls, but she has left early to get back to work. There is still a Senate vote ahead. There is no time to waste. She thinks they are in "these final weeks of the suffrage struggle."[1]

One good thing about democracy is that most of the time, in most cases, it keeps people from massacring one another. Men and women who feel driven to change the world, to make it accord with their ideals, can satisfy that desire without reaching for their rifles or machetes: To change the world, in a democracy, means changing minds. True, the strongest and richest members of a society often manipulate democracy to their advantage, and you do sometimes get a civil war, but the prospects without democracy are much worse: The strong and rich would *always* prevail, or you'd have nothing *but* civil war.

Another good thing about democracy is that it expresses the mind of a society, however imperfectly and incompletely, in numbers. In a democracy, you can keep score. In 1915, the House defeated the suffrage amendment by one hundred votes, and the measure looked as forlorn as it always had. In 1918, it passed. What happened in the interim? The meaning of the suffragists' long fight for their political rights depends on who changed those minds, and how.

The Suffragist declares that the House vote is a complete vindication for Alice Paul. An editorial claims that Wilson's endorsement "slipped the keystone into the political building-up of the suffrage question into a national political issue begun by the National Woman's Party in 1913." He gave the word, they argue, because of the pressure applied by the pickets, and his fear that they would menace him again. Max Eastman agrees, giving all the credit to Paul and her militants: "They won a victory which was very definitely their own."[2]

Catt had guessed that Paul would hog the credit for her militants this way. "You may assure any who make that claim that it was accomplished in spite of them," she told her officers. She knows that fifty-six of the one hundred decisive votes came from states that had won suffrage in the intervening years.[3] This is why her "winning plan" had focused so much time and energy on state-level campaigns instead of the go-for-broke federal approach of the National Woman's Party. And those dozen congressmen who voted yes after meeting with the president? She's the one who suggested they go see him.

Neither Paul nor Catt would want to hear this, but the evidence suggests the House victory required both of them. The part they'd hate the most is that each was effective *because of the other.* Catt is right to think that winning suffrage at the state level was the chief determinant of congressmen voting for the amendment. But Paul is right to think that raising the cost of opposing suffrage instilled a productive amount of fear in elected officials, including the one in the White House. The pressures intersect and double up. Elizabeth Bass, an influential member of the Democratic National Committee, is affiliated with NAWSA, but she repeatedly alerts Wilson to the dangers posed by the militants: "The so-called Woman's Party are engaged in active propaganda to discredit us."[4]

Catt and Paul couldn't acknowledge each other's contributions even if they wanted to (and didn't they want to). Catt couldn't defend the militants without losing the confidence of the president. Paul couldn't motivate the militants to risk their lives if she gave them reason to think a bigger, better-funded organization could win their freedom. Catt gave Wilson and other tremulous leaders a way to support suffrage without condoning unladylike militants; those militants, left cold by NAWSA's stately approach, could be galvanized into action by a leader who declared, as Paul did, that the political equality of women "is worth sacrificing everything for, leisure, money, reputation, and even our lives."[5]

Although both suffrage leaders are confident that the House vote clears the way for victory in the Senate—Catt even has a new dress made—they do not celebrate together. And though both organizations deploy the full arsenal of their lobbying techniques—Paul having instigated a sophisticated persuasion machine, one that NAWSA has duplicated—they do not coordinate their work.

It would have been better for them both if they had.

For, before long, February slips away, as do March and April, and somehow the summer is gone, and still the senators haven't voted on suffrage. If the congressional session ends before two-thirds of them vote for it, the amendment will have to start over in the House. Nobody wants that.

A sense of urgency grows: gradually, then rapidly, then precipitously. Could the suffragists come so far and still lose?

Catt stretches the bounds of her relationship with Wilson, asking him to write more and more letters to recalcitrant senators. He proves surprisingly obliging. But writing letters isn't good enough for Alice Paul. She tells a reporter that if the president would really stand up for women, and give one rousing speech in favor of the amendment, "it would pass at once."[6] With the congressional session dribbling away and Wilson showing no signs of addressing the Senate directly, she does what she always does in such situations: She escalates.

After nearly a year of detente, the militants of the National Woman's Party resume their protests in front of the White House. There are full-on melees in the streets—sprains, bruises, broken fingers.

The arrests resume.

The prison superintendent, having anticipated that the suffragists would be back in his charge, had reopened a dank, abandoned jail on the banks of the Anacostia River. The plumbing is open; the water tastes strange. Soon many of the women feel weak, nauseous. The air or the water or both is poisoning them. One visitor describes the women lying on straw pallets "stricken, in pain, like soldiers brought in from the field of battle."[7]

Again Alice Paul and her suffragists are pushed to their last resort: a hunger strike. The authorities cave and let the women go free. But now their time is nearly up.

The Senate schedules a vote for October 1, 1918, at the end of the session. The lobbyists in both suffrage groups think they're still two votes short. Catt makes one last plea to the president, telling him that a defeat for the amendment would imperil his war effort: "It will take the heart out of thousands of women, and it will be no solace to tell them that 'it is coming.'"

A day later, on the eve of the vote, Wilson takes a dramatic step. Is it because of Catt's warning about the war effort? Or because his son-in-law, William McAdoo, told him that Democrats would suffer in the midterm elections if he didn't do more? Is it fear of Alice Paul and the untold havoc she might wreak? Maybe his suffragist daughter Jessie, in some quiet moment, really did push him to a change of heart: Maybe he actually believes what he is about to say.[8]

On September 30, the suffrage leaders reconvene on Capitol Hill. It's the Senate side this time, not the House, but the dry mouths and rapid heartbeats are the same. Paul, Catt, and their associates crowd into the gallery. So does the First Lady—so does her mother.

Wilson speaks that day with what one reporter calls "unusual earnestness." It's the only way he *could* speak, considering what he had come to say. He wants to persuade the senators—especially his fellow southern Democrats—to vote yes. He is careful to say that "foolish and intemperate agitators do not reach me at all"—in other words, the pickets haven't forced his hand. He can dismiss them all he wants: He still sounds like Alice Paul.

"If we be indeed democrats, and wish to lead the world to democracy, we can ask other peoples to accept in proof of our sincerity and our ability to lead them whither they wish to be led nothing less persuasive and convincing than our actions," he says. "Our professions will not suffice."

At the end of fifteen impassioned minutes, Wilson finishes to a standing ovation. Even Paul, his chief tormentor, cheers him. Why shouldn't she? After five often excruciating years, he has finally done what she wanted him to do all along. She calls it "so glorious a thing for suffrage."[9]

The Senate votes on the amendment the next day—and defeats it. The suffragists needed two votes before the president's speech. The amendment fails by two votes. Wilson didn't persuade anybody.

In democracy, progress comes from changing minds. It's a better mechanism than the alternatives. But there's a catch. Sometimes minds won't change.

The parades, the pleading, the lobbying, the petitions, the brawls in the streets, the hunger strikes, the presidential arm-twisting, the dramatic last-minute wartime appeal, the sacrifice of time and money and health and even women's lives: All of these forces combined are no match for the knot of prejudices that makes southern Democrats vote "no."

Chapter 26

One winter night in 1918, Randolph Bourne meets a friend for dinner—a friend who is distressed by what she sees.

Bourne has always been a neat, fastidious dresser. His fellow Greenwich Villagers have grown used to seeing him in a hat pulled low and a long student cape. They don't mask his deformed features, but they confer what this friend calls "an awkward sort of dignity." But now Bourne looks worn—a little shabby, even. And he has grown terribly sad.

"The door was opening onto promise," he tells her. Great advances in thought, in politics, in ways of communicating had been so close. Radio. Airplanes. "Now comes this irrelevance of war. The monster has slammed the door. It will be a thousand years before it opens again."[1]

Bourne is in mourning. He has lost the ideal that he thought held great promise for the nation's life—and for his own. A year earlier, his essay on trans-national America had won him an invitation to speak at Harvard: "I was introduced in the most cosmic terms; never have I ever conceived myself such an international figure," he marveled at the time.[2] But by going to war, America had surrendered its special ability to serve as a neutral meeting ground for different nationalities. It would be absurd to talk about America being "trans-national" while orchestras refused to play Beethoven, and German shopkeepers were being tarred and feathered.

Bourne is too much a realist to deny the painful truth. The road that might have led to the creation of a Beloved Community, where people would reach across their differences and work together to fulfill their individual potential, has been blocked. The phrase "trans-national America" drops out of his lexicon.

Bourne's friend Beulah Amidon leaves dinner that night to resume her work securing political rights for women: She is one of Alice Paul's most reliable lieutenants. Bourne wants to see them win their fight, but politics holds little interest for him now. The rapid expansion of the wartime government—all those bright boys dining at the House of Truth—has led to an unhealthy inflation of the political sphere. He thinks it has become a "cult." Politics means compromise, and after watching his mentor John Dewey make peace with a grotesque war, Bourne has seen enough of compromise. He seeks a new ideal to replace the one he lost, a new star to steer by.

Since his college days, Bourne has worked out his philosophy one long essay at a time: "Youth," "The Experimental Life," "Trans-National America," "Twilight of Idols." Nobody wants to publish such essays now, not by a writer known to be so antagonistic to flag and country. He makes his living by reviewing books, mostly novels. Some of these still run in *The New Republic,* but most appear in *The Dial,* a general-interest magazine in Chicago. The would-be prophet has come a long way down.

But in these novels, he finds clues to what he has been seeking. In wartime, when everybody's choices are compelled, and thought itself is conscripted, artists have a chance to remain free. Literature, he thinks, could incubate "an idealism which is not full of compromises, which is more concerned with American civilization than with American politics, which is more desirous for American life, liberty and the pursuit of happiness than for a model constitution and a watertight political-democratic system." He has good reason for putting his faith in novels as a source of ideals: his own youth. In the uptight world of Bloomfield, his reading of adventurous modern fiction prepared his mind for radical thought.

In spring, his prospects seem a little less forlorn. *The Dial*'s proprietor, Martyn Johnson, announces that the magazine will grow. A rich young man named Scofield Thayer admires Bourne's writing, and the prospect of Bourne's playing a larger role in the revamped publication leads him to invest $25,000. In the fall, the magazine will move to Greenwich Village, where it will find Randolph Bourne waiting for it.

Bourne knows that if he is to do the work he has set for himself, and help find the new creative ideals that will aid in the reconstruction, he needs to keep the war at a distance. He is blessed and cursed with an acute sensitivity to the world around him. He knows how the keys should feel under his fingers when playing Brahms. He knows, from seeing the heartening sights of Paris or Berlin or Basel, that civic beauty is not the accidental by-product of good planning, but its ultimate goal. He knows, from a lifetime of belittling experiences, what it means when somebody looks away from him an instant too soon—or, worse, stares an instant too long.

It's not easy for such a person to stay sane in what he calls "a mad and half-destroyed world." But it can be done. Bourne offers a mantra for the dreamer in a menacing world, a passage as consoling as anything he ever wrote:

Let us compel the war to break in on us, if it must, not go hospitably to meet it. Let us force it perceptibly to batter in our spiritual walls. This attitude need not be a fatuous hiding in the sand, denying realities. When we are broken in on, we can yield to the inexorable. Those who are conscripted will have been broken in on. If they do not want to be martyrs, they will have to be victims. They are entitled to whatever alleviations are possible in an inexorable world. But the others can certainly resist the attitude that blackens the whole conscious sky with war. They can resist the poison which makes art and all the desires for more impassioned living seem idle and even shameful. For many of us, resentment against the war has meant a vivider consciousness of what we are seeking in American life.[3]

In 1918, in a country losing its mind, even a literary critic who spends his days amid the sheltering streets of Greenwich Village is going to be broken in on.

In summer, she returns. The beautiful, mercurial, much-loved Esther Cornell drifts back into Bourne's life as unexpectedly as she'd drifted out. With a few months until his new editorial duties begin—when "the gates of Martyn Johnson close about my soul," as he puts it—they decide to take a trip.[4] With their friend Agnes de Lima, they take a two-week walking tour up the coast to Massachusetts. Sometimes they ride trolleys; usually they stay in little inns along the coast.

This is when Bourne's real trouble begins.

One evening, walking along the beach, Esther decides to demonstrate the "rhythmic dancing" that she has learned. She jumps onto some rocks and begins to sway.

"Don't do that," says Randolph. He can see a gunboat offshore. There has been a submarine scare recently. "They'll think you're signaling the enemy."

Esther thinks this is funny. She keeps doing it.

The gunboat swings around. It begins tracking them.

The three of them flee back to their inn.

On Martha's Vineyard, Randolph and Esther say goodbye to Agnes, who needs to return to New York. They are out for a walk when a man wearing a naval uniform confronts them. He demands to know their business.

Randolph flusters. He can't say much. He is afraid of exposing Esther to opprobrium—a single woman, alone with a single man, very far from home.

Esther, keeping cool, explains they have come from New York on a trip.

"There were three of you when you arrived here," the officer says.

"Yes," says Esther. "My friend had to go back to her job."

He wants to see Randolph's notebook, the figures he has been scribbling. Randolph, meticulous as ever, has been tabulating their expenses. He hands it over.

"Would you be willing to have all documents in your possession examined?" he asks.

"Documents? What documents?"

"The mail you received this morning, for example," he says. For they had received letters.

"Certainly," says Esther, still staying calm, which means she is giving the performance of a lifetime.

When they leave the Vineyard the next morning, the officer is on their ferry. When they reach the mainland, he sits behind them on the train. When they reach South Station in Boston, he orders them to wait while he telephones for instructions. When he can't locate his superiors, he refuses to let them leave.

This is excruciating. Randolph can't bear the thought of prisons.[5]

Esther once again fills the breach. She invites the man to join them for lunch. Once seated at a counter, she turns on her very powerful charm, trying to disarm him.

"Tell me how come you are able to get *two* girls to walk with you," the officer says to Bourne. "I can't even get one!"

He lets them go.

They return to New York deeply shaken, but the news there is even more unnerving. While Bourne was away, government officials had come to the offices of *The New Republic,* asking about him.[6]

To the paranoid mind—and wartime hysteria has taught radicals the value of paranoia, knowing you are being followed, wondering if

THE REAL AND THE IDEAL 227

someone at the next table is listening—certain incidents in Bourne's life begin to suggest a pattern. A few months earlier, he had gone to visit his friend Van Wyck Brooks, and a trunk full of his letters had gone missing. Has it been taken by government officials, maybe the same ones who asked about him at *The New Republic*? Why was that naval officer so interested in him? Is his name on a list somewhere?[7]

A few years earlier, Bourne had roused his contemporaries with the limitless possibilities of the modern world. Now he refers to "this ever-frightening military-industrial era." It gets more frightening all the time.[8]

Bourne must feel a sense of déjà vu. Four years after climbing the steps to the handsome townhouse of *The New Republic* for the first time, he does the same at the new offices of *The Dial*. They are only eight blocks apart.

Martyn Johnson is well aware of how crowded the magazine field has grown. To improve the odds for his revamped publication, he recruits high-profile contributors, stars that will bring instant cachet. And who could bring more cachet than the country's foremost philosopher, John Dewey?

Johnson approaches Dewey and finds him agreeable—with one exception. Being a business-minded publisher, a practical sort of man, Johnson dispatches the problem quickly enough. He does what Dewey asks.

Johnson summons Bourne and informs him that *The Dial* won't need his editorial services after all.

Scofield Thayer is furious. He reminds Johnson that his investment in the magazine had been contingent on Bourne playing a major role. His fury may be the only thing that keeps Bourne involved in even a writing capacity.

Bourne writes his mother a letter. He assures her that though he has been relieved of his editorial duties, he is still to receive a salary. "I prefer it this way as it leaves me much freer."[9]

That is hard to believe. There may be a truer record of his feelings in an essay he wrote around this time, one that suggests that as much as he struggled to stay "below the battle," the war had broken him: The last trace of RANDOLPH BOURNE, the bold young idealistic hero of the *Youth and Life* essays, might be gone.

In "Old Tyrannies," he disavows virtually everything he once proclaimed. He now argues that trying to change society is foolish, considering people can't control their own base impulses: fear, anger, hate, love. Individuals have no agency in society, because society controls them at every turn. The men and women who try to live as individuals anyway end up jailed or killed.

Why this pretense of individuality in the first place?

"We all enter as individuals into an organized herd-whole in which we are as significant as a drop of water in the ocean, and against which we can about as much prevail," he writes. "Whether we shall act in the interests of ourselves or of society is, therefore, an entirely academic question."[10]

Tacitly rejecting the optimism of William James (he has been reading a lot of Nietzsche), he argues that no one changes anything in this world. By the time a young person marshals his or her "puny strength" to make a so-called difference, it's too late. "You are now a part of that very flaming rampart against which new youth advances. . . . So you have never overtaken the given. Actually you have fallen farther and farther behind."

"You have not affected the world you live in; you have been molded and shaped by it yourself."

"While you thought you were making headway, you were really being devoured."

On and on it goes, angry and despairing.

Friends note that Bourne seems bitter in the fall of 1918.[11] If he is still playing the piano, none of them mention it.

Chapter 27

"**W**ell, Art, got your grip packed for Atlanta?"[1] asks Jack Reed, dropping into a chair next to Art Young at the defendants' table.

It is September 30, 1918, the first morning of the *Masses* trial. The second *Masses* trial, to be exact, though it's the first one for Reed. The State Department had proven so obnoxious about letting him come back from Russia that he missed his court date. His welcome-home party in Greenwich Village had given him a chance to hear macabre details of the just-concluded fiasco, which had ended in a mistrial: "a scene from *Alice in Wonderland*, rewritten by Dostoevsky," according to his co-defendant Floyd Dell.[2]

Earl Barnes, the assistant district attorney—"a bald-headed hawk-faced clothes-pole of a man with a perpetual tight little smile under his nose," according to Max Eastman—relishes having another chance to send Eastman, Reed, Young, Dell, and the business manager Merrill Rogers away. In the first trial, he had faced two of the sharpest lawyers in America: Morris Hillquit, co-founder of the Socialist Party of

America, and Dudley Field Malone, adept defender of Alice Paul's suffragists. Barnes nearly proved their equal, persuading ten of the twelve
jurors to vote to convict. This time, Hillquit has fallen ill and Malone is
traveling.[3] The best the defendants can do on short notice is Seymour
Stedman, who had represented Eugene Debs in his trial for violating
the Espionage Act—a trial that Debs had *lost*.

The man who had won 6 percent of the vote for president in 1912
had been sentenced to ten years in jail. If Gene Debs isn't safe, then no
radical is safe. Especially not the *Masses* defendants—not after Stedman falls ill, too.

Eastman and Reed think they're going to jail this time for sure.[4]

For Jack, who is no stranger to the defendant's table, the trial is bizarre, bewildering. He faces twenty years in prison because he had written seven words. The August 1917 issue of *The Masses* included an
item from the *New-York Tribune* that called the enormous surge in
mental illness—what we now call shell shock—"the unexpected and
staggering factor of the present war."[5] Reed had given this item the
provocative headline "Knit a Strait-Jacket for Your Soldier Boy."

When Barnes calls Reed to the stand, he argues that the headline is
a plain attempt to obstruct enlistment, and therefore a violation of the
Espionage Act.

Reed explains it differently. To describe his state of mind, he offers
a harrowing account of what he'd witnessed in three years as a war correspondent: a French hospital full of women raped by German troops;
a German hospital full of soldiers gone mad; rats running across soldiers' faces in muddy trenches; wounded soldiers shrieking as they sink
into the mud.

"Didn't you think it was time we got into it if you saw all of that?"
asks the judge.

"No, I did not think—I do not see the analogy," he says, stunned. "I
think it was a reason to keep *out*."

Judge and prosecutor alike keep pressing, trying to get Reed to convict himself. Other defendants are pressed the same way.

By the time the government has finished making its case that *The*

Masses intended to obstruct recruitment—more generally, that the magazine is a conspiracy of godless kaiser-sympathizing America-hating socialists—it's clear that Stedman is in no shape to deliver a closing argument. He's feverish; he has been missing dates. It's also clear that only one person can do it for him.

What's not at all clear is what in the world Max can say.

Martyrdom doesn't appeal to Eastman. He had demonstrated as much in the first trial. On the witness stand, Barnes had pressed him about a grimly comic spectacle that unfolded on the trial's first morning. Below the windows of the courtroom, a brass band struck up the national anthem, so everybody stood. But the band was part of a Liberty Loan drive, so a few minutes later, they played the anthem again, and when Merrill Rogers leapt to his feet, everybody else had to do the same. This went on happening until the judge finally made Rogers knock it off. Barnes used the incident to challenge Eastman: Had he stood out of a genuine sense of devotion? After all, he was under indictment for writing an essay that denounced "the religion of patriotism."

Eastman could have gone down guns blazing, decrying the war as a crime and patriotism as a sham. Instead he said that his feelings had changed, now that American soldiers were on the way to the front.

Was this prudence or cowardice?

In the six months between his court dates, the dilemma was never far from Eastman's mind. For in spite of his frustrations with editing—the fundraising, the contributor stalking, the legal pressures—he had launched a new magazine, *The Liberator*. Most of the *Masses* stalwarts have reassembled in its pages: Art Young draws cartoons, Floyd Dell writes some of the country's sharpest book reviews, an extraordinarily gifted illustrator named Frank Walts contributes cover designs. The freewheeling democratic character of *The Masses* doesn't survive the transition: no more collective ownership, no more kaleidoscopic editorial meetings. And now everybody gets paid.

Still they are all dancing across a minefield, with opportunities for prudence and cowardice on every page. The magazine wants workers' control of industry, full equality for women (with special praise for "Alice Paul and her young army of militants"), and the distribution of information on birth control. It also strongly condemns the official indifference to the lynching of black men, a scourge that has been growing amid the dislocations of the war. The featured story nearly every month is a long report from John Reed on what he had seen in Russia. On only one point does the magazine stand on solid ground, at least where post office inspectors are concerned. Eastman strongly supports President Wilson's war aims, as expressed in the Fourteen Points. The international peacekeeping organization that Wilson wants to create after the war seems to Eastman a step toward "an age of freedom and happiness for mankind." He even calls on the Socialist Party to offer "generous recognition" of Wilson's war aims in its platform.[6]

To some of Eastman's fellow radicals, this position looks even more ignominious than his testimony. Is he toeing the administration line just so Postmaster General Burleson doesn't get him again? Eastman swears he is sincere. He claims that he is only applying a principle that Leon Trotsky had articulated: that Wilson and the socialists can be fellow travelers on the same train, sharing a car until they depart at their respective stations.[7]

Unfortunately for Eastman, that sentiment isn't shared by John Reed.

One warm night in July, after Max and Florence finished their dinner, Reed had come for a visit. They were spending much of their time that summer in Croton-on-Hudson, a little town north of New York City. Bohemians had reconstituted their bohemia in the tiny houses that line Mount Airy Road, curving up a wooded hillside. Jack and Louise lived just down the lane.

Florence straightened up. Max fussed at his desk. Jack paced, restless. It was like his fidgety first meeting with Max, back in 1912.

"Max," he said, "I think I've got to resign from the magazine."

It struck Max "like a gunshot." He knew what it must be about: his not-very-Bolshevist editorial in the current issue telling the socialists to back Wilson. Tears sprang to his eyes.

"Well, it's your fault!" said Max. "I showed you my editorial. . . ."

Voice wavering, constitutionally averse to confrontation, he rushed outside.

Reed had changed in Russia; Eastman had seen it. He had come home leaner, sharper edged, more serious. It had surprised Max, because he thought that anybody who had seen the glories of the revolution would be overjoyed—Jack more than most. But until that night in Croton, Eastman hadn't fully grasped the depth of Reed's transformation, the way he had absorbed the hard lesson of the Bolsheviks: The most dangerous enemy of the revolution isn't the capitalists; it's the moderate socialists. There must be no compromise.

Max walked back inside. Gingerly he joined Jack and Florence's conversation. He thought that Jack hung around an unusually long time, perhaps hoping that they would talk about what he'd said.

But Max didn't want to talk about it. Eventually Jack left.[8]

The next issue announced his resignation.

"I cannot in these times bring myself to share editorial responsibility for a magazine which exists upon the sufferance of Mr. Burleson," Jack wrote. He assured Eastman that he'll keep contributing stories. "And in the happy day when we can again call a spade a spade without tying bunting on it, you will find me, as you have in the past, Yours for the Profound Social Change."[9]

In his reply, Eastman offered no protest, just "a deep feeling of regret." He explained that they had weighed their options when Reed was in Russia, and came to a hard decision. "It was our duty to the social revolution to keep this instrument we have created alive toward a time of great usefulness."

He added a more personal note, too: "Personally I envy you the power to cast loose when not only a good deal of the dramatic beauty, but also the glamour of abstract moral principle, is gone out of the venture, and it remains for us merely the most effective and therefore the right thing to do."[10]

In October, in the nervous days when he can't eat and the nights when he can't sleep, racking his brain to come up with a closing statement, Eastman is still ruminating on that painful episode. Reed's defection has made him feel insecure about his revolutionary bona fides. And he really does feel ashamed of himself for not having said what he felt in the first trial. But he also sees no point in marching himself into a jail cell. He is responsible for the well-being of his four friends and comrades—in fact, his responsibility runs deeper than that. Roger Baldwin, who leads the organization that will soon become the ACLU, says that no case involving press freedom has more significance than that of *The Masses*.[11]

Before the month is out, Baldwin will be in jail, too.[12]

Closing arguments begin on October 4, 1918, amid a very dark stretch for the young radicals. It's a few days after Alice Paul loses in the Senate, a few days before Randolph Bourne gets demoted at *The Dial*.

Stedman staggers to his feet, challenges certain aspects of the government's case, and retires.

Eastman rises, gathers his notes, steps forward. Dell admires the way that he conducts himself with "grace and savoir faire," so he must do a splendid job of masking the fact that he is anxious as hell.[13]

Eastman tells the prosperous gentlemen of the jury that despite what the prosecutor would have them believe, he and his colleagues didn't intend to obstruct the United States military. To understand what they *did* intend, it's necessary to understand the true nature of the magazine. He is going to try to help the jurors grasp what has eluded the magazine's critics, some of its readers, and even some of its contributors.

"We were artists and literary men in a state of revolt from the commercial magazines," Eastman says. They published exactly what they wanted to publish in "a mood of extreme and proud and rather obstreperous individual expression."

"We were most of us young, and most of us enthusiastically dissatisfied with the present state of affairs in art and politics and society. And we had this one place in which to say so, and we were accustomed from the beginning to say so in extremely vigorous and sometimes extravagant language."

In other words, the magazine's highest principle isn't pacifism or socialism or anti-Americanism—it's a belief, and a delight, in saying what they think is true.

There's a deeper charge to rebut as well: That they are "Bolsheviki." Barnes never precisely defined what he meant by the term, assuming that its mere connotations would be scary enough to win a conviction. Eastman could respond narrowly, and say that their political views are immaterial to what they published about the war. Or he could hedge, as he had in the first trial. Instead, he does the opposite: He stakes his freedom on a ringing defense of his ideals.

"The Socialists believe in liberty and democracy," he tells the jury:

And they believe in liberty and democracy exactly in the same way that Thomas Jefferson and Patrick Henry and Samuel Adams, and all the rest of the true revolutionary fathers whose hearts are in the Declaration of Independence, believed in liberty and democracy. Only it is their opinion that real democracy does not consist merely in letting the people elect the officials who shall govern them, and they believe that true liberty is not guaranteed to a citizen merely by the possession of the right to vote. They think that democracy will begin when the people rule in industry as well as in politics. And they believe that true liberty involves the right to work and to possess all that you produce by doing your work.

People can only be free, he argues, if they don't have to worry about falling into poverty. They can't be free if they're dominated by another person, "or some corporation which holds their luck and their happiness in its power. That is so obvious that I think you might say the Socialists are the only ones who take the word 'liberty' very seriously, and really mean the thing definitely when they say it."

Reed is impressed. "Standing there, with the attitude and attributes of intellectual eminence, young, good-looking, he was the typical champion of ideals—ideals which he made to seem the ideals of every real American," he writes. He notices how silent the courtroom has grown, how tense.[14]

Eastman now shifts to bolder, riskier rhetorical ground, considering the propertied nature of the gentlemen he is addressing. Some people say that the industrial democracy that socialists demand can't be implemented. He counters with the example of the railroads, which President Wilson had nationalized the previous December.

"It was the simple, quick, sensible thing to do in an emergency," says Eastman. "But Socialists believe that the fact that 10 percent of the people own 90 percent of the wealth, and that 2 percent of the people own 60 percent of the wealth, is an emergency, and that we ought to do the simple, quick, sensible thing on that account, and do it everywhere, and do it a little more thoroughly."

In preparing his speech, Eastman had thought of Eugene Debs, and drawn courage from the example of that brave man insisting on the truth of his ideals, no matter what a war-mad jury might do to him. It had inspired Max not to go quietly, but to lean into the point he wished to make. So he does.[15]

> And so I ask you that, whatever your own judgment of the truth or wisdom of our faith may be, you will respect it as one of the heroic ideas and ardent beliefs of humanity's history. . . . It is either the most beautiful and courageous mistake that hundreds of millions of mankind ever made, or else it is really the truth that will lead us out of our misery, and anxiety, and poverty, and war, and strife and hatred between classes, into a free and happy world. In either case, it deserves your respect.[16]

He concludes with a remark that sounds like he's trying to reassure himself that he has done the right thing: "I am not afraid to spend the better part of my life in a penitentiary, if my principles have brought me to it. I have decided, after experimenting a little in the inside of my own mind and heart, that I am more afraid to betray my principles."

Eastman sits down.

Barnes says his piece.

The jurors go away.

For eleven hours, Max and Jack and the others wait. A knock on the jury-room door signals that a verdict has been reached.

Max and Jack return to their seats.

The foreman stands.

He tells the judge that they want to go home. Like their predecessors, they have deadlocked. They can neither convict nor acquit.[17]

The judge gavels the trial closed, and Max and Jack and the others go free.

The stupefying final count is eight to four—*in favor of the defense.* With the addition of Reed's testimony, and on the strength of Eastman's closing argument, they fared *better* the second time around.

Eastman's closing argument circulates widely in the months that follow. *The Liberator* publishes it as a pamphlet. An official in the district attorney's office, who has every reason to resent its success, tells him that "as an address of a man accused of a crime, it would probably live as one of the great addresses of modern times."[18]

"Your speech before the court was a masterpiece, and will stand as a classic in the literature of the revolution," writes Eugene Debs.[19]

For a magazine as cockeyed as *The Masses,* it's only fitting that the story ends with a twist. While throwing the full arsenal of his oratorical powers into his closing argument, defending the essential Americanness of his socialist creed, Eastman had noticed that one juror sat unmoved. After the adjournment, as the courtroom emptied out, the juror approached Eastman and extended his hand.

"Mr. Eastman, I am familiar with your book on poetry, and I was on your side from the beginning."[20]

Chapter 28

Seventeen months after President Wilson sent the country into war, the U.S. Army is ready. One million three hundred thousand American soldiers have arrived in Europe. General John J. Pershing makes final preparations for the first major offensive that the Americans will launch on their own.[1]

"History awaits you," French premier Georges Clemenceau wires him. "You will not fail it."[2]

At dawn on September 12, 1918, a half million American soldiers rise from their trenches and storm the front line. For four years, the Germans had held a salient, a bulge of territory, around the town of Saint-Mihiel. Two French offensives had failed to reclaim it. Pershing's two-pronged attack on that salient leads to the largest American battle since the Civil War. It is the biggest air engagement fought to that time.[3] Luck is on his side: The Germans are in the midst of withdrawing, and thus out of position. So does raw reckless tenacity: Brigadier General Douglas MacArthur leads a brigade; Lieutenant Colonel George Patton commands the tanks.

The victorious Americans liberate two hundred square miles of France. They're not done. In less than three weeks, the army shifts sixty miles and sets itself for another attack. On September 26, the Allies launch a coordinated offensive along the entire length of the western front. The French, Americans, British, and Italians seek to drive Germany off the Hindenburg Line and right out of the war. The Meuse-Argonne campaign remains, even now, the largest offensive in the history of the U.S. Army.

German morale collapses. The country has no more blood to give, and now a million young Americans, apparently indifferent to death— apparently able to stomp through heretofore impenetrable barbed-wire redoubts—are swarming all over them. "Singing slangy Americans," somebody calls them. Softened up by months of Allied propaganda, the exhausted Germans surrender in waves.

As they stream across no-man's-land, hands raised in surrender, one of the first faces they see belongs to Captain Walter Lippmann. It pleases the young intelligence officer to see so many Germans arrive clutching a leaflet about the food they'll get as prisoners of war: He wrote it.[4]

Lippmann has come to Europe with a new military intelligence unit, assured by Colonel House that there is "no one who could serve the government so well in such a capacity."[5] To keep working with the Inquiry would have been anticlimactic after the Fourteen Points address. Now, instead of helping Wilson frame his ideals in speeches, he weaponizes those ideals and sprays them across enemy lines. He writes, prints, and arranges the distribution of millions of pieces of propaganda. One little sign of a world gone mad is that Walter Lippmann and Jack Reed, Harvard friends and classmates, both end up doing propaganda in 1918—but for different governments.

On October 5, 1918, a week into the Meuse-Argonne battle, Germany asks President Wilson to open peace talks on the basis of his Fourteen Points. Though Lippmann hasn't done any fighting in the trenches—hasn't been gassed, hasn't slashed anyone with a bayonet—he has experienced some of the anguish of a soldier's life. Like a million other young Americans, he dreams of going home: no more camp life, a whole world throwing off its chains.

"No one knows what it will be like to walk out of the prison house into the sunlight again," he tells Faye.

He thinks of their unborn children—"the nine little golden Fayes"— and how horrible it would be for them to live through a war like the one that he has seen. "I've done something, thank God, to put into the hands of those who will have the power of decision the intellectual instruments and the clarifications they need," he writes. "Whether they will use it or not, I do not know."[6]

It sounds like a reverie—a man looking back on a job that's finished. But Lippmann's job isn't finished.

On October 28, he is summoned to a private conference with Colonel House at his residence on the Left Bank. House tells Lippmann that he has been talking to political and military leaders from all the Allied nations, and he is at an impasse. He needs them to agree on the Fourteen Points as the basis of the armistice, but nobody can figure out what the points mean.[7]

"You helped write these points," House tells Lippmann. "Now you must give me a precise definition of each one. I shall need it by tomorrow morning at ten o'clock."[8]

Lippmann says yes—the only thing he *can* say. He flings himself into the work. It is already late afternoon.

He rushes around Paris, seeking any materials that might help. He must long for Inquiry headquarters—all those books, all those maps, all those scholars. In Paris, he doesn't just lack his supporting documentation; he lacks *the points themselves*. He finally locates a copy in the newsroom of the *Paris Herald*.

Frank Cobb, the editor of *The New York World*, had accompanied House to France, and tells Lippmann that he can handle explicating the last point, about the League of Nations. Otherwise, Lippmann is on his own.

It is a challenge to Lippmann's capacities, everything he has learned how to do: his ability to synthesize; his knack for writing quickly, clearly, and well. To succeed, he has to find ways to translate lofty Wilsonian ideals to the realities of European conditions.

In other words, he has to execute, in a super-distilled form, the essential challenge of all the young radicals.

An idealist, to have any chance of winning the world to his or her ideal, needs to be a translator: A vision only gains power if enough people share it. Shakespeare understood this. In *A Midsummer Night's Dream*, Theseus, the practical-minded leader, dismisses every variety of dreamer who "gives to airy nothing / A local habitation and a name." But Hippolyta, his new bride, sees things more clearly: She points out that when many people come to share a dreamer's vision, it "grows to something of great constancy."

That constancy—that conversion of a dream to a fixed reality—is the essential movement of human progress, in every place and time.

Lippmann dashes off his final notes at 1:30 A.M. While he sleeps, House's communications team encodes his words and transmits them to the White House. President Wilson reads Lippmann's commentary on his work. He wires back his approval.

This clarified version of the Fourteen Points doesn't have any magical properties. Negotiations drag on for two days, then three, and keep dragging. House uses every inducement and threat in his very formidable repertoire, but American ideals are a hard sell to Allied premiers, no matter how clearly articulated.

Lippmann has done all that he can do. Now he can only wait with the rest of the troops, and their families, on both sides of the line. He knows the stakes. "Either we shall raise the souls of men the world over or . . . we shall break their hearts."[9]

The arguing stretches into November, so the shooting does, too, and the body count keeps climbing. After fifty-one months and tens of millions of deaths, the Great War will not die.

Chapter 29

When peace comes, it comes like a dream. A siren wails over the city din, then another, then another, then jubilation in the streets. The *New-York Tribune* calls it "the greatest spontaneous celebration the city was ever to see."

Car horns, whistles, and paperboys shriek. Women kick off impromptu parades; old men dance; Caruso steps onto his balcony and belts the national anthem; on the street in front of the Waldorf, a crowd of a thousand men and women sing for an hour. Books are ripped to shreds and tossed from high windows. [1]

In Washington, it's the same: shrieking, crying, dancing, laughing. Fifteen hundred women from the State and War departments stand outside the White House to wave flags and cheer. President Wilson, usually so diligent about ignoring women at his gates, steps onto his portico and waves a handkerchief back.[2]

Except they are wrong, all of them. When peace comes that day, it really *is* a dream: a false report. The celebrations in cities and towns around the world had been inspired by a single intensely contagious error made in France.[3] Soldiers are still fighting and dying while their families are celebrating their deliverance. As if the whole war hasn't been sadistic enough.

It is November 7, 1918.

Four days later, news of peace comes again. There is suspicion, naturally, but then comes confirmation, and after that, joy. Again and again, people say that the revelers have lost their minds: "mad with joy," "temporarily insane," a "wild mob," and so forth.[4] After everything that the world has lived through, this seems to put it backward. If anything, the world has gone sane.

President Wilson addresses Congress. His face shows no traces of the disrupted sleep he suffered the night before, according to one reporter: "He seemed the personification of physical vigor and did not look his 61 years." He reads the terms of the armistice. Everybody cheers when he says "The war thus comes to an end."[5]

Wilson carries a message to the rest of the country, too. It goes across the wires that morning: "Everything for which America fought has been accomplished. It will now be our fortunate duty to assist by example, by sober, friendly counsel, and by material aid in the establishment of just democracy throughout the world."

The air of finality is understandable, but what Wilson says can't possibly be true. Some aims have been accomplished, but the big one— making the world safe for democracy—hasn't. The world isn't safe: It's just exhausted, broken, and bled nearly dry. It will take years to know if what America fought for has been accomplished. Longer than that, maybe, to know if it was worth the cost.

But then no ledger book is big enough to tabulate that cost. The infrastructure of Europe is destroyed, though you can always rebuild infrastructure. Millions of people are starving, but you can find ways to feed them. You can't do anything about battlefields strewn with fifteen million corpses.

Maybe it's fewer than that. Probably it's more. Nobody knows. Partly it's because the number is very, very high, and once a number has enough zeros after it, how precise do you really need it to be? What's another hundred thousand, unless someone you love is among the hundred thousand?

The other reason is that half of the soldiers who die in the war are never found.[6] Those families—let's take the least upsetting estimate, and say there are seven million of them—have the most extraordinary wartime experience of all. The warm and living certainty of a husband, son, or father is replaced by a void, an abstraction, a treasured memory. It is the saddest of all the ways that the real gives way to an ideal.

All of this dying—this death on a scale never encountered before in the West—makes for the grimmest irony in a decade unusually full of ironies. The radicals had plunged into the world feeling confident that they could speed up the tempo of progress. In some respects, the world did make leaps into the future. But the aspect of life that sped up most incontrovertibly was the tempo of sorrow. There's a natural ebb and flow of life and death, of growing up and growing old and saying good-bye, and it's just barely endurable in the best of times. The war piled a century's worth of grief into four years. Young men who should have lived long enough to be puzzled by their grandchildren's rap music were bayoneted on the Somme.

All of those sane happy people around the world celebrate on November 11, 1918, because the monster that civilization had set loose on itself is gone. Except that it's not gone. They are wrong again. The war has spawned. Impossibly, the worst isn't over.

Soldiers returning to their homes that year bring a virus that knows more about killing than all the generals combined. Civilians spread this virus, too. In fact, one in every five people in the world falls ill from it. The world war, humanity's first truly planetary project, gives this virus the vector it needs. The 1918 influenza pandemic kills more people than the war does.[7] Possibly three times as many.

In an era that loves the new, this flu is very, very new. There are recognizable symptoms: headache, chills, fever. But in its extremity, the flu kills in ways that almost nobody has seen. Sometimes it forms air pockets under the skin, so patients crackle when you move them. Sometimes people cough until their muscles shred; their lungs look like the victims of a poison gas attack.[8]

One breath is enough to catch it; one cough is enough to spread it. Sometimes it takes only a couple of hours to show symptoms, sicken, and die.

The first wave hit America early in the year, and it was catastrophic; when it returns in the fall, it's apocalyptic. People die in such vast numbers that health systems collapse. In Philadelphia, the dead are left to rot in their homes, because there's no one to remove them. In New York, nurses are kidnapped.[9] Churches, schools, theaters, are closed. The life expectancy in 1918 drops twelve years, to what it had been fifty years earlier. By the time it burns itself out, the flu kills 675,000 Americans. Entire neighborhoods smell like the western front.

The flu, like the war that fosters it, has a particular craving for the young and healthy. Most years, the mortality curve for the flu is "U" shaped, with deaths clustered among the very young and very old. In 1918, the curve is a "W." Men and women in their twenties and thirties are culled in appalling numbers. For some of these young people, the gravest damage is wreaked not by the virus but by the body's response to it, the "cytokine storm" unleashed by the immune system as it throws its entire arsenal at the threat. In many cases, they suffocate as their lungs fill up. Here, too, is an echo of the war. Ask a radical trying to live through the hysteria of wartime America: The overreaction to a threat can be worse than the threat itself.

The young radicals are not immune.

John Reed catches the flu a few days before the armistice. He gets through it, which is lucky, considering his generally bad health and missing kidney. His comrade Max Eastman avoids it, though his hypochondria must have kept him sweating for months.

In Paris, Walter Lippmann catches it, but recovers with his usual ease. He improves just in time to keep a vigil at the bedside of Willard Straight, the young owner of *The New Republic,* who is with the army in Paris. Straight dies there one Saturday night.

In Washington, the National Woman's Party headquarters becomes a field hospital once more. Alice Paul falls ill but soldiers through it. Across the street, President Wilson stays healthy—for now.

In Manhattan, Randolph Bourne's friends notice that he isn't looking well.

"It was most touching, the mood in the streets," Bourne writes to Van Wyck Brooks the day after the armistice. That is not how most people would describe the bacchanal, but Bourne sees something sublime in the public celebration. "As a pacifist, I rejoice at the innocent uprising of the unconscious desire on the part of the populace for peace, and the throwing off of the repressed reluctance for the war. . . . How much blither and freer the air!"[10]

Bourne has been translating a French novel. It is a bad book, and he thinks he's doing a bad job with it, but he could use the money. He finds it too cold to work in his apartment, so he asks Merrill Rogers for the use of his place. Rogers says yes, but Bourne soon returns the key: It's too cold there as well.[11]

Things aren't good but they'll get better. *The Dial,* his employer/tormentor, is about to get a new editor, who considers it his first task to attempt a reconciliation between Bourne and John Dewey.[12] An even brighter prospect is Esther Cornell—his beloved Esther, at last and for good. He has proposed; she has said yes. They have met each other's families. They plan to be married soon.

"Now that the war is over people can speak freely again and we can dare to think," Bourne writes to his mother a week after the armistice. "It's like coming out of a nightmare."[13]

The cough is just a cold, probably. Still, Esther doesn't like the sound of it. She and her roommate, Agnes de Lima, convince Randolph to move into their apartment at 18 West Eighth Street sooner than planned. (They'll live there after the wedding; Agnes will move out.)

By the time he arrives, Esther thinks he looks worse. She and Agnes put him to bed. His temperature is 102.

A doctor visits and the news isn't good. He says Bourne's illness could prove serious, given his existing physical difficulties, especially his small lungs. He puts Bourne's chances at fifty-fifty.[14]

The man had who tried so hard for so long to stay "below the battle" can only lie helpless as the battle crashes in on him. Beyond the physical problems—the pain behind the eyes, the chill that can't be warmed, the bloody crushing cough—this spectacular flu is a disease of the mind. You are racked with nightmares. You have delirious dreams.

Bourne's friends huddle to his side, but what can they do? They watch him shiver on the narrow iron bed in the front room.[15]

"I don't want to die," he tells one of them. It is getting harder to speak.[16]

On Saturday night, Bourne tries to be cheerful. He is considerate of his caretakers, especially Esther. He worries that perhaps he should go to a hospital, but a friend who visits him—a nurse—tells him he is getting better care at home than he could in one of the city's overcrowded emergency rooms.[17]

What Bourne's friend doesn't say is that his location doesn't matter. Nobody has a cure for the flu. Nobody even has a treatment. You can try to keep a patient comfortable, but that's all. Esther has been doing it for thirty-six hours straight when she goes to sleep in the next room. Agnes stays by his side through another long night.

Bourne's lungs are filling with fluid now. His systems are failing now. But his mind is clear, so with his exquisite sense of irony, he might contemplate how absurd it is—how *stupid*—to be drowning not on some brave seafaring adventure, but on a narrow bed in a walk-up apartment on Eighth Street.

He opens his eyes. He asks for an eggnog. He takes it, drinks it, praises its pale yellow beauty, and dies.

It is five o'clock in the morning on Sunday, December 22, 1918. New York is quiet at that hour; it will be dark yet for quite some time. Esther comes into the front room and sees Agnes cradling the small body of her fiancé. She sobs while she listens to the troopships steaming up the river, carrying the victors home.[18]

V. LONELY UTOPIA

(1918–22)

Our hour of triumph is what brings the void.

—WILLIAM JAMES

Chapter 30

Gawkers lean out every window; they cram the rooftops; brave boys dangle from the spindly trees. The crowd, hundreds of thousands strong, dims away into the morning mist. It's the biggest gathering in the history of Paris, some say. The boulevards are jammed with workingmen, saucer-eyed kids, widows in black.

At midday, on the far side of the Seine, cannons boom. The people begin to surge and sway. Two lines of soldiers in pale blue uniforms open a path through the crowd that fills the Place de la Concorde. Brass-helmeted cavalrymen appear on the bridge, leading a horse-drawn carriage into the newly opened path.[1] The carriage is what makes everybody begin to scream.

It is the man himself. Not his words this time, but flesh and blood. He smiles at them, waves his hat to them, as they smile and shout and wave their handkerchiefs back. "Honor to Wilson the Just" say the banners.[2]

Three stories above the plaza, Walter Lippmann watches the great human pageant unfold. From a balcony of the Hôtel de Crillon, he looks straight down on the president's head as the carriage rolls by.

Nobody, not even the aviators pulling stunts in the cloudy sky, can see the president more clearly. Nobody describes him more concisely. On December 14, 1918, the day of his arrival in Paris, Woodrow Wilson is nothing less than "the incarnation of human hope."[3]

The president has come to Paris to fashion a treaty that will end the war—and, in ending it, attempt to redeem it. Tens of millions of people have died. In Europe alone, two hundred million go to bed hungry that night, if they have beds.[4] It is impossible to think that the West, at the height of its power and sophistication, could have invited its own devastation for no purpose, only to end up worse than before. If Woodrow Wilson, the idealist from across the sea, can force the Allied leaders to fashion a permanent peace, then all the dying and suffering and grieving will not have been in vain. And if he can't—well, that is too terrible a thought for a traumatized world to bear.

The carriage disappears into the Champs-Élysées, but the celebration continues. All day long and well into the night, there is dancing in the streets, happy crowds singing, plentiful kisses for the doughboys.

Why, then, does Lippmann have such an ominous feeling?[5]

Look at the men and women thronging Wilson down there. They cheer him in unison, but they want different things. And that's just in Paris. What about Rome, London, Constantinople, Berlin? Lippmann thinks that winning the war was "a thing of extraordinary moral simplicity" compared to forging a peace that will satisfy all of them.[6]

Wilson does nothing to temper people's expectations. Supremely confident in his own abilities, and of the role chosen for him by God and history, he calls the peace conference "this great—may I not say final—enterprise of humanity."[7]

After the most shattering war in history, in a world strewn with bodies, maybe it's understandable that a religious man would describe a diplomatic negotiation in terms of eschatology. The fact that he thinks in those terms suggests that he missed the meaning of the war starting in the first place: There is no final enterprise, and there never will be. It never stops.

No young radical, in the late days of 1918, would make that mistake.

Not after seeing the comforting illusions of their school days blown to pieces. Not after watching a country that had been arcing toward progress pitch into madness and reaction. Not after feeling their pursuit of ideals devolve, at times, into a bare struggle to survive.

What next? After all of that, what do they do now?

For Max Eastman and John Reed, the armistice and the end of the *Masses* trial ought to mean less danger—but they don't. Almost overnight, the country switches from hysterically pursuing German sympathizers to hysterically pursuing Bolshevik sympathizers. They will or won't find a way to reconcile socialism with American life.

Alice Paul has to reckon with the fact that she got what she wanted—a ringing suffrage speech by the president—and it didn't work. (She says that it came too late—that it wasn't enough—but the president was as embarrassed by the defeat as the suffragists were. He really did give it his all.) What more can she do, especially now that Wilson is on the other side of the planet?

Even Randolph Bourne's experiments will conclude. He won't be there to see it, but he also hasn't vanished without a trace. He touched many more lives through his writing than he ever did in his life. People go on arguing with him, and being inspired by him, and finding truth in what he says. Bourne's voice will be heard again, but first his friends have to contend with the dilemma that always plagued him: what to do with the troublesome body that gave rise to those luminous ideals.

A week after Wilson's arrival in Paris, they gather on a cold, wet day to bid him goodbye. The service is led by Norman Thomas, who admired him but didn't really know him. Then his mortal remains are carried away from Greenwich Village and consigned to earth.

They bury him in the place that he had spent much of his brief life trying to escape: Bloomfield, in a family plot, next to his hated uncle.

It is a final insult to his luckless bones.

For Lippmann, who thrives in proximity to power, the president's arrival in Paris ought to kick off a string of halcyon days. Instead, a friend reports that Lippmann is "much troubled" because "he has been puttering about here on a multitude of things without being given any definite and sizable job."[8]

How can that be? After all, Lippmann is one of the architects of the Inquiry, which was created for this precise moment.

Part of the answer lies in what he's done in the few months since arriving in Europe. He took his turn to answer the question that had bedeviled so many of his contemporaries—the one that he himself had posed: *What do you do with freedom when you get it?* It turns out that sometimes you do all the wrong things, and then you pay for it.

He had landed in France with an astonishingly free hand. Newton Baker, the secretary of war, had sent a letter to General Pershing alerting him that his young captain would be working for the War Department, the Inquiry, *and* the State Department.[9]

Left mainly to his own devices, he began to investigate how propaganda from the Committee on Public Information was working in Europe. He did not think it was working well. So he'd written a scathing letter to Colonel House calling the work of the CPI "very bad" and proposing the creation of a new organization to assume its duties.[10] Lippmann had thought he was writing solely to House, but by sending the letter in a diplomatic pouch, he guaranteed that it would spread like fire when it reached Washington. House compounded the problem by *sharing it with the president.*

"I am very much puzzled as to who sent Lippmann over to inquire into matters of propaganda," Wilson fumed. "I have found his judgment most unsound, and therefore entirely unserviceable, in matters of that sort because he, in common with the men of *The New Republic,* has ideas about the war and its purposes which are highly unorthodox from my point of view."[11]

(Wilson was mad because the magazine had criticized the antidemocratic effects of the war effort. Lippmann had warned Herbert Croly it would happen, but Croly had ignored him, and *Lippmann* suffered the consequences.)[12]

House had defended Lippmann, but before he could tell his opinionated protégé to be more discreet, Lippmann sent another scathing memo that was read even more widely. This time Wilson, who was very busy trying to end a war, intervened directly with two cabinet secretaries to make it stop. Lippmann had created a mess as vast as it was toxic.

Lippmann apologized to House, but soon found another way to overreach. He had interpreted his job to include visiting with high-ranking officials in European capitals and sussing out their views on Wilson's plan for a League of Nations. But it confused the hell out of the Allies. The French were embarrassed and puzzled by his questions, unsure whether he spoke for President Wilson, for Colonel House, or for himself. The British, equally perplexed, contacted their emissary in New York to figure out who this young American was. "I do not think that Lippmann has given you quite the right impression," replied Sir William Wiseman, explaining that Colonel House would never let Lippmann set up his own political intelligence department in Europe. Wiseman seemed surprised, for he knew and liked the young American, "but he does not seem to have the knack of fitting into a Government Department."[13]

And then it was open season on the golden boy. It might just be gossip, but one report said that only the fortuitous arrival of Newton Baker, his most reliable protector, kept Lippmann from being sent home from France, or worse—maybe even to Texas for the duration of the war.[14]

When Wilson arrives, Lippmann's final humbling still awaits. What role will he play in arranging the peace conference? The division of responsibilities is hopelessly tangled. To find a solution, Lippmann spends most of an afternoon in what he calls a "very frank" conversation with Isaiah Bowman, the geographer who took control of the Inquiry after Lippmann departed. Bowman despises him, much more than Lippmann realizes. Only after the meeting does Lippmann learn something that none of his Inquiry colleagues would tell him to his face: On the night before they left New York, Bowman had sent out a press release revealing the existence of the Inquiry, describing its secretive nature, explaining how it had come to exist, and even naming eighteen of its members—but never once mentioning Lippmann.[15]

"Bowman is perfectly aware that a gentleman does not attack another man while he's away, and then continue to write him cordial letters in the manner of a colleague," Walter fumes to Faye. He thinks about complaining to Colonel House but decides not to bother. He says he will leave Bowman "to his conscience."[16]

In late January 1919, he leaves for New York. He wants to go back to writing. He assures Faye that he is "very happy" to not be staying in Paris; the decision had been made before Wilson even arrived. But friends don't treat him as a conquering hero. Felix Frankfurter tries to console him for his "recent difficulties." And his *New Republic* colleague Francis Hackett commiserates with him about the "tough experience" he'd had. "I sometimes feel you haven't had many. But I feel you'll field this one perfectly in the end, and be twice as rounded for it."[17]

Like so much in 1919, that depends on what happens in Paris. Lippmann had given up his youthful socialism without losing a night's sleep, had shed his bohemian friends to enjoy the congenial company at the House of Truth, had stopped attacking the president to join his administration—at every step, accepting more responsibility, broadening his vision, growing up. If Wilson prevails in his negotiations, and the peace treaty yields a new, more rational, more peaceful, more democratic world order—one that enshrines in international law the Fourteen Points that Lippmann had helped to frame—then a young man's diligent service on behalf of his ideals will pay off. He is acutely aware of how many men and women have invested their hopes in Wilson, because he is one of them.

"I trust him beyond any statesman in the world today," Lippmann writes in his return to political commentary.[18]

How, then, does Walter Lippmann hear the news that will upend him?

Is he at breakfast one morning with Faye, in their new apartment uptown, when he glances at the morning paper, coffee cup frozen half-way to his lip? Maybe he's riding the subway, rumbling south to the office/clubhouse of *The New Republic*, holding a strap with one hand (they are still straps in 1919), clutching the *Times* or *The World* with the other, as his fellow commuters wonder why the handsome young man has turned so tense, so pale. Perhaps an individual as superbly well connected as Walter Lippmann doesn't need a newspaper to get the news. A touch on the arm at the Harvard Club might suffice. "Are you sitting down?" a well-placed friend might ask him, risking a phone call late one night. "Because you're not going to believe this."

President Wilson has done something like what Lippmann did: arrive in Europe full of hope, only to squander his chances, disappoint a lot of people, and create an enormous, toxic mess.

Wilson succeeded in getting his League of Nations covenant into the treaty that the Allies present to Germany. But what happened to the rest of the lofty aims that justified America's declaration of war? Lippmann thinks that Britain, France, and Japan have used the peace-making process to grab control of a hemisphere, and the United States has promised to guarantee their security. The ideal of self-determination has become an instrument of exploitation, cited as a reason to take territory away from Germany but not to give it back. Lippmann is particularly appalled at the decision to hand the Saar Valley to France, an idea that he had labeled "a clear violation of the President's proposal" in his overnight explication of the Fourteen Points.[19] On the other side of the world, but in the same spirit of victors dividing up the spoils, the Shantung Province was taken from China and given to Japan.

Where are the ideals in this? Where is the peace without victory?

The Germans might sign such a treaty, but they'll never abide by it. They can't. The astronomical indemnities they are being asked to pay will simply never be paid. It will only create an impulse for vengeance. It will start another war.[20]

The editors of *The New Republic* swallow their pride. The president they supported has failed. Their ideals have miscarried: "We were wrong. We hoped and lost."[21]

Lippmann takes it as hard as any of them. "I was the typical fool determined to hope till the bitter end," he tells a friend that summer. "Well it's bitter."[22]

As ever, the question is not what to think, but what to *do*. The president comes home that summer to get two-thirds of the Senate to ratify the treaty. That debate, Lippmann thinks, will be "the most important political decision that any one now living has ever been called upon to make."[23]

Which side should he take?

It's Schenectady all over again, but with stakes so much higher. He has been disappointed by the miscarriage of an ideal. Does he stay at his post and make the best of it, or does he burn the place down? Doing nothing isn't an option: Even though he has left government, he is a party to Wilson's failure. "His pen has served the President ably and well," editorializes the *New-York Tribune* that summer.[24]

So many people have worked so hard, and fought so much, and suffered. How has it come to this?

Lippmann, bewildered, commiserates with a friend: "Sometimes I think we are a damned generation."[25]

Chapter 31

John Reed hammers at his typewriter day and night, fired by cigarettes, caffeine, and revolutionary zeal. He spends frantic weeks that winter of 1919 in a rented room above Polly Holliday's restaurant writing his book on the Russian Revolution. "A slice of intensified history," he calls it, "history as I saw it."[1]

He doesn't have much human contact in those weeks—he tells only a few people where he is—but one morning Max Eastman runs into him on Sheridan Square while he is out getting something essential, such as coffee. Max recoils from his friend's greasy, sleepless appearance.

"Half-crazy," Max thinks.[2]

He might be right. Despite having a fireplace in his room, Jack keeps trying to flush his notes down the toilet. Polly shouts at him to stop wrecking her plumbing.[3]

He can write the book because he finally has his papers back from the State Department: all the notebooks and posters and newspapers he had brought home from Petrograd. He's not really sure how that happened—nobody gave him an explanation—but he is very goddamn glad to know how it *didn't* happen.

A few months earlier, in a moment of despair, he had asked Lincoln Steffens for help. Steffens tried. He made a suggestion. Reed rejected it outright.

"I wouldn't ask Walter L. for anything for the whole world."[4]

It's not *The Harvard Monthly* anymore, or 42 Washington Square, or even Jack's hospital room in Baltimore. He'd chased his ideals to Russia and had seen the new world born. But Lippmann? Lippmann had gone to work for the hateful war. He had helped to line the pockets of the financiers. He had put on captain's bars and joined the same army that was waging an unconstitutional war in Soviet Russia. If Reed is sure enough of his revolutionary convictions to resign the masthead of *The Liberator*, he's not going to think twice about casting off Lippmann without a backward glance.

From all the evidence, it seems that Walter has done the same to Jack.

"Wherever his sympathies marched with the facts, Reed was superb," Lippmann wrote of his friend before they grew apart—or, rather, before their diverging ideals flung them apart. It is never truer than in January 1919, when Reed steps onto a Village sidewalk, blinking in the white winter sun, the great work of his life complete, the manuscript of *Ten Days That Shook the World* under his arm.

The book is partisan to the Bolsheviks, and it gets things wrong, and even in 1919, readers knew the broad strokes of what was coming. It's riveting anyway. Reed, ever the man of the theater, conceives of his story as the "pageant of the Rising of the Russian Masses." Today, when better-behaved accounts of the revolution gather dust, its drama is still warm on these pages.

Reed is glad to be done writing about the revolution. Now he has more time to start one.

The prospect of American society cracking in some fundamental way doesn't seem crazy in 1919. "The springtime of revolution," John Dos

Passos calls that year. When soldiers come home from Europe, unemployment skyrockets. The cost of living rises so quickly that even the people who manage to find jobs can't feed their families. The economic dislocation leads to the greatest labor unrest in the country's history: 3,600 strikes that year alone.[5]

In Seattle, a general strike shuts down the city. In Butte and Portland, workers don't just walk off the job: They form *soviets*.[6] The Boston police go on strike, inviting lawlessness on a mass scale, until Governor Calvin Coolidge sends in the militia. A steel strike, stretching the breadth of the country, sees four hundred thousand workers walk out. Work stoppages spread to the mines and the railroads and beyond, sometimes with the blessing of unions, sometimes in spite of them. Workers feel they can't take it anymore—that they're on their own.

The organization that ought to harness that discontent, the Socialist Party, has been growing rapidly. Its opposition to the war and the reflected glory of the Bolsheviks' success drives its membership from 80,000 to 104,000. Reed has no use for it. He sees power accruing to people who don't have the knowledge or the conviction to use it. "Fully a third of the Socialist votes in normal times are, I think, cast by middle-class persons who think that Karl Marx wrote a good Anti-Trust Law."[7]

The most impatient socialists have formed a Left Wing Section, explicitly opposed to the party's slow-going moderate leaders. "It is a struggle to the end. No compromise, no hesitation," reads the Left Wing Manifesto. At Socialist Party meetings that spring, Left Wingers jump on desks to protest points of order, trying to win control of their locals. There are fistfights. There are *chair* fights.[8]

This is Jack's kind of politics.

He gets himself elected to the Left Wing's city committee. As usual, once he commits to a cause, he can't stop himself. Soon he is working twenty-hour days. He becomes editor of the New York Left Wing's newspaper, *The New York Communist*. He even dabbles in becoming a theorist. It doesn't work, but the Left Wing doesn't need him to theorize. They need him to wield his star power, his charisma, to lend his imprimatur to the way they apply the lessons of Lenin and Trotsky's triumph. A crucial one is "The center must be smashed as a necessary means of conquering the party for the party, for revolutionary Social-ism."[9]

Reed does so gladly—but it leads to some surprising consequences.

On April 23, 1919, the Left Wing's executive committee rules that *The Liberator* must conform to their manifesto and that Max Eastman must "submit himself to party discipline."[10]

Here is something new.

The Bolsheviks have had no more faithful supporter in the United States than *The Liberator*. Eastman boasts that it is "the only popular magazine of revolutionary socialism in America."[11] He had published Lenin's "Letter to American Workingmen." But like its freewheeling prewar predecessor, *The Masses*, the magazine also includes poems, stories, and illustrations that have nothing to do with the class struggle. Imposing a party line would make it a different magazine—and make Eastman a different radical. While Reed was pouring body and soul into writing his account of the Russian Revolution, Eastman had put the finishing touches on *Colors of Life*, a collection of poems so aggressively detached from the class struggle that he felt compelled to explain himself in the preface:

> Life is older than liberty. It is greater than revolution. It burns in both camps. And life is what I love. And though I love life for all men and women, and so inevitably stand in the ranks of revolution against the cruel system of these times, I loved it first for myself. Its essence—the essence of life—is variety and specific depth, and it cannot be found in monotonous consecration to a general principle. Therefore I have feared and avoided this consecration, which earnest friends for some reason always expect me to exemplify, and my poetry has never entered, even so deeply as it might, into those tempests of social change that are coloring our thoughts today.[12]

Four days after the Left Wing's leaders vote to demand Eastman's submission to party discipline, they accept his membership. Whatever transpired in those ninety-six hours had passed.

They're all comrades again. For now.

The spectacle of Jack speeding past Max in commitment to socialism amuses them both. During a contentious conversation around this time, Max blurts out: "Jack, the trouble with you is you're getting too damned adult!"

After that, whenever Jack wants to make a serious point, he prefaces it by saying, "If you will pardon my bringing this up in the presence of children—"[13]

Later that summer, they take a break from their labors, playing tennis in the morning and planning to sail with friends in the afternoon. It's supposed to be a jolly excursion, but by the time they reach the pier, they're both sad.

Max is sad because the wind has died down.

Jack is sad because an intricate maneuver to seize control of the Socialist Party—electing Left Wing members to the national executive council, a strategy that had *actually worked,* yielding twelve of the fifteen seats—had been thwarted by the underhanded tactics of the goddamned moderates, who had summarily expelled the Left Wing, choosing to save the party by *casting out most of its members,* a problem compounded when the Left Wing itself split in two, no discipline, no strategic sense, no goddamned vision.[14]

The wind picks up. It's a good day to sail after all. But by that time, Max and Jack's friends need to go. That leaves the two of them. Should they take the boat out anyway?

Max begs off. He tells Jack he ought to go work. (He has begun another book that's almost aggressively detached from the class struggle: a semi-scientific treatise on humor.)

They say their goodbyes and separate. But Max had lied to Jack.

That night, Max writes a penitent letter to Florence, who is away in Hollywood, beginning to succeed in the new field of motion-picture acting. He *wishes* he were wrapped up in his book, he tells her. He'd made up the excuse because he didn't want to spend any more time with his increasingly militant friend.

"He depresses me too much," Max writes. "I'm fond of Jack but his impersonality, his conversational remoteness, has a terribly depressing effect on me."[15]

It's the opposite of how he used to describe Reed.

Louise Bryant can see her husband struggling. A few days after the abortive sailing trip with Eastman, she takes him to Cape Cod, where they'd spent such happy days in the theater with their friends.

Three years have passed since that summer. Reed thinks of it often. He had found time to write a bitter little satire about the Paris Peace Conference, which the Provincetown Players had staged that spring. Even now, he wants to write, to create, to play.

"I wish I could stay here," he tells Jig Cook and Susan Glaspell on that trip to the Cape. "Maybe it will surprise you, but what I really want is to write poetry."

It doesn't surprise them. "Why don't you?" they ask.

Sitting there on the Cape, in the ocean air, with his fellow artists, it must have been tantalizing. Harriet Monroe gives Reed's "Proud New York" an honorable mention in that year's *Poetry* contest: He is torn between two viable lives. "This class struggle plays hell with your poetry," he complained to Eastman as his revolutionary commitment grew.

But he shakes his head. He tells them he can't stay: He has "promised too many people."[16]

A few days later, he leaves Provincetown for the last time.

"The way to get the hall," Reed explains, "is to go and get it."

On August 30, 1919, he leads several dozen members of the expelled Left Wing up the stairs to the second floor of Machinists Hall in Chicago. That is where the Socialist Party, of which they had recently been members, is having its national convention.

They have not been invited. That's why they've come.

At the top of the stairs, the door is blocked by Comrade Julius Gerber, though not for long. An eyewitness says that "Gerber could have licked Reed, if Reed hadn't held him so far up in the air that he couldn't reach down."[17]

The other Left Wingers follow Jack into the sunny, high-ceilinged hall and make themselves comfortable. Comfortable and *loud:* When party officials try to open the convention, Reed and his comrades catcall and hiss.[18]

This leads the chairman to commit a major revolutionary faux pas: He calls the cops, the people who had been making life miserable for so many socialists that year. The machinists are furious when they find out, but by then Reed and the others have been tossed onto the street.

Their scrapes and bruises mark the birth pains of American communism. The eighty expelled members of the Left Wing reconvene downstairs, in the machinists' pool room, and after singing the "Internationale" and offering three cheers for revolutionary socialism, and three more for Russia, and three more for Eugene Debs, and three more for the IWW, they vote to form the Communist Labor Party.[19]

Reed and the other leaders of this party do not want to break into the American political system, the way Alice Paul had. They reject "the present fraudulent capitalist democracy" in its entirety. They are not interested in extracting concessions for workers from the ruling class, one measly labor law at a time. They want the workers to *become* the ruling class. The laboring masses will "make and enforce the laws; they shall own and control land, factories, mills, mines, transportation systems and financial institutions. All power to the workers!"[20]

The new party elects a slate of officers, including Reed as its international delegate. They also make up a song:

Men of thought and men of toil
Men whose labor tills the soil

Stand together, tyrants foil

Rise! Rise! Rise![21]

"We've got it!" Reed exults to Elizabeth Gurley Flynn, a leader of the IWW. "A real American working-class Socialist party at last!"[22]

The jubilation is tempered by the fact that the Left Wing hasn't patched up its internal split. The day after Reed's Left Wing faction forms a party, the other Left Wing faction does, too: the Communist Party.

The doctrinal differences between the two new parties are thin. And Reed's group is only one-third the size of the Communist Party. Shouldn't they just merge? Reed doesn't think so. Partly he's still furious about that split over the summer and feels that the other Left Wing faction had betrayed him. But there's also a principle at stake.

Reed has traveled the country, spending time with every kind of laborer, and he has come to believe that socialism will never accrue power as long as an American worker can regard it as "a system worked out in foreign countries, not born of his own particular needs and opposed to 'democracy' and 'fair play,' which is the way he has been taught to characterize the institutions of this country."[23] The Communist Labor Party might be small, but it has a stronger claim to being an *American* party. Unlike the Communist Party, which is dominated by Russian immigrants, Reed's group can present itself as an ideological descendant, however distant, of the radicals in the founding generation—the argument Eastman used in his closing address.

But the decision isn't up to the American comrades. In Moscow, the Bolsheviks have created the Third Communist International, an organization to steer the global revolution. The Comintern is unlikely to recognize two parties in one country. Which American group will prevail? Somebody will have to risk a trip halfway across a dangerous planet to plead their case to Lenin and Trotsky in person.

Every member of the Communist Labor Party knows who has the best chance of convincing them.[24]

Louise is appalled by the idea. She doesn't want to lose Jack for months and months; she doesn't want him to run the insane risks of trying to get to Russia in the middle of a civil war, not even for the revolution that means almost as much to her as it does to him.

It must be a relief, then, to consider that there is no way Reed can leave the country. Since returning from Russia, he has given one fire-breathing speech after another. A few months earlier he had claimed that since his family "has sacrificed everything in fighting what battles for liberty this nation can boast," he has "a perfect right to stand up here and damn the whole government of the United States if I please."[25] The Justice Department, unmoved by his pedigree, has indicted him yet again for violating the Espionage Act. There is no way Reed can get a passport stamped.

Back, then, to Greenwich Village: the cafes, the crooked streets, the theater. The place has changed since Reed wrote the epic poem that did so much to define it. Seventh Avenue, which used to stop at Greenwich Avenue, now cuts clear through the neighborhood's heart. There are tourists now, too. The "merry villager" has become a marketable type, a species of urban fauna that uptown folks enjoy observing in the wild. Its poverty has become fashionable; rents are going up. A young newcomer to the Village that year is struck by the joylessness of the place, "its pervading atmosphere of middle-agedness." People are already waxing nostalgic for the glory days of 1916, when the political rebels and cultural rebels fought the same fight.[26]

If anybody embodied the unity of the old Village, it was Jack Reed. But he embodies the divisions of the new Village, too. Nobody faces a more absolute choice between art and revolution than he does. Nobody, in picking one or the other, has more to lose. He makes his choice anyway.

One day he is palling around with Village friends. The next day he is gone.

Overnight, a sailor nobody has seen before—a sailor wearing a flannel shirt, hat cocked to one side—walks up the gangway of a Swedish freighter in New York harbor. He presents some authentic-looking documents that allow him to work in the ship's engine room. It will be a long trip to Scandinavia—he will stoke the fire.[27]

It takes the government more than a month to locate John Reed. Informants in Moscow report that an American has been overheard bragging about his escape from New York. He's been calling himself Tom Paine.[28]

Chapter 32

eave aside the qualities that make Alice Paul a formidable champion of a noble ideal: her adroit grasp of political strategies; her physical courage; her uncanny capacity to inspire women to give up their time, money, status, and health for the sake of her campaign; her smiling insistence that if the whole world opposes her, it just means she has more work to do. She also happens to be an extraordinary impresario—a genius of street theater. Put her up there with Barnum and Ziegfeld and DeMille: an adept of the American spectacular.

By 1919, her knack for putting on the right show for the right crowd at the right time tells her that the old shows aren't enough. For one thing, the pageant movement is dying. During the war, these affirmative displays of what a community believes had been co-opted as a tool for building and reinforcing national loyalty.[1] Anyway people don't feel the same need to create their own entertainment now that mass media makes it cheap and easy for professionals to do it: ragtime on the radio, screen idols in the movies, Babe Ruth.

Pickets aren't enough anymore, either. She knows she needs a new and bolder demonstration to illustrate the hypocrisy of a president who gives lofty speeches about democracy abroad while failing to do enough to foster it at home. A campaign of mass persuasion, like any good drama, doesn't just roll forward: Once you start escalating, you have to keep escalating.

One winter day, late in the afternoon, an honor guard of women carrying purple, white, and gold pennants lines up on the sidewalk outside the White House, arrayed on either side of a stone urn. An audience gathers.

A suffragist lights a fire in the urn. The wood that starts it burning comes from Independence Square in Philadelphia. They use the fire to burn four of the president's recent speeches on democracy.

This is the start of Paul's audacious demonstration "The Watchfire of Freedom." She plans to keep the fire burning around the clock, every day, until women win the vote, with a bell ringing at suffrage headquarters every two hours to announce the changing of the guard.

In the weeks to come, the Watchfire burns through snow and sleet and winter wind. Suffrage headquarters begins to reek of kerosene. (It takes the cops a while to figure out that water isn't enough to defeat those logs—they need to spray chemicals.)[2] Dragged into court, the suffragists refuse to give their names, to answer questions, to have anything to do with a system that denies their rights. Then it's off to jail again: the rats and bedbugs, the hunger strikes now a matter of course. No quarter asked or given.

"They have done the very worst they can, short of turning guns on us, and still our determination flames," says a suffragist from Kansas City. "They have no chemicals strong enough to quench our fire."[3]

In the seventh year of her all-out fight for the vote, Paul has become the leader of what one historian of feminism calls "an epitome of coalition politics." Though the Woman's Party still draws its main strength from middle-class white women, it now spans races, national origins, tax brackets.[4] All of their agitation is concentrated on winning the support of a single senator, for there is still a chance—a slim, vanishing chance— that the Senate might vote for the amendment, sparing the need to go back to the House after all. Time dwindling, the logic of escalation leads Paul and her suffragists into their most extreme spectacle yet.

On February 9, 1919, on the eve of what looks like the final Senate vote of the session, nearly a hundred women stream out of suffrage headquarters, making their way through a crowd of two thousand spectators and several dozen cops, all of whom will have a role to play in what *The Suffragist* calls a "little drama of freedom."[5]

They burn Woodrow Wilson in effigy.

The ensuing melee happens in the fog of war. Eyewitnesses don't agree on the most basic descriptions of what occurs. The effigy of Wilson is either a small plaster statue, a three-foot-tall paper likeness, or a two-foot figure stuffed with straw. It does or doesn't burn before the cops intervene. The one detail that all the accounts share is that the police undertake a spate of "wholesale and indiscriminate arresting," in the words of *The Suffragist*. They arrest thirty-nine women, including Louise Bryant, who is grabbed off the sidewalk as she begins a speech.[6]

The imprisoned suffragists are in court the next afternoon when the Senate convenes. They need sixty-four votes. They get sixty-three.

By spring 1919, suffragists who have stood by Alice Paul's side from the beginning must feel that they've seen everything. But there is one more phase, as surprising as anything that had come before it: anticlimax.

On May 21, in the new congressional session, the House takes up suffrage again. This time the outcome is so foreordained that most suffrage leaders don't bother to show up. A reporter is struck by how "remarkably little interest in the outcome was evidenced today by the public or the Senate." The galleries don't even fill up until the end of the roll call.[7] After a few perfunctory hours of debate, the final count is 304 to 89, a huge advance on the last vote.

Two weeks later, the action once again shifts to the Senate. In the midterm election, suffragists from both parties had helped to defeat two anti-suffrage senators. A constant barrage of lobbying has kept the pressure on the new arrivals. The math ought to work.

And, for once, it does. Needing sixty-four votes for passage, they get sixty-six.

"It was all very dull," according to one of Paul's lobbyists.[8]

When the results are announced, Paul is in Michigan, lining up the thirty-six state ratifications they'll need to enshrine woman suffrage in the Constitution. She has declared victory many times for many reasons over the years, both legitimate and for the sake of women's morale. This time her instinct for the right word at the right moment leads her to make a statement that is unexpectedly profound: "Freedom has come not as a gift but as a triumph, and it is therefore a spiritual as well as a political freedom which women receive."[9]

Paul is suggesting that the value of an advance toward an ideal depends in part on the struggle to realize it. By dramatizing women's desire for freedom, she demonstrates that women want their political rights badly enough to fight for them. This also demonstrates that those rights are worth fighting for. Paul ennobles democracy at the same time that she ennobles the women who seek it. And because she does so with a supreme sense of stagecraft—using symbols in powerful, emotionally resonant ways—we can still be galvanized by her campaign many years later. Women burning their president in effigy on his own doorstep for the sake of equal rights would be shocking if it happened *today*.

It's fitting that Paul would choose fire for her last great act of suffrage stagecraft. Ideals aspire to the condition of fire. An ideal helps us see a dim and confusing world more clearly, and decide how we ought to proceed. It can be dangerous: an ideal, like a torch, can singe the person who waves it around. Most of all, it spreads. Fire is the only element that, with the addition of a little oxygen and a little fuel, will replicate itself infinitely, just as an ideal can leap from mind to mind inexhaustibly.

John Reed, another rebel with an impresario streak, described the Russian Revolution in terms that apply just as well to Paul's suffrage campaign: Its triumph would create a "pillar of fire for mankind forever."[10]

Chapter 33

Walter Lippmann keeps uncharacteristically quiet in the summer of 1919. He waits, watches, bides his time.

He wants to hear President Wilson admit that in spite of his confidence, his eloquence, his capacity to inspire, he has failed.

"The world can endure honest disappointment, and no one can complain of a failure confessed. For such confession is good for the soul and keeps alive the truth, and it permits other men to go on where the work is unfinished. But I see nothing but pain and disorder and confusion if this first act of honesty is not performed."[1]

Colonel House, the recipient of Lippmann's lament, doesn't bother to point out that the president is never, ever going to do that, because he is *trying to convince sixty-four senators that the treaty is worth ratifying.*

In July, Wilson delivers the treaty to the Senate in person—literally, he carries it into the chamber tucked under one arm—in hopes that a dramatic gesture will jolt them into action. The senators decline to be jolted. There is plainly something wrong with him: He gives a bad speech, dropping words, repeating himself.[2]

He needs a rest, but duty keeps him in swampy Washington, trying to talk skeptical senators out of their reservations to the treaty—trying to convince them that for the good of the nation and the world, the United States must approve this peace and join this league. He holds twenty-six such meetings. He doesn't gain a single vote.

In August, when Henry Cabot Lodge, the chairman of the Foreign Relations Committee, opens hearings on the treaty, Wilson thinks he sees his chance. He offers to testify, something no president has ever done.

The senators visit him in the East Room. He tells them that he has secured every adjustment they requested, including recognition for the Monroe Doctrine and wider prerogatives for their ability to declare war and peace. He makes a new concession, saying that he would be willing to accept interpretative amendments—that is, statements spelling out what they think the treaty means—as long as they aren't included in the treaty itself. That would mean renegotiating the whole thing.

The senators listen politely. Four days later, they vote to strike the Shantung provision from his treaty anyway.

Wilson has one last card to play. Everyone who loves him is against it. He plays it anyway.

The president announces that he will deliver forty major speeches in twenty-one days—more than ever before in his life. He will travel across the Midwest to Washington State, then down the Pacific Coast, then through the Rockies, then back to the East. Wilson's doctor, Admiral Cary Grayson, thinks it might kill him. His secretary, Joseph Tumulty, thinks he's on the verge of a nervous breakdown.[3] But what choice does he have if he wants to see his ideal prevail?

Alice Paul would be a noble woman not to relish the irony of this plan. Her great antagonist is about to undertake the kind of exhausting, demoralizing campaign to rally public support that he had forced her to sustain for seven years.

Because Paul misses nothing, she might notice that Wilson's itinerary looks a great deal like the one that killed Inez Milholland.

Columbus, Kansas City, Sioux Falls, St. Paul: At every stop Wilson gives a rousing speech about the American origins of the league, about the need to make good the sacrifices of the honored dead. His head aches from shouting to thousands of people day after day, but he draws energy from the crowds. And Tumulty acts as a one-man wire service, circulating Wilson's speeches to hundreds of newspapers. A cheerful report from the White House greets them at the Pacific: The treaty's enemies are panicking. "Generally conceded all amendments will be beaten and that our position strategically will be strengthened as result when fight comes on reservations."[4]

Those bright prospects last less than twenty-four hours.

The next morning, a young ex-diplomat named William C. Bullitt takes his seat to testify before Senator Lodge's committee.

"I do not think that Secretary [Robert] Lansing is at all enthusiastic about the League of Nations as it stands at present," says Bullitt.

It is a powerful charge, but the senators don't think much of it. They had pressed the secretary of state for *hours* without getting him to say a single unkind thing about the league.

Bullitt insists that it's true. He reaches into a dispatch bag, holds up a paper. *Proof.*

Bullitt had spent five months working with Colonel House before resigning out of disgust with the treaty, which he found a sorry reflection of Wilson's ideals. Between his resignation and his departure from Paris, high-ranking members of the American delegation tried to talk him out of quitting—including Lansing. And he has notes to prove it.

He has barely begun to read when Lodge cuts in, disbelieving.

"This is a note of the conversation made at the time?" he asks.

"This is a note which I immediately dictated after the conversation."

According to Bullitt's note, Lansing had called "many parts of the treaty thoroughly bad, particularly those dealing with Shantung and the League of Nations."

He had also said: "I consider that the League of Nations at present is entirely useless."

He had also said: "I believe that if the Senate could only understand what this treaty means, and if the American people could really understand, it would unquestionably be defeated, but I wonder if they will ever understand what it lets them in for."

Lansing made some unkind remarks about individual senators—some of whom are sitting right there, listening to Bullitt read them aloud—but everybody can share a laugh about it.

Why shouldn't they laugh? They've got the president now.[5]

The news that Wilson's own secretary of state has denounced his treaty runs on dozens of front pages all across the country and around the world. The treaty's allies are reported to be in "a real panic" and its opponents "delighted . . . over what they regarded as the most powerful blow yet given the treaty." One paper says Bullitt had "ripped to shreds the curtain of secrecy Woodrow Wilson drew to hide the proceedings of the American delegation to the Paris Peace Conference." *The New York Times* says that Wilson's enemies "were in great luck" to discover Bullitt, who was in a rare position to make such embarrassing revelations.[6]

Wilson's enemies are indeed fortunate, but it's not luck: It's Walter Lippmann. He's the one who told the committee to call his friend Bill Bullitt to testify.

Lippmann had gone to Washington to give Hiram Johnson, the Republican senator from California and one of the treaty's fiercest opponents, a confidential briefing on the league's vulnerabilities. Johnson used that information to frame his questions to the president during his testimony. The committee's invitation to Bullitt had gone out soon after.[7]

Johnson must have been impressed by Lippmann's antagonism toward the president. While the committee was waiting for Bullitt to reply to their invitation, he asked if Lippmann had any "wish to be a martyr." That is, did he care to testify for himself?

"You are the only man I know who could demonstrate how we abandoned our ideals," the senator told him.[8]

Lippmann declined, feeling that the committee would gain little from anything he could add at that point. "It has been a gallant fight against enormous odds and no man deserves more honor for it than you," Lippmann said.[9]

It's the kind of verbal bouquet he had recently given to Wilson and the men who worked for him, not the men trying to defeat him. But then Lippmann has always been nimble with his reversals. When socialism didn't seem to be working in Schenectady, he had quit his job and broadcast the mayor's failure in *The New York Call*. Now that the treaty is failing to live up to his ideals, he doesn't just complain, he *acts:* He arms the people who are trying to defeat it, even though he had been arguing the other side just a few months before.

There is a weird integrity to Lippmann acting this way, or at least there would be if his stands on principle didn't coincide with the optimal moments to disembark a sinking ship. For Hiram Johnson isn't any old senator. He had been Teddy Roosevelt's running mate in 1912, and is a leading contender to run on his own in 1920.

"I was for you in 1912 and I am for you now, though I guess you will not have any difficulty in understanding why I cannot be a Republican," Lippmann tells him. "I do not know why I should wander off into that, but it is pleasant to be candid with you."[10]

The president is in Spokane when he learns of Bullitt's testimony. Reporters press him for a comment. He declines to make one, but Tumulty describes him as "incensed and distressed beyond measure."[11]

Wilson can't afford to get sidetracked. He still has hope. In city after city, he keeps shouting his message to enormous crowds under the hot Pacific sun: Portland, Los Angeles, San Diego. His headaches get worse and last longer; they come close to blinding him. He says things that don't make sense.

On September 25, in Pueblo, Colorado, the champion of equipoise, who asked his fellow Americans to stay neutral in thought as well as deed, who warned against strong passions, who insisted that even a terrible war must be fought like gentlemen, goes over completely to demagoguery, paranoia, self-pity. Like Roosevelt at his most jingoistic, he lashes out at the "hyphenated" Americans—those who came here from another country.

"And I want to say—I cannot say it too often—any man who carries a hyphen about with him carries a dagger that he is ready to plunge into the vitals of this republic whenever he gets ready," he shouts.

The crowd eggs him on.

"If I can catch any man with a hyphen in this great contest, I will know that I have caught an enemy of the republic," he continues. "My fellow citizens, it is only certain bodies of foreign sympathies, certain bodies of sympathy with foreign nations that are organized against this great document, which the American representatives have brought back from Paris."[12]

He recounts how he had secured every change that the Republicans had wanted in Paris. Still they deny him.

"What more could I have done?" he asks. "What more could have been obtained?"[13]

It is a poignant question. Nobody in Pueblo has an answer.

Wilson goes back to his train.

A few hours later, he wakes up coughing and choking, unable to breathe. It is an asthma attack, compounded by intense nausea and terrible agitation.[14] Tumulty and Dr. Grayson beg him to give up the trip for the sake of his life.

Against all his instincts, Wilson agrees. Depending on whose account you believe, he looks out the window and cries.

Tumulty tells the conductor to clear the track and make all speed back to Washington. More than once, they have to slow down because the swaying pains Wilson: The machine exceeds the limits of what a fallible human can bear.[15]

On the president's fourth day back at the White House, Edith wakens to find him sitting up in bed. His left hand is limp.

"I have no feeling in that hand," he tells her. "Will you rub it? But first help me to the bathroom."

She helps him to the toilet, then runs for help. While she is gone, the brain that had been charged with too many duties for too long, that incubated a world-spanning dream of democracy and sacrificed his failing body to try to realize it, finally cracks under the strain.[16] A massive stroke sends the president tumbling to the floor.

Chapter 34

And then there is no one to stop it. No centripetal force to keep the pieces from flying apart, no firebreak to stop the inferno. The president lies incontinent, half-paralyzed, speaking in Lear-like jokes and riddles, as the country falls apart around him.[1]

The intense economic dislocation of 1919 is only the start. A steel strike in Gary, Indiana, leads to the imposition of martial law: an army division, armed with cannons, shuts down the city.

All that summer, race riots had swept up from the South to northern cities—at least twenty-five major ones, leading to the lynching of at least fifty-two black men. Chicago had burned for four days. "One by one the idealistic war dreams are vanishing, and as they vanish the solid outlines of the old, prewar conditions loom up clearer and clearer," writes James Weldon Johnson, a leader of the rapidly expanding National Association for the Advancement of Colored People.[2]

He thinks federal action is necessary to stop the violence, but the government doesn't take it. W.E.B. Du Bois refers to the Wilson administration as "the dominant southern oligarchy in Washington."[3]

Left to defend themselves, black men returning from the war for democracy are less and less inclined to turn the other cheek. Max Eastman publishes "If We Must Die," a sonnet of defiance by the then-unknown Jamaican poet Claude McKay: "Like men we'll face the murderous, cowardly pack / Pressed to the wall, dying, but—fighting back!"[4]

That summer, coordinated terror attacks strike nine cities. An enormous bomb blows the front off the home of A. Mitchell Palmer, the attorney general. When his ears stop ringing from the detonation and from the screams of his terrified daughter and wife, he sets the government on a plan of reprisal. The next morning, there are security checkpoints around Washington; there are armed guards at churches. The perpetrators were almost certainly Italian anarchists—an Italian dictionary is found at the blast site—but Palmer turns loose the Department of Justice to retaliate against radicals of every stripe.

As with the flu, the American people have no resistance to what afflicts them. Three hundred thousand vigilantes spy on their neighbors, denying liberty in the name of liberty.[5]

In Washington, Victor Berger, a socialist elected to Congress by the people of Wisconsin, is denied his seat because he is under indictment for violating the Espionage Act. Before long, in Albany, the state assembly will expel five legitimately elected legislators for being socialists.[6] In Greenwich Village, men wearing no identification break into Max Eastman's apartment. He's not there—he has gone to Hollywood, to visit Florence—but a friend is. He tells the men that if they don't stop rummaging in his desk and leave immediately, he'll call the cops.

"We *are* the cops," they reply.

A rational concern about Bolshevik infiltration can't drive a country to this kind of paranoia, any more than isolated episodes of wartime sabotage explain why upstanding citizens felt it was time to murder their German-speaking neighbors. The same leaps ahead that thrilled the young radicals in the prewar years, the breaking of so many old ties, left many of their fellow Americans bewildered. The stress and fear of sending a million young men to fight only added to the trauma—as did two years of unremitting wartime propaganda. An adroit president, like the first-term Woodrow Wilson, might have helped the American people regain their bearings and acclimate to a changed reality. But in late 1919, the United States has no such president, just an incapacitated old man whose condition is hidden by his doctor and wife. There have been too many new ideas and new programs and new foreign faces and new things to fear. They all should be stopped. Or smashed.[7]

Walter Lippmann reels at these depredations, what he calls a "reign of terror." He cannot stomach the sight of the government that he had supported instituting "the complete Prussianizing of American institutions"[8]—a charge he would have dismissed as foolish if John Reed had made it.

"You know what hopes were put in this administration, how loudly and insistently it proclaimed its loyalty to the cause of freedom," he writes to Newton Baker. "Well it was possible to fail in those hopes. It was credible that the wisdom and the strength to realize them would be lacking. But it is forever incredible that an administration announcing the most spacious ideals in our history should have done more to endanger fundamental American liberties than any group of men for a hundred years."

He begs Baker to do something—anything—to stop it. "I plead with you not to fail us at this time, not by your silence to seem a party to an hysteria which a few years hence will make us ashamed."[9]

The liberal-minded Lippmann, worrying himself about the intersection of realities and ideals, is speaking the language of a world that's gone. A new young man has the ear of official Washington now—as widely admired as Lippmann had been in the prewar days, but even more precociously successful and vastly more powerful. Attorney General Palmer, responding to the attack that nearly killed his family and dozens more like it, created a Radical Division at the Bureau of Investigation. He put it in the hands of his twenty-four-year-old special assistant, J. Edgar Hoover.

Hoover doesn't fraternize with the bright boys at the House of

Truth. He has no time to spout ideals. He *works*. He looks for threats, finds them, and stops them. He is very, very adept at his job.

To Hoover, the intertwining rebellions of the prewar years are not exciting expressions of a common desire for liberation, but a spiderweb of threats to the American way of life. He creates a nightmare version of the Inquiry, one turned inward, toward American radicals, not outward to European states. He wants to know everything: He opens mail, taps phones, bugs meeting halls, and tabulates it all in a filing system that's efficient beyond the wildest dreams of Alice Paul and her squadron of lobbyists. Within a few months, he is tracking 150,000 people. Nor is this knowledge accrued for the mere sake of having knowledge: As Max Eastman has been saying, the purpose of knowledge is to furnish more efficacious action. And so Hoover acts.[10]

The fruit of his diligence is a pair of enormous raids. They are called the Palmer Raids, but they are really Hoover's. In November 1919, and again in January 1920, hundreds of agents launch raids in dozens of cities, largely to stamp out the Communist Party and Communist Labor Party. The standards for arrests are so porous that nobody is sure how many people get rounded up. Five thousand? Many are held incommunicado, sometimes for months. Hoover misses John Reed by a couple of weeks, and immediately starts seeking another way to get him.

Palmer and Hoover are not interested in locking up most of these people: They want to be rid of them. One cold night that winter, 249 men and women are herded onto the SS *Buford,* a creaky ship that will transport them to Russia. Emma Goldman, the country's most visible anarchist, is among the deportees. From a tugboat in New York harbor, Hoover watches her go. The attorney general, with one eye on the upcoming presidential election, promises the public more of these "Soviet arks." Hoover is certainly capable of filling them.[11]

Only the national fever has just about run its course. One brave bureaucrat, Louis F. Post, sees appalling overreach and reckless violation of civil liberties in those arrests: Using every bit of his authority as assistant secretary of labor, he cancels thousands of warrants, nearly getting himself impeached in the process. Zechariah Chafee and eleven other lawyers assemble a powerful brief against the actions of the Department of Justice, an early demonstration of the power of fighting legal fire with legal fire. Mostly the Red Scare collapses from its own destructive momentum. The authorities lash the country to a frenzy about the imminent threat of widespread terror attacks on May Day 1920. And then nothing happens.[12]

Certainly this is embarrassing for Hoover. But as Lippmann had written, it's possible to turn our mistakes into wisdom. Bright boys often do. The madness and dislocation of the Red Scare had given Hoover a chance to establish himself. He had learned some valuable lessons. He would find many opportunities to apply them in the forty-eight years he would spend hunting radicals as director of the FBI.

Amid the roundups, the raids, the deportations, a reckoning begins. How could a war for ideals have spawned what Lippmann calls "the blackest reaction our generation has known"? Nobody faces the questions more squarely than John Dewey.

"Were not those right who held that it was self-contradictory to try to further the permanent ideals of peace by recourse to war?" he asks. "Was not he who thought they might thus be promoted one of the gullible throng who swallowed the cant of idealism as a sugar coating for the bitter core of violence and greed?"

He refuses to be consoled by the "scant though true" argument made by Lippmann, among others, that the world situation would be even worse if America had stayed out and Germany had won the war. Dewey had declared his support for Wilson's war effort because he thought it would *advance* certain liberal ideals.

He doesn't disavow his essays in support of the war. He thinks the Wilson administration erred severely in how it prosecuted the fight. Still he makes a large concession. "The defeat of idealistic aims has been, without exaggeration, enormous," he writes in *The New Repub-*

lic. "The consistent pacifist has much to urge now in his own justification; he is entitled to his flourish of private triumphings."[13]

That is generous on Dewey's part, but much too late. The person who most deserves a flourish can't enjoy it, because he is dead.

That Randolph Bourne made a singularly exact prediction of what would happen because of the war isn't the verdict of future generations; his own contemporaries see it. In 1919, the critic Lewis Mumford attacks pro-war liberals for having failed to anticipate "the virulence of the animus" that had been set loose by the war. "Perhaps the only writer who gauged this imponderable element at its full worth was the late Randolph Bourne," he writes. In 1920, the editors of *The Nation* write: "You may remember that you lost your head in 1917, and you are intellectually ashamed; but you take comfort from the assurance that practically everyone else did also. Randolph Bourne did not lose his head."[14]

Bourne had predicted that leaders stupid enough to start a world war would be too stupid to end it. The Allied leaders are, in fact, unable to conclude a peace. He said that President Wilson had given the Allies a blank check, which would lead to a peace much less liberal than his vaunted Fourteen Points. Lippmann's disgust shows that this was correct, too.

The consequence of war that scared Bourne the most was the spiritual and psychological damage it might inflict, the chance that it would endanger "the only genuinely precious thing in a nation, the hope and ardent idealism of its youth."[15] That prediction seems difficult to verify: People don't come right out and say that they've lost their ardent idealism. Or do they?

The war "killed individualism out of our generation," says Amory Blaine, the callow young protagonist of a book written just after the armistice. "Oh Lord, what a pleasure it used to be to dream I might be a really great dictator or writer or religious or political leader. . . . The world is so overgrown that it can't lift its own fingers, and I was planning to be such an important finger."

This Side of Paradise bears out Bourne's warnings about disillusioned American youth as neatly as the race riots fulfill his prophecy of hatreds being unloosed by the war. Amory and his friends belong to what their creator, F. Scott Fitzgerald, calls "a new generation dedicated more than the last to the fear of poverty and the worship of success; grown up to find all gods dead, all wars fought, all faiths in man shaken."[16]

The young men and women of that generation—the Lost Generation, it would come to be called—recognize themselves in Fitzgerald's characters. They make his book the first literary hit of the new decade. It helps to establish a mood of ironic despair as the defining tone of the postwar era.

At a stroke, the distinctive tone of the prewar years, the urgent hopeful experimentalism of Bourne's own *Youth and Life,* comes to seem as dead as the man who wrote it.

Chapter 35

Even amid the constant stream of calamitous news in 1920, the story leaps off the page: John Reed is dead.

The brief item on the front page of New York's *Evening World* for April 9 says that he had been arrested while trying to sneak out of Russia. He'd been caught with thousands of dollars' worth of diamonds, false identification, and microfilmed Soviet propaganda. Now he has been shot by the Finnish authorities. *Executed.*[1]

A dead American, however red he might be, is still a dead American. The State Department contacts the Finns to undertake the usual inquiries.

The inquiries reveal that Jack is alive.[2]

Some of the story is true. He really did get caught by the Finnish police, stowing away in the coal bunker of a boat bound for home: hair slicked back, dust all over his face. And he really was carrying forged papers, as well as 102 loose diamonds and dozens of letters written by Russians who had been deported on the *Buford*, intended for their friends and relatives in the States.[3] But the part about being dead isn't true—at least not entirely.

The police in Abo had put Reed in solitary confinement, cut off from the outside world in a cold wet cell, kept alive on salted fish. After five weeks locked in a little cage, feeling his mental and physical health fraying, Reed had dreamed up the story of his death and bribed somebody to circulate it, knowing it would catch the attention of friends who might set him free.[4]

The Finns don't set him free, but they do let him write to his wife.

"The thought of you drags at me sometimes until my imagination plays tricks, and then I almost go crazy," he tells her.[5]

Louise Bryant rallies every friend who might have any influence left with the Wilson administration to press for Reed's release. But the height of a Red Scare is a bad time to seek help for a communist in distress. By June, after Reed has been locked up for more than three months, the police in Abo are eager to be rid of him. If the United States won't issue him a passport, the Finns might ship him to a concentration camp.[6]

With their anxiety climbing, Reed's friends receive another report: He has gotten free. It's not clear even now how he does it. The most picturesque version, if not the most likely, is that the Soviets trade two imprisoned Finnish professors for his release. This version ends with Lenin saying that the Finns had made a bad deal: He would have traded a whole college faculty to get Jack back.[7]

However Reed escapes, he arrives in Russia badly damaged. Emma Goldman, stuck there after her deportation on the *Buford,* is shocked by the sight of him. Before his attempt to get home, he had seemed to her "a sudden ray of light, the old buoyant, adventurous Jack that I used to know in the States." Now his arms and legs are swollen, his body covered in sores, his gums ravaged by scurvy. Medicine is scarce in Russia because of the ongoing Allied blockade—even soap and hot water are hard to come by. She nurses him as best she can.[8]

Convalescence means another couple weeks of staring at the ceiling, brooding on his failure. Reed had come halfway around a dangerous world to win recognition for the Communist Labor Party. The leaders of the Communist International, after listening to his argument, had ordered the party to merge with its antagonistic twin. This will put Reed's group, the smaller of the two, at a disadvantage. The dominant voice in American communism would likely belong to the Russian-born leaders of the Communist Party, who denounce what they call the "treacherous ideology of 'Americanism.'"[9]

He had failed coming over with his party's mandate and he had failed going back with the Soviets' jewels. It's a haphazard (but, some-how, characteristic) prelude to Reed becoming the foremost American communist in the world.

From the far corners of the globe Reed watches them come: a tough-looking bunch "of real proletarians, of actual workmen-fighters-strikers, barricade-defenders and of active leaders of the revolutionary national-ist movements in the backward and colonial countries." They march through crowds of cheering Russians, sporting the red carnations they'd been given as they stepped off their trains.[10]

Reed meets them, listens to stories of their voyages, joins them to watch an enormous pageant—five thousand performers strong—on the history of revolution. And they do the same with him. He is one of them now: a delegate to the Communist International like all the rest.

In July 1920, in the monumentally ornate throne room of the Krem-lin, Lenin opens the Second Congress of the Third International. (A small and sparsely attended meeting the previous year was technically the First Congress.) Reed and the 168 other delegates face a new ver-sion of the old dilemma: how to translate a vast, gleaming ideal into precise realities. They must find a way to convert the idea of an inter-national workers' revolution to specific structures, well-organized bu-reaus, disciplined chains of command.

The settlement of these difficulties lies in the hands of someone who inflames them at every turn. Grigory Zinoviev is humorless and unsmiling—"a vain and fluid thing of shifty mind and tongue," according to Max Eastman, who would meet him in later years and grasp at once why Reed despised him. (Shaking hands with Comrade Zinoviev, Max would say, is "like receiving the present of a flattened-out banana.")[11] He is the chairman of the Comintern but is also the president of the Petrograd Soviet, a combination of roles that makes the limits of Russian control of the session hard to judge. He is also a demagogue, an autocrat, a tyrant in training—exactly the sort of authority figure that Reed felt a congenital obligation to take down a peg. He starts making trouble shortly after Zinoviev calls the congress to order.

Reed asks that English be declared an official language. Zinoviev refuses. So Reed asks again. When that doesn't work, he asks yet again.

"Comrade Reed, you are making this proposal for the third time, while the question has already been settled," says Angelica Balabanova, the secretary.[12] She chides him despite being his friend.

The Russians put up with him for some reason—or lots of reasons. The Comintern has nothing like the power over its members that it will one day wield. Also Lenin likes Reed—he even supplied a blurb for *Ten Days That Shook the World*. ("Here is a book which I should like to see published in millions of copies and translated into all languages.")[13] And it helps their cause to have a charismatic American around, even an unruly one. It helps so much that in spite of the presence of more docile American communists, the Russians pick Reed for a position of rare authority.

When the congress ends, all Comintern matters will be handled by an Executive Committee drawn from a dozen nations. American communism may be wobbly, divided, and insolent, but America itself is enormous and powerful. Somebody has to speak for it. The Russians pick Reed.

It ought to be an honor, but as Reed spends day after day in meetings chaired by Zinoviev, his frustration and dismay grow. For Reed, who was never a champion theorist, the test of an ideal is how it works. "Revolutionary Socialism, above all other kinds, must be *practical*—it must *work*—it must make *Socialists* out of workers, and make them quick."[14] Yet in these meetings, he keeps feeling baffled by the unreality and obstinacy of his comrades. He watches them trying to impose Russian solutions on countries where conditions are different—even as they say they are doing the opposite. The Comintern's policy on trade unions is to infiltrate them. Reed knows that the American Federation of Labor, led by Samuel Gompers, will never be infiltrated. These clear-eyed engineers of revolution are being obtuse.

He is working very long hours and still hasn't recovered from his ordeal in the Finnish jail.[15] And now he finds himself in a position not so different from Lippmann the previous summer, trying to decide what to do about Wilson's botched treaty: He believes in the ideal but he cannot abide the way it is being realized.

What should he do? He resigns.[16]

Probably something like this was bound to happen. Reed is good at quitting things, like *The Liberator*. It's also a family tradition of sorts—his father had turned his back on Portland society when he began curtailing its corruption. That independent streak might be one of the reasons why C. J. Reed asked Lincoln Steffens to look out for Jack, and not let convictions lead him astray.

Steffens knows by this point that he has failed. He and Jack had a tense conversation in 1918, when Jack was in his first flush of revolutionary zeal. Steffens remembered him as the most joyous creature he'd ever seen. Now Jack didn't smile anymore.[17]

The conviction that Steffens had seen in 1918 is still there in 1920. For some reason that's lost to history, Reed takes back his resignation. He decides to stay on the Executive Committee.

And that is what takes him to Baku.

The heat rises in waves, and through the black air Reed hears a half dozen languages he doesn't understand. In the middle of the night, a week after leaving Moscow, the communists' train has arrived in Baku, in present-day Azerbaijan, on the shore of the Caspian Sea.

Jack is as far from home as he would ever be.

A huge crowd has been waiting in the grand theater of the city. The comrades from Moscow make their way to the stage, where they are greeted by a roar. When it's Reed's turn to speak, he gives the crowd a mocking hello from the United States.

"Don't you know how Baku is pronounced in American? It's pronounced *oil*."[18]

The Russians have organized an Oriental congress to rally new recruits to the cause. Two thousand delegates from the breadth of the Eastern Hemisphere are there: Persians and South Asians and Egyptians, men who had crossed deserts and mountains, who rode camels and stowed away on ships, who wear fezzes and turbans and every kind of mustache. Some carry swords. His whole life, Reed had been drawn to what was different from him. Now *he* is the exotic one: the comrade from the other side of the planet. Photos show him lean and sunbrowned in a collarless white shirt.

The communists have organized the congress to outflank the imperialists and their American-devised League of Nations. That's why Zinoviev insisted that Reed come, even though Reed didn't want to. Reed writes a speech warning his listeners not to trust the Western capitalists, especially not the Americans. Look at how his countrymen treat the people in the Caribbean. Would America be less exploitative in how it treats people living atop an ocean of petroleum? Or look at black men and women living in the American South—and, increasingly, in northern cities—and how they are denied the rights that should accompany their citizenship. Why expect better treatment than that? (It's not just a talking point for the sake of his listeners: Reed feels strongly that communists need to reach out to oppressed black workers and make common cause. They should be organized in the same unions as white workers, "the best and quickest way to root out racial prejudice and awaken class solidarity.")

It's a rousing speech, but he never gets to deliver it. On the fourth night of the conference, Zinoviev declares that because time is short, only the British and the French representatives will speak; the remarks of other comrades will be printed.[19] There had been plenty of time for Zinoviev's own speech, though.

Reed's friend Alfred Rosmer watches a change come over him. He is disturbed by the high-handed conduct and demagoguery of Zinoviev. Rosmer suspects that Reed, with his journalistic curiosity, knows more about the Russians' activities than the rest of the delegates do. Jack loses interest in the conference, spending more time wandering down the dim alleys of the town. He returns with precious silks and tales of god-only-knows what other adventures. And he broods. If he was disenchanted enough to quit before leaving Moscow, he can only be more so after Baku.[20]

The communists leave for Moscow amid great fanfare. The train snakes north, sun pounding down on the armored cars. During the trip Reed has a furious fight with Zinoviev. Maybe it's because of Zinoviev's high-handedness in denying him a chance to speak; maybe it's the privileges the Bolshevik leaders arrogate to themselves in a country full of poor and starving peasants; maybe it's Reed's disgust with the demagogic appeals Zinoviev had made, telling his listeners to wage "a true people's holy war against the robbers and oppressors," driving them to scream and wave their weapons—so unlike what Reed thinks a real revolutionary would say.[21]

This isn't the only fight on the trip back to Moscow. Counterrevolutionary forces have sabotaged the tracks. The guards detach the engine from the rest of the train and venture ahead, scouting the terrain to make sure the route will be safe. Reed goes with them. He may not be the burly youngster who rode into battle with Pancho Villa, or even the eager reporter who sprinted into the Winter Palace alongside the Red Guards, but if there's going to be trouble, there's no way John Reed is going to miss it.[22]

Jack walks arm in arm with Louise under the white birch trees. Bands play; children run everywhere. His appearance had shocked her when he ran shouting into her room on that first day back in Moscow. He

had looked so thin and tired, in clothes that were darned and patched—
little better than rags, really. He had grown gentle—ascetic, even.[23] Not
like the old Jack, but just like the old Jack.

Oh, it is good to see his honey again.

They go to the ballet and the opera. Jack tells her about a novel he'd
like to write, one that started to come to him in that Finnish cage. A
young man named Robin arrives in New York full of ideas and determined to have adventures—adventures that would be just like Reed's,
to judge from the notes he scribbled: "Max and Florence. . . . Pageants,
the People's Theater, the village. . . . Harold Stearns and Randolph
Bourne. . . . Walter Lippmann. . . . The coming of Gene O'Neill." Jack
is full of ideas. Another one is to write a book about the vast pageant of
revolution he had seen at the beginning of the congress, before it all
started going wrong with the Comintern.[24]

They visit Lenin and Trotsky, which pleases Reed, and he tells her
of his frustration with the Comintern, which pains him. He had written a story for an American communist newspaper giving a largely lau-
datory account of the Second Congress, but one that makes plain his
disappointment with the policy on unions. "At the next Congress, these
theses must be altered." He tells Louise he has much more to say, and
he intends to say it: He will write an article attacking the Comintern
when he gets home.[25]

Louise pleads with him not to leave too soon. J. Edgar Hoover and
his agents are waiting for him. Reed will almost certainly go to jail. She
wants him to regain his strength first.

"My dear little Honey," he says, "I would do anything I could for
you, but don't ask me to be a coward."

She bursts into tears and says that's not what she meant, and that
she'll go with him anywhere. He smiles at that.[26]

They spend a happy week together before Jack falls ill. His head is
pounding and his fever climbs, but no one can tell them what's wrong.

The flu? It takes days for a doctor to land on the right diagnosis. When he does, it is the worst diagnosis.

Reed knows all too clearly what's going to happen to him, the consequences of a tick bite in Baku. He had seen it five years earlier in Serbia, "the Country of Death." He had walked through the typhus ward in Chere Kula, smelled the dying men as they sweated and rotted in their cots: some moaning, others raving, delirious. He knows that surviving typhus is often no reprieve: the gangrene, the organs wasting away. Some people ask doctors to amputate the sick parts of themselves so the healthy parts have a chance to live. But sometimes they die anyway.[27]

Reed is taken to the typhus ward at Mariinsky Hospital and isolated for the sake of the other comrades. Bryant defies the quarantine and stays by his side. The nuns light candles for him, as they do for every sick man. They are surprised at how many candles they need to light—how hard and persistently this young American fights.

He gets thinner and weaker. His beard grows in.

Sometimes he is a disciplined revolutionary, asking Louise to make sure that one of the American comrades will revise his speeches from the congress, since the translators garbled them.[28] At other times, he is a dreaming poet, floating free of politics. He tells Louise that the water he drinks is full of little songs.

She holds his hand and doesn't let go.[29]

The second report of John Reed's death—the one that can't be taken back, because it's true—runs on October 18, 1920. He has died in Moscow at age thirty-two.

A week later, poets and artists and revolutionaries and would-be revolutionaries—Jack's friends—gather in New York to do the unthinkable: mourn the death of the most vibrantly alive person they'd ever known. So many people want to take part that the organizers have to add a second memorial.[30]

The larger event is at the cavernous Central Opera House on Sixty-seventh Street, which accommodates thousands. The grieving men and women sing the "Internationale," then fall silent. A reporter hears brief, sudden sobs, and then the effort to stifle the sobs, which leads to gasps.

A big crayon drawing of Jack by Hugo Gellert, one of the *Masses* artists, is displayed at center stage. Max Eastman stands next to it to deliver his eulogy.[31]

Eastman acknowledges the handsome tributes that have appeared in the papers since their friend's death, but says they were a little lacking, a little coy. They skirt the fact that Reed had died an outlaw.

"We know what his crime was—it is the oldest in all the codes of history, the crime of fighting loyalty to the slaves," he says. "And we pay our tribute to him now that he lies dead, only exactly as we used to pay it when he stood here making us laugh and feel brave, because he was so full of brave laughter. Our tribute to John Reed is a pledge that the cause he died for shall live."

Eastman tries to explain what made Reed "a very unusual phenomenon." He thinks Reed himself never really understood it: the balance he struck between being a dreamer and a man of action. "He was a poet who could understand science. He was an idealist who could face facts."

The pursuit of those ideals had led Reed to Moscow, where he died for them. But his life is only the last and dearest in a long series of things Jack sacrificed for his convictions, Eastman says. When America went to war, the bourgeois world offered him every sort of temptation— fame, riches, glory—but he refused them all to keep writing for *The Masses*. Reed didn't miss the material rewards that might have come his way, but he did wish he could write more poems.

Max hopes that Jack's verses won't be lost because the man who wrote them "chose to make a great poem of his life."[32]

Chapter 36

Max Eastman's tribute to John Reed is the last transmission from a ship before sinking. Its weaving together of poetry and revolution, its personal point of view mixed with flat defiance of authority, captures the distinctive ring of the 1910s, an era when all these things seemed to have some relationship to one another.

Exactly one week later, the American people declare the decade over with as much force as a democratic republic can muster. James Cox, the Democratic candidate, manages only 34 percent of the vote. It's the most lopsided margin in a hundred years—a savage rejection of Woodrow Wilson and his ideals.

The young radicals who live to see Warren G. Harding inaugurated are no longer young. It's not just the number of years they have spent in the arena; it's the scarifying nature of what they've seen and done. All of them have argued and fought, run risks and faced setbacks, persisted and changed course.

They have learned that there are things called catastrophes, not just in their history books, but right here, in their own time, all around

them. They have learned how it feels to live through one, and then live
through another, and another. They have seen an entire civilization destroy itself, and a country savage itself, for nothing. Many Americans in
1920 perceive the enormousness of the failure all around them; only the
most perceptive among them see what lies ahead. Every baby learning
to walk that year will have his or her life upended in late adolescence,
when the war returns to claim another generation.

Who can say in advance what you'll do, or how much you'll with-
stand, for the sake of what you believe? The young radicals know that
now. The government's determination to silence dissent surprised Max
Eastman, but not as much as his own determination to face down a
mob and go on dissenting in Fargo. Suffragists returning from picketing the White House were surprised to find gashes on the backs of
their hands, where the mob had tried to wrench their banners away, but
more surprised to find the gashes on their palms, from their own fin-
gernails, because they'd refused to let go.[1]

They learned how far they would go to defeat barriers to realizing
ideals—but they also learned about the ideals themselves. Sometimes
those ideals turn out to be false, in whole or in part. The election that
ends the decade has a different meaning for each of the no-longer-
young radicals, but it finds all three of them reassessing their ideals in
light of all that they've seen and done and learned. Do they keep fighting? If so, how?

And, above all, for what?

For Alice Paul, the election of 1920 means deliverance, citizenship, victory. She is one of many millions of American women who cast a vote
for the first time.

The suffragists had secured the amendment with no time to spare.
Through the sweltering summer of 1920, Tennessee—their last hope
for the thirty-sixth and final state ratification they needed—had become what they called "Armageddon." Paul directed her forces from
headquarters in Washington. Carrie Chapman Catt had traveled to

Nashville with an overnight bag and ended up staying six weeks. In her thirty-year career she had never seen anything like the vitriol or intrigue of that place, as all of the country's anti-suffrage artillery was trained on one small town: "I was flooded with anonymous letters, vulgar, ignorant, insane."[2]

The state senate voted yes, focusing even more pressure on the closely divided house of representatives. After four generations of organized lobbying, careful persuasion, ingenious pressure tactics, and heroic suffering, the decisive vote in the fight for woman suffrage fell to the youngest state representative, twenty-four-year-old Harry Burn. He voted yes because his mother told him to.

In Washington, Paul stepped out on the balcony of National Woman's Party headquarters. She unfurled an enormous suffrage flag, with stripes of purple, gold, and white, and a newly sewn thirty-sixth star.

A photo captured her beaming.[3]

Paul issued a statement, and for once it was what she always claimed to be: nonpartisan. She said that credit didn't belong to Democrats or Republicans.

"It was won by the thousands of women who sacrificed health and careers, who suffered physical violence and every other indignity, even to imprisonment, in the long, weary struggle to secure that freedom which should belong to every one of our citizens."[4]

Paul knew how powerful it would be to include women in a photo capturing the moment that the Nineteenth Amendment was certified. She and several fellow suffragists sat up almost all night waiting for word that the official document from the Tennessee legislature had reached Bainbridge Colby, the secretary of state, so he could sign it and make it official. But on the morning of August 26, 1920, she was told that Colby had already signed it. In his official statement, he explained that he didn't want to give the enemies of suffrage a chance to make a legal appeal. He also wanted no part of the dispute about which group of suffragists would get to be on hand.

Later that day, Paul's hopes were revived: She received word that there might be a photo op after all. She and some lieutenants hurried

to the State Department. They were walking down the hall outside
Colby's office when his door opened and out stepped Catt.

Everybody froze. Catt and several of her colleagues had been invited to see the precious document. She hadn't expected to see Alice
Paul, and vice versa. They had continued to antagonize each other
throughout the closing stages of the campaign. Still, this was a day of
triumph, wasn't it? Nobody alive in 1920 deserved more credit for enfranchising women than Paul and Catt. Nobody could sympathize
more completely with the special sense of gratification the other must
have felt.

They faced each other in the hallway. It was not a large hallway. Paul
stepped to one side. Her associates followed her lead.

Catt and her group walked by.

Nobody said a word.[5]

Even as she casts her first ballot, even as she celebrates, Paul is
thinking about the future of her movement. One faction within the
National Woman's Party wants to reorganize on behalf of disarmament.
Another, led by Crystal Eastman, wants to broaden their focus to a
wide slate of feminist reforms: to open more jobs to women, to make it
easier for them to run for office, to let them control their own income,
to give them access to birth control, to reform the male-dominated
divorce laws and guardianship laws and laws of inheritance.[6]

All sides of this debate work from the premise that the fight for
woman suffrage is fully, truly won. But that premise is false. And they
know it.

Throughout the South, black women attempting to vote for the first
time in 1920 are subjected to what a reporter for *The Nation* describes
as "not only injustice, but rank insult": waiting all day until every white
person has registered, needing to answer impossibly difficult questions,
outright threats. Three-quarters of the country's black women live in
the South: The complete victory that Paul and other suffragists have
been claiming isn't close to complete.[7]

In early 1921, sixty of these disenfranchised black women rally to protest the denial of their rights. They follow a time-tested strategy. They congregate in Washington—in this case, at the Nineteenth Street Baptist Church, under the auspices of the NAACP. They ask a powerful official for a hearing. When it is denied, they persist, climbing the long flights of stairs to make their appeal in person. Only in this case, the official who tries to stonewall them isn't the president or a senator— it's Alice Paul.

They present her with evidence of their disenfranchisement. They tell her they can't believe that the National Woman's Party would allow the amendment for which they had fought so long and so hard to be trampled—excluding millions of their sisters from the vote.

They turn Paul's own argument against her: *"No women are free until all are free."*[8]

Paul feels that the National Woman's Party has already exerted itself on behalf of disenfranchised black women: It pushed for an "enforcement" bill for the Nineteenth Amendment to be introduced in the Senate after the election.[9] Her visitors know about that. They also know what it looks like when the indomitable Alice Paul fully commits herself, and her party, to redressing an injustice. The delegates make a specific request of her, as she once did of the newly elected President Wilson: to use the upcoming National Woman's Party convention to press for a Congressional investigation of their disenfranchisement.

For Paul, securing the Nineteenth Amendment hasn't changed the essential logic of women's empowerment. Standing up for the rights of black women will cost her the support of southern legislators, maybe even southern members of her own party.[10] Paul will need that support to achieve the party's next goal: not disarmament, not a broad-based program of feminist reforms, but a narrowly focused intervention against laws that discriminate against women. Paul faces a choice between two courses, two ideals: fighting to ensure that a woman's race does not exclude her from political freedom, or attacking legal barriers that afflict all women—at least in theory.

Leaders make choices. Paul makes hers. She agrees to let an advocate of black women speak from the floor of the party's upcoming convention, though not to make a formal presentation from the lectern. The party will make no demand for an investigation.[11]

Mary Church Terrell, the leader of the National Association of Colored Women, can see Paul's point. She makes a public statement that of all the women's organizations in America, Paul's is "the most broadminded and friendly in its attitude to the colored people." Still she calls herself "grievously disappointed" by the failure of the National Woman's Party to stand up more effectively for black women.[12] She is not alone. Paul gives some members of that delegation the impression that she is "indifferent" to their plight and "resentful" of their request.

"There is danger that because of a great victory women will believe that their whole struggle for independence ended," Paul writes in the final issue of *The Suffragist*. "They have still far to go."[13]

Some have farther to go than the rest.

To Max Eastman, the significance of the 1920 election is that it has no significance whatsoever. Four years earlier, he had endorsed Wilson. Now he abides by the manifesto of the Third International, which calls political democracy nothing more than "the dictatorship of the bourgeoisie."[14]

Cox or Harding: Who cares?

The choice that matters to Eastman in 1920 isn't between Cox or Harding; it's whether to accept the Twenty-one Conditions. These are the principles outlined by Lenin to control who can affiliate with the Comintern. They insist on strict adherence to the decisions of the Executive Committee, regular purges of centrists, secret agitation in the armed forces, and a commitment to working in both legal and illegal parties.

Many American socialists reject these conditions, even some who support the Russian Revolution. Morris Hillquit, still the leader of what people now call "the old Socialist Party," decries them as an attempt to destroy the socialism in America. (It's not entirely surprising that Hillquit would object, since he is denounced by name in one of the conditions.) Eugene Debs, locked in his federal prison cell for violating the Espionage Act, rejects them, too. He supports the Soviet Republic but thinks that Russians are trying to dictate the course of American radicalism in a way that is "ridiculous, arbitrary, autocratic."

Eastman has ties to both of these men. Hillquit had defended him in the first *Masses* trial; Debs had inspired the peroration of his closing argument in the second. Now he condemns them both. They are ignorant of true socialism, he says.

He accepts the Twenty-one Conditions without reservations. "In a lump," he will say later.[15]

Enthralled by the success of the Russian Revolution, which he regards as "the supreme social achievement of mankind," Eastman's ideals change and keep changing. When a correspondent returns from Moscow complaining about infringements of civil liberties, Eastman calls him bourgeois, and stakes out his most extreme position yet: "The most rigid political tyranny conceivable, if it accomplished the elimination of wage-slavery and continued to produce wealth, would increase the amount of actual liberty so much that the very sides of the earth would heave with relief."[16]

This startling rearrangement of his priorities has some real-world applications. When *The Liberator* refuses to run an ad for some anti-communist propaganda, he gets mocked for it by the *New-York Tribune*. Now Eastman, who stood up for civil liberties even in the face of the Espionage Act, says he doesn't believe in free speech. He says that nobody does.

"I know it to be a fact that as soon as my speech becomes again a menace to the absolutely vital interests of the ruling business men, they will suppress me again if they can," he writes. "And I know also that only one thing would please me better than to suppress the *Tribune*, if I had the power, and that would be to suppress the *Times*. So long as our civilization consists in its economic essence of a war between two classes, Free Speech will exist only at such times, or to such extent as may be harmless to the interests of the class in power."[17]

The Soviet example even makes Eastman rethink his most treasured ideal of all—about the relationship between poetry and politics. Henri Barbusse invites *The Liberator* to align with "Clarté," a new group of writers and thinkers aiming to provide intellectual assistance to the revolution. Eastman declines. He thinks it's unwise for poets and intellectuals to create a group separate from the party apparatus: "These particular people, I should say, are more in need of guidance and careful watching by the practical and theoretical workers of the movement than the members of any other trade."

Eastman isn't suggesting that poets submit to official party censorship. He wants artists to be "very free and irresponsible." But he puts a surprisingly exact boundary on that freedom and irresponsibility: "We have not only to cultivate the poetry, but keep the poetry true to the science of the revolution—to give life and laughter and passion and adventures in speculation, without ever clouding or ignoring any point that is vital in the theory and practice of communism."[18]

The essay jolts the critic Van Wyck Brooks. He replies to Eastman in the pages of *The Freeman,* staking out a position like the one his late friend Randolph Bourne would have taken. Their views are so close in those years that H. L. Mencken calls Brooks the "heir and assign" to Bourne. In fact, Brooks keeps a replica of his friend's death mask in his office: Horatio to his Hamlet.[19]

When Eastman says "free and irresponsible," Brooks writes, he really means "free within necessity." The only freedom worth having for artists is *absolute* freedom, to write with no regard for revolutionary doctrines. That is the only way to enlighten people's desires, which does more good for the human condition than any politically approved stand.

Eastman claims, then and later, that Brooks was misreading him; he had no thought of subjecting poetry to the discipline of apparatchiks. But he also acknowledges (not then, only later) that he spent the years after the Russian Revolution in a state of "half-fanatical glassy-mindedness"—nothing truly critical of Lenin or the Soviet regime was going to reach him.[20]

Why did someone as naturally rebellious as Max Eastman commit this way to Moscow? He would never bend his knee to a king; he didn't let a mob in Fargo shut him up. The answer is the magical word "science."

When Lenin speaks, Eastman doesn't hear the voice of a political chief; he hears an engineer of social structures, a man who thinks in terms of tested hypotheses, of ideals ratified by an unsentimental appraisal of facts. He pays Lenin the highest compliment that a disciple of John Dewey can offer: "It seemed as though the instrumental theory of knowledge was at last actively understood."[21]

His mistake, he would realize later, was in thinking that the Russians behaved any differently than the Americans. One person could have made him see reason, but John Reed died before he got the chance.

Max doesn't write much about Jack in the years after his death. After all, for the last few years, they had spent much of their time in different places. Eastman had spent some of that time in Hollywood, with Florence Deshon. It was a lovely life, as they got to spend time with Charlie Chaplin in a charmed circle of artists—like Greenwich Village, only without the politics or the poverty. For a time, Eastman, Chaplin, and Deshon found themselves in a love triangle. Through it all, Max loved Florence desperately. The end of their relationship seems to have affected him more than Jack's death did.

By 1921, Eastman's fair hair has gone prematurely white. He seems tired of it all. Tired of the magazine, tired of watching his prewar hopes fall to ash—at least in his own country. He think it's delusional to expect a revolution anytime soon, and nothing short of revolution will redeem a country that has grown "ruthless and savage, untamed either by law or culture." In its annual report that year, the American Civil Liberties Union declares "Never before in American history were the forces of reaction so completely in control of our political and economic life." After years of government crackdowns and amid persistent infighting, no group on the left has the power to stand against them.

J. Edgar Hoover publishes a report claiming that the Palmer Raids led to "the wrecking of the communist parties in this country." They certainly helped.[22]

Eastman decides to go to Russia. In the sour years that follow the idealistic heyday of the Wilson years, he is far from alone. "The dreamers and revolters against tyranny are traveling East instead of West," Eastman writes, "and the eyes of all the true lovers of liberty in all the world are turning in the same direction as they go."[23]

He publishes an announcement that he will leave for Russia soon, and when he does, he will step down from *The Liberator*. He doesn't know it, but he is announcing the magazine's demise: It won't last long without him.

A few weeks before he is supposed to depart, he goes to a play. A man crouches down in the dark next to him and whispers terrible news. Eastman never finds out who the man was or how anybody knew where to find him.

He rushes to the hospital to find Florence clinging to life. She had been discovered in her apartment, unconscious, with the gas turned on. He takes off his shirt and lies down on a table next to hers. The doctors begin a transfusion, pumping blood from his body into hers, hoping that his vitality might save her life.

Her breath comes in horrible ragged gasps. She dies at twenty-nine.

The story makes the papers. Grim rumors circulate that Florence and Max had a falling-out, and this is what had led her to end her life. Eastman refuses to accept that she had taken her life; the official report calls it an accident. A friend of Florence's tries to assure Max that he has nothing to feel guilty about. Florence did feel despair, but it was about her career, which had flourished for a while in its early days but then had lost its way.[24]

"I cannot give up my bright hopes," Florence had written to him a couple of years earlier. "I would die first."[25]

She, too, has a vision of how the world should be.

Eastman is too grief-stricken to attend her funeral. A few weeks later, he is in on his way to Moscow.

For Lippmann, the 1920 election brings a blessed end to his boredom. "This is the dullest political campaign on record," he told a British friend that fall. "Nobody cares who is elected. Nobody believes in anything. Nobody wants anything very badly that he thinks he can get out of politics. If the thing keeps on, *The New Republic* will have to transform itself into a fashion journal."[26]

President Wilson had tried to make the election a referendum on the treaty, but he'd already ruined his chance. As he recovered a little of his strength, his old insistence on sticking to principle mutated into a terrible obstinacy; his trust in the people became a form of populist megalomania. A stroke can exaggerate certain character traits—rarely with such terrible consequences for the world.

When Wilson had needed the greatest tact and flexibility to make a deal with Republicans and secure ratification—when winning had depended on that cool discipline he was forever extolling—the volcano had erupted again. He declared that altering a few sentences in the League covenant would mean the difference between "an ideal of democracy" and "an ideal of imperialism."[27] Anybody who disagreed with him was breaking faith with the honored dead. And so on.

The final vote in the Senate wasn't close. "He has strangled his own child," concludes one of Wilson's opponents.[28]

Lippmann had helped to defeat that treaty, but that doesn't make him feel any better about how the decade turns out. Just before the election, he tells a friend, "I sometimes think that the terrific morale we developed during the war exhausted the public spirit of this country for a generation, and that nobody will be enthusiastic about anything until a generation grows up that has forgotten how violent we were and how unreasonable."[29]

When the enfeebled Wilson leaves the White House, Lippmann reflects on his administration. In *Vanity Fair,* where he has begun writing a stylish monthly column, he offers an autopsy for the era.

When Wilson took office in 1913, Americans believed they understood their problems and had confidence in how to fix them. "Not so today," he writes. "There is no agreement as to what the difficulties are, much less about how triumphantly to resolve them."[30]

He has come a long way from the confidence that rings on every page of *Drift and Mastery.* And he now feels the impulse to write another book—one drawing on the experiences of his past few years: journalist, propagandist, and appalled bystander to an election in which every issue was "distorted beyond recognition."[31]

After all that Lippmann has seen, he argues that it's a mistake to think that people operate directly on their environments. A middle layer intervenes between the two: a "pseudo-environment," an image of what we *think* the world is. That's what determines our behavior. The trouble is that this image can be shaped by fictions as well as facts—fictions that can be constructed by, say, government agencies of propaganda.

Leaders can get away with it because in the modern world, life has become too immense and complicated for people to have direct experience of almost anything. He never liked "the village view of life," but now he sees that the global view is too sprawling and complicated for people to manage. It's impossible for anybody to know all that must be known to fulfill the duties of citizenship. It calls into question what he calls "the original dogma of democracy"—the belief that individual citizens have the mental faculties to be capable of self-government.

Public Opinion (as Lippmann calls his inflammatory treatise) draws a somewhat awed review from John Dewey in *The New Republic.* The book is "perhaps the most effective indictment of democracy as currently conceived ever penned," he writes. "It shivers most of our illusions, and this particular Humpty Dumpty can never be put together again for anyone who reads these chapters with an open mind."[32]

It's poignant that a decade that offered glimpses of a bolder, braver, more vibrant American democracy ended with such a slashing critique of it. It's tragic that the man who offered that critique had been one of the most hopeful of democracy's messengers. He writes now as one "who has lived through the romantic age in politics and is no longer moved by the stale echoes of its hot cries . . . a man back from a crusade to make the world something or other it did not become."[33]

Lippmann is not alone in this. In the months and years after the election, as America veers away from what it had tried to become, many writers produce books like this one, an account of ideals thwarted. He has written a work of social science, but it still belongs on the same rueful shelf as Fitzgerald and Hemingway and the rest: a Lost Generation book without the jazz and the spilled champagne.

Epilogue

T he Americans who came of age after World War I knew that something vital had passed from the scene. They had watched idealists fight to realize their lofty hope for a better world and, to a great extent, fail to get it. Why repeat that ordeal? "We were content to build our modest happiness in the wreck of their lost illusions," one of the new arrivals wrote, "a cottage in the ruins of a palace."[1]

I started writing this book because I wanted to visit those palaces. Living in an era of dysfunction and gridlock, of shrinking voter turnout and widespread cynicism about American possibilities—in other words, an era of cottages, as far as the eye could see—I wanted to know how it felt to live in a country vibrating with hope, supremely confident in its prospects, charging into the future, not just in its politics, but socially and culturally, too. Without a time machine, I had no expectation of experiencing it for myself. We'll never see a recurrence of that prewar moment when socialism, progressivism, modernism, and feminism all exploded at once.

Nor did I expect to see Americans revive the spirit of that era's idealists, the art rebels and political rebels and social innovators discovering how much they had in common, and deciding to fight together on behalf of a more vibrant democracy. But now, to my surprise, in the last days of working on this book, I've seen that kind of union. I *am seeing* it.

On January 21, 2017, four million Americans took to the streets on behalf of their ideals. Outraged by a new president who transgressed their values and threatened their institutions, they marched in big cities and small towns, defending American democracy itself. The spirit of 1913 was everywhere you looked that day. Like Alice Paul's suffrage parade, the marches were conceived, organized, and largely populated by women; like John Reed's Paterson Strike Pageant, the marches were vast, audacious, and heterogeneous; and like Max Eastman's *The Masses,* the marchers championed their ideals with humor and wry self-awareness. (One marcher's sign read: WHAT DO WE WANT? EVIDENCE BASED SCIENCE. WHEN DO WE WANT IT? AFTER PEER REVIEW.)

American conditions feel so precarious as I'm writing this in February 2017 that any prediction might seem foolish by the time you read it. It might seem foolish by the time I finish typing it. But the scale and the zeal of the Women's March suggests that we've entered a new phase in the history of American idealism. Facing a challenge to the most essential parts of the national character, an enormous number of men and women are picking up the weapons of citizenship for the first time, joining the activists already in the field.

What do we inherit from the idealists who preceded us? The question seems less abstract than it did even a few weeks ago. To assess the legacies of the young radicals, to find out what they've left us, we don't have to reach a full century into our past. The idealists who survived that era had decades to live out its lessons. (For the young radicals, as for the early astronauts, surviving the adventures of youth seemed to bring a guarantee of long life.) Those who didn't survive the era had their legacies debated and pursued by the idealists of intervening generations.

A glimpse of the later lives and afterlives of the five figures in our story suggests that our inheritance is very near at hand. Which is lucky for us, now that we need it most.

Alice Paul spent eight years fighting to secure a suffrage amendment for women and the next fifty years fighting to make women equal under the law. In 1923, she introduced the Equal Rights Amendment, a single sweeping measure designed to end discrimination based on gender. Close allies begged her to stop, told her that it would do more harm than good. She persisted anyway. There were no more mass arrests, none of the urgent drama of the suffrage campaign. Mainly there was lobbying, and more lobbying, year after year, with friends dwindling, and opponents laughing, all the way up to 1972. That's when the ERA passed both houses of Congress.

The amendment failed to secure the state ratifications it needed before its time limit expired, but Paul didn't live to see it. She died in 1977, in a modest Quaker nursing home, at age ninety-two. It's up to the activists of a new generation to push the ERA now—and they do, year after year after year. They know what persistence looks like.

But there's another side to Paul's legacy, a more meaningful sequel to her suffrage fight. It's a case study in how the idealists of one generation build on the work of their predecessors.

When Paul was seventy-eight, Congress began to frame the landmark Civil Rights Act of 1964. At the instigation of the National Woman's Party, the section designed to counteract racial discrimination in employment was broadened to include gender discrimination. To everybody's surprise, this amended version of Title VII passed the House. But—the perennial radicals' refrain!—it wasn't clear that the provision could pass the Senate. Plenty of people thought that racial discrimination and gender discrimination were separate issues. That's why Paul could declare a complete victory for the suffrage movement in 1920, despite the fact that millions of American black women still couldn't vote.[2]

Alice Paul's agitation for Title VII created an opening, and into it stepped Pauli Murray. The fifty-three-year-old lawyer from North Carolina was not a member of the National Woman's Party in 1964; she didn't even support the ERA at the time. But with the fate of those gender protections in doubt, she drafted a groundbreaking memo that framed the civil rights struggle and the campaign for women's equality as twin strands in the long fight for freedom.

"The costly lesson of American history is that human rights are indivisible," she wrote. "They cannot be affirmed for one social group and ignored in the case of another without tragic consequences."[3]

The arguments in that memo were the product of a brilliant legal mind; their moral force came from her own experience. Murray had spent a lifetime battling what she called "Jane Crow," the compound discrimination that afflicts black women. Had she been a little older, she probably would have been turned away from the polls in 1920: She might have been one of the women protesting her disenfranchisement in Alice Paul's office.

To Murray, it was perverse for one oppressed group to improve its condition at the expense of another—for women to seek equality through expedient ties with segregationists, as the suffragists had. She thought that by 1964, the time had come for a richer, fuller definition of freedom, and she helped convince members of Lyndon Johnson's administration to feel the same. When he signed the gender protection of Title VII into law, Marguerite Rawalt, one of the most influential women in Washington, gave Murray "a real measure of credit" for the victory.[4]

Today, a century after the Nineteenth Amendment, half a century after the Voting Rights Act, the newspapers are filling up with reports of voter suppression, of stories that describe widespread disenfranchisement. It almost makes you think we need a suffrage movement again. Any such movement will need a more nuanced understanding of how different groups relate to one another than the National Woman's Party possessed a century ago. It will need precisely the insights that Murray articulated in her Title VII memo: that an identity group isn't a fixed bloc, but a coalition that includes many different kinds of people, with many different experiences, priorities, desires.

That new movement, if it is to succeed, will also need leaders with foresight, courage, and "a single-mindedness bordering on fanaticism"— all qualities that Pauli Murray attributed to Alice Paul in the warm tribute she delivered a few days after the heroic suffragist's death.

When Max Eastman left for Russia in 1922, he said he was going to find out if the things he had been saying were true. It took him twenty years to give a definitive answer: *No.*

The break didn't come all at once. He spent the 1920s and '30s in a slow, unsteady retreat from the convictions that he had risked his freedom and even his life to defend. Two years in Russia convinced him that Joseph Stalin had hijacked Lenin's revolution. He even arranged the first English-language publication of "Lenin's Testament," the warning against Stalin that had been suppressed by his successors. But the horrors of the 1930s convinced him that the problem wasn't a single brutal ruler, it was the nature of the Russian regime itself. (His wife, Eliena Krylenko, was the sister of an Old Bolshevik: Her entire family disappeared in the purges. Eastman worried that he might be next. You would worry, too, if Joseph Stalin denounced you by name as a "gangster of the pen.")[5] By the early 1940s, his observations of Soviet conditions and a rigorous study of Marxist literature convinced him that the problem was deeper than Stalin, deeper than Russia: It lay in Marxist thought itself. The collectivizing action of socialism would always lead to tyranny. Socialism was an enemy of freedom, "a dangerous fairy tale."[6]

This decision "to let go of an idea around which one has organized a lifeful of emotions" didn't lead him to retreat from the field of rhetorical combat. Feeling a share of responsibility for having propagated socialism in America, he attacked his old allies, and was attacked in return. Even Art Young, much-loved comrade of his youth, dropped him for life. Eastman traveled so far from his youthful socialism that he ended up in Joseph McCarthy's camp: The man hounded and harassed during the first Red Scare became an advocate of the second. When his young friend William F. Buckley, Jr., founded a magazine to articulate a forceful new version of conservatism, Max was glad to offer advice. This is how the editor of *The Masses* turned up, forty unlikely years later, on the founding editorial board of *National Review*.[7]

If Eastman's story ended there, you could read it as a parable about the wisdom of age correcting the delusions of youth—especially since he also spent these years as a roving editor of *Reader's Digest*, the squarest and least radical magazine in America. (At last, he really was writing for the masses.) But Max's life was messier and more interesting than that.

As he swung from one ideological pole to the other, he went on writing and publishing his poems. He and Eliena had a happy, devoted marriage that was very, very open. His papers are full of letters from lovers, ex-lovers, and prospective lovers, stretching from his youth into his seventies. And his stay on the editorial board of *National Review* proved to be short-lived. Eastman couldn't abide the overlay of Christian theology in its struggle against communism. Less than three years after the magazine's founding, he told Buckley to remove his name from the masthead.[8] Impossible Max!

By his eightieth birthday, in 1963, Eastman was a pagan libertarian poet living on a hilltop in Martha's Vineyard—the fruit of that *Reader's Digest* sinecure. Having nursed Eliena through her final illness, he had married a young third wife. He was, in almost every way, free beyond the furthest dreams of old Greenwich Village: healthy, still handsome, and convivial in company. But he was distressed.

Eastman had come to feel that he had betrayed his talents. A poem that he intended to be his epitaph ended with the despairing self-assessment: "I am not science, and I am not song."[9] His dismay had a social dimension, too. He gave a revealing interview to a *New York Times* reporter in 1969, a few months before his death (at age eighty-six, in Barbados, sun-chasing to the end). He said that he recognized the militant attitude of that era's rebels, but he pitied them.

"They want to make a revolution but they have no ultimate purpose," he said. "We had a program and a purpose, which was to make over capitalism into socialism, and it was based on an ideal and on an ideology."[10]

It's odd to hear him sound nostalgic for a phase of his life that he had spent the last few decades denouncing as a fogbank of error. It's strange to see him speak fondly of "a program and a purpose" after years of arguing that in a world of continual change, we must forgo all doctrines, and take each crisis as it comes. One way to interpret Eastman's remark is that it's not enough to abandon false theories. Without a *true* theory, a viable explanation for how to effect change, we are left with resignation—and resignation is never satisfying. "We have to patch up the world as it is and accept it," he told his interviewer, "although I don't feel very happy about it."[11]

Eastman almost never felt very happy. (As his readers pointed out, there wasn't much enjoyment in his memoir of his early years, which he called *Enjoyment of Living*.) But it's easy to see why, at the end of his life, he'd feel nostalgic for his radical youth. Though he often felt burdened by the demands of running *The Masses,* and wished he had more time for his own pursuits, it was the only phase of his long, strange career that offered full scope to his abilities. Eastman was, like Alice Paul, that rarest of specimens: not just a radical, but a radical *leader—* a genius at nurturing the political and cultural expressions of dozens of gifted contemporaries.

In his youth, Eastman had shown how to fight for freedom, and help others do the same. In old age, after he abandoned his theories, and his comrades, and so many other encumbrances, he offers a second lesson, equally vital to us today, when so many Americans are looking for a cause greater than themselves: that freedom is essential to the good life, and freedom isn't enough.

John Reed was a legendary figure while he lived; death turned him into a symbol. The Soviets honored their American comrade with a hero's burial under the Kremlin wall, commending his dedication to the revolution. A few years later, American communists honored him, too. The John Reed Clubs were formed for artists and writers who were committed to the Soviet regime.

But not everybody was prepared to make Reed the embodiment of communist devotion. Max Eastman denounced the first biography of Reed, claiming that its Stalinist author misrepresented its subject. Eastman claimed that Louise Bryant had said that Reed died a dissenter from Moscow, not a true believer. The biographer, Granville Hicks, knew all about Bryant's stories—he just didn't think they were reliable. By the 1930s, she had fallen on hard times, drinking too much and saying wildly conflicting things. She died before the book appeared in 1936.

We'll never be sure what Reed believed on his deathbed. But one clue that wasn't available in the 1930s bolsters Eastman's case. A few months after Reed's death, Bryant got stuck in Riga for several weeks. An intelligence agent for the American military gained her trust and asked her about Russia. His report—which found its way to J. Edgar Hoover, whose fervid interest in Reed outlived him—gives us Bryant's *contemporary* view of Reed, not the dissipated stories of her final years. It's also a private account, not one she intended for public consumption. She said that Reed had been so disgusted with the Soviet leaders, and the way they took advantage of their authority, that it contributed to the illness that killed him. That corroborates an account given by Angelica Balabanova, a friend of Reed's who knew him well in his final year. She, too, described him as disgusted to the point of despair.[12]

So did Reed die an apostate and not a martyr? Maybe it's the wrong question. For no matter what he felt on his deathbed, it's hard to imagine him staying true to Moscow for long. Stalin disliked *Ten Days That Shook the World*, specifically its kind words about Trotsky and its lack of words about him. Reed had shown exemplary discipline in the service of the revolution: He'd shouldered a rifle, he'd traveled to Baku, he'd defended the violence of the regime. But could he support a government that *banned his book*? Eastman's final word on the question of

Reed's politics rings true: "His grave beneath the Kremlin wall is not a tribute, but a reproach to the regime within."[13]

If we can't be sure how to interpret Reed's death, then we have to look elsewhere to reckon with his legacy. We have to ask: *What would Reed have become if he'd lived?*

Balabanova thought that if he'd returned to America, he would have become "an independent honest revolutionary."[14] That sounds right, though it is hard to know what it might mean in practice. A labor organizer? For the rollicking boy from the West was always loved—genuinely loved—by all kinds of people, artists and workers alike. The left could have used him in the despairing years after the Red Scare.

Max thought that if Jack had lived, he would have rededicated himself to creative work. Max was thinking of Jack's poetry, but it seems at least as plausible that a post-revolutionary Reed would have adopted a different persona: impresario. His adventures in Russia obscure the fact that while still in his twenties, he played a key role in two of the watershed events in American theater history: the Paterson Strike Pageant of 1913 and the formation of the Provincetown Players in 1916. His dramatic instinct might have led him back to the theater. His love of spectacle might have led him West. Honestly: Could any power on earth have kept Jack Reed out of Hollywood?

Politics or art? Picket lines or opening nights? For Reed, both courses are equally plausible. So equally, in fact, that maybe he wouldn't choose at all. The fusion of art rebels and political rebels in the years just before the war only happened because some gifted individuals could straddle those worlds. Reed was one of them. There's no telling what new fusions he might have dreamed up if he'd had the chance.

But he helped give somebody else a chance. In 1965, Cesar Chavez led migrant farmworkers on a strike in the Delano grape fields of California. A student of theater named Luis Valdez, himself the son of migrant farmworkers, wanted to support the strike. He had been studying political theater—Odets, Brecht, the *carpa* tradition of Mexican theater—and devising a new style of short satirical plays. Out of this rich array of influences and traditions, Valdez says that the inspiration that sent him into the grape fields, where his company, El Teatro Campesino, helped workers devise plays for their fellow workers, and raise money for their struggle, was John Reed's strike pageant.[15]

In Paterson, the strikers lost; in Delano, they won.

In the fall of 1958, Walter Lippmann paid his first visit to Soviet Russia. He walked along the Kremlin wall until he found the stone that marked his friend's final resting place. He and Jack had come a long, long way from Harvard Yard and 42 Washington Square.

Lippmann had traveled to Moscow to interview the Soviet premier, Nikita Khrushchev, but it might as well have been a state visit. For the past quarter century, Lippmann had been writing a column syndicated in hundreds of newspapers for millions of readers. That year, *Time* called him "the most widely quoted and acclaimed pundit in the world."[16] He was more than that: He was an authority, a personage, an institution.

"Lippmann always has his own foreign policy," President Kennedy would say a few years later. "Sometimes it coincides with ours."[17]

This long career writing about public affairs for a general readership might seem to contradict the disparaging things he said about democracy in the sour years after the war. It doesn't. Lippmann's column gave him a platform, and the platform gave him power. He often took part in the events he described, heading off a war here, getting somebody nominated to the cabinet there. The journalistic ethics of our decorous age wouldn't let him get away with these collaborations, even though he didn't do them to enrich himself. (His only scandal was a personal one: In 1937, he divorced Faye to marry his best friend's wife. It was not very Olympian.)

The contemporaries who doubted Lippmann's liberal convictions found fresh reasons for suspicion as the years went by. He wrote for a conservative paper; he hung around with bankers and magnates; he opposed FDR in 1936. "A good deal of his sensitiveness has gone," Harold Laski reported to Oliver Wendell Holmes, Jr., after spending time with him. "And he has arrived at the stage where he is not eager to take intellectual risks."[18]

When Lyndon B. Johnson awarded Lippmann one of the inaugural Medals of Freedom in 1964, it seemed like the capstone to a dignified career. But it wasn't. At age seventy-four, one last time, Lippmann had to answer the old question: *What do you do with your freedom when you get it?*

In 1965, President Johnson took steps to Americanize the war in Vietnam, rapidly increasing the country's military involvement in Southeast Asia. He was so eager to have Lippmann's support that he and his advisers invited the aging columnist to the White House for personal consultations. But all their persuading failed to persuade him. Lippmann didn't see how any vital national interest would be worth the enormous material or moral cost that was bound to follow the kind of escalation that Johnson wanted.

For a man in Lippmann's position, it would have been easy to toe the administration line, or to soft-pedal his doubts. He did neither. He wrote a column declaring his opposition to the buildup. When Johnson escalated the war anyway, Lippmann escalated his opposition. Lippmann had chastised presidents before, but never as personally or directly as he began to attack Johnson week after week, month after month, charging him with "flagrant abuses and unchallenged power," insufficient "moral courage," and wasting the money that the country desperately needed for his Great Society programs. "In the atmosphere of war it is impossible to pursue the tasks of peace," he argued.[19]

When Randolph Bourne attacked the pro-war liberals in 1917, he accused them of being too intoxicated by their proximity to power to ever give it up. Lippmann gave it up. Johnson, furious at Lippmann's defiance, ordered researchers to scour his record for embarrassing comments. "The War on Walter Lippmann," *The Washington Post* called it. A half century after his days in Greenwich Village, he found himself aligned once again with the motley outsiders, antiwar protesters who mainly lived on the far side of a wide social gulf—a strange sensation for the ultimate establishment figure.[20]

By 1967, *Life* magazine was calling Lippmann "the embodiment of meaningful opposition" to Johnson's management of the war. But he no longer found Washington tolerable. Lippmann was used to presidents attacking him. What hurt was the loss of friends in and around the administration. He decided, at long last, that he'd had enough. He decided to give up his regular column. The president declined to offer a gracious send-off, using his speech at the White House Correspondents' Dinner that year to belittle an unnamed but easily identifiable "political commentator of yesteryear."[21]

Lippmann spent the last seven years of his life in his native New York. He outlived his wife; he even wore out his potent dynamo of a brain. Sometimes, in those final years, in his nursing home, his mind drifted strangely, and carried him back to old friends. In his imagination, if not in real life, he could have settled an account with John Reed.

In their angry exchange of letters in 1916, when their friendship broke down, Reed had accused him of abandoning his radical hopes. By the 1960s, that was certainly true. Lippmann had come to think of his generation's history as a record of democratic defeat, of possibilities foreclosed. But Lippmann had made a defiant promise that he would still be fighting long after Reed had quit, and in at least one prominent and costly way, he fulfilled it: He felt a sense of resignation about American prospects, and he knew what he stood to lose, but he wrote those columns anyway.

Of all the young radicals, Randolph Bourne's legacy is the least clear—partly because he died so young, partly because the meaning of his life was distorted by what happened next.

On one of those dark December days after they took his body away, a friend looked in a trash can at Esther Cornell's apartment and spotted a stack of paper. It was a fragment of a long manuscript called "The State." It was Bourne's attempt to frame a political theory that would account for the violence and repression of American life in 1918.

How did the manuscript end up in that trash can? Had Bourne been working on the manuscript when he died? Or had he abandoned it long ago, and only remembered to throw it away when he moved into Esther's apartment? Whatever its provenance, however much he would or wouldn't stand by it, that manuscript included a sentence that would overshadow everything that he published in his lifetime: "War is the health of the state."

In compact fashion, Bourne was arguing that in the modern world, a national government needs the material demands and psychological atmosphere of war to thrive. Once this sentence found its way into a posthumous volume of Bourne's work, it was on its way to an eventful career in the bloody twentieth century. Pacifists and assorted opponents of America's wars found it very useful—terse, stern, aphoristic. President Eisenhower's warning about a military-industrial complex ratified part of what Bourne was trying to say.

It is good to be remembered when you're gone. Still, the emphasis on Bourne's most famous sentence changed the meaning of his life. The marvel of Bourne's brief career is how many vital and wide-ranging insights he offered in only a half dozen years: about the radicalism of youth, the experience of being handicapped, the vitality of a distinctly American culture, the promise of progressive education, the lack of an ideal at the center of America's reigning philosophical tradition. He is certainly the antecedent of all those antiwar protesters who quote his famous sentence, but it would be more just to Bourne, and more useful for us today, to see him in full. Then we would come face-to-face with one of the greatest champions of democracy that the country has produced, a spiritual heir of Walt Whitman.

Like Whitman, Bourne thought the meaning of America lay in the future, not the past. Like Whitman, he celebrated a kaleidoscopic polyglot America. Both of them saw the coming-together of unlike peoples—a "spiritual welding," in Bourne's phrase—as the essential challenge of American democracy, and its greatest reward. The essay in which Bourne makes the fullest account of this vision, "Trans-national America," is how *Democratic Vistas* might read if Whitman had lived a half century later, and written with a head full of up-to-date social science.

In that essay, Bourne became the first person to apply Josiah Royce's vision of the Beloved Community to American conditions. He argued that mere tolerance isn't good enough for a country drawing on as many different kinds of people as ours does. We need to *love* what's different. If we do, we get a society richer and more dynamic than any false vision of a melting pot could allow it to be. What makes this connection to Royce more than a footnote in Bourne's intellectual pedigree is the identity of the *second* person to make that connection: Dr. Martin Luther King, Jr. In the culminating days of the Montgomery bus boycott, he announced the ultimate aim of the civil rights movement: "The end is reconciliation, the end is redemption, the end is the creation of the Beloved Community."[22]

King probably didn't get the phrase from Bourne, but the fact that he used it—especially as one of the cornerstones of his life's work—should make us pay more attention to Bourne's essay and its implications for American life. Today, the country is on the verge of the most colossal demographic change in its history: It is about to become majority-minority. Bourne's idea that America's cultural tradition is, paradoxically, something that lies in the future—the joint product of what all of us will make together—could be the vision that guides us through that change.

Nor does Bourne's essay need a demographic shift to be timely. While writing this epilogue, I've watched thousands of Americans rush to airports to protest a ban on immigrants from majority-Muslim countries. Bourne wasn't an absolutist on immigration policies—he acknowledged there was a limit on how many new arrivals could be absorbed how quickly—but the core of his vision is that people who come to this country can't be discriminated against because of who they are or what they believe. The protesters who showed up in terminals and baggage claims to chant "Let them in!" and to shout "Welcome home!" probably never heard the name Randolph Bourne. All the same, they were doing what World War I prevented Bourne from doing: realizing an ideal of an Americanism that's equally available to all. They were standing up to be counted as citizens of trans-national America.

———

From one day to the next, it's hard to tell what kind of America we're living in. When the news is full of threats, and saber-rattling, and rumors of pending repression, it seems like 1917. And that is ominous, because 1917 showed how much damage the government and its militant-minded citizens can inflict on foreigners, dissenters, and anybody who declines to abide by a strict old standard of Americanism. On good days, when marchers are on the streets, or some potent new alliance forms, then it feels like 1912. Then it's possible to daydream, even if only for a moment, that the forces of idealism are discovering their strength, and that one day they'll help this country make another leap into the future.

Whatever happens, we ought to be braced by the example of the young radicals: how they discovered their ideals, made a decision to fight for them, and went on fighting even when the battle turned against them. Their defeats were painful, but not final. Battles for ideals never are.

Ruins stop being ruins when you build with them.

Acknowledgments

Immersing in the lives of five complicated figures was only possible because of the generosity and diligence of archivists and librarians beyond counting. I am particularly indebted to the staffs of Beinecke and Sterling Memorial libraries at Yale University; Rare Book & Manuscript Library at Butler Library, Columbia; Houghton Library at Harvard; the Lilly Library at Indiana University; Schlesinger Library at Radcliffe; the Tamiment Library at NYU; and the Swarthmore College Peace Collection.

At Random House, Jon Meacham gave me the chance to begin telling this story and my editor Ben Greenberg was the perfect partner in finishing it. Thanks also to Susan Kamil, Caitlin McKenna, Christine Mykityshyn, and Molly Turpin.

Edel Rodriguez designed this book's stunning cover. Check out his website—there is more where this came from.

Jennifer Joel's kindness, judgment, and dedication throughout this process are more than anybody could ask of an agent, or a friend.

I was fortunate to draw on contributions of books, insights, feedback, wisdom, and various forms of logistical and moral support from Jeff Beals, Jamie Bennett, Drew Broussard, Jackson Bryer, Oskar Eustis, Sonia Pressman Fuentes, Jason Grunebaum, Beverly Hallberg, Mark Harris, Serena Mayeri, Jen McDonald, Nami Mun, Floyd Skloot, Rebecca Skloot, and Tappan Wilder. All views in this book and any errors are my own.

Julie has more of my love and my gratitude, for this and for everything, than a book could ever convey.

Notes

AG	—	Alyse Gregory
AP	—	Alice Paul
JR	—	John Reed
MD	—	Mabel Dodge Luhan
ME	—	Max Eastman
PWW	—	The Papers of Woodrow Wilson (Princeton University Press)
RB	—	Randolph Bourne
WL	—	Walter Lippmann
WW	—	Woodrow Wilson

Chapter 1

1. Henry Farrand Griffin, "The Rising Tide of Socialism," *The Outlook,* 2/24/12, p. 440.
2. WL, "Political Notes," *The International,* 11/11, p. 85; Henry F. May, *The End of American Innocence* (New York: Columbia University Press, 1992), pp. 22–23.
3. *Reminiscences of Walter Lippmann,* Columbia University Oral History Collection, p. 50.
4. WL, "Two Months in Schenectady," *The Masses,* 4/12, p. 13.
5. WL to Jacob Lippmann, 4/30/08, WL papers, Manuscripts and Archives, Yale University Library.
6. WL to Hazel Albertson, 1/8/12, WL papers.
7. WL, *A Preface to Politics* (New York: Mitchell Kennerly, 1913), p. 183.
8. WL, "The Privileged Classes: A Reply," *The Harvard Illustrated,* 11/08, p. 56; WL to Jacob and Daisy Lippmann, 11/22/09 and 11/17/09, WL papers.
9. WL, "Schenectady the Unripe," *The New York Call,* 6/9/12.
10. Correspondence, *The New York Call.* Emphasis added.

11. Christine Stansell, *American Moderns* (New York: Metropolitan Books, 2000), p. 44.

Chapter 2

1. Nina Lane Faubion, "Kremlin Bound!" *The Sunday Oregonian,* 6/7/36.
2. JR to Edward Hunt, 4/1/12, JR papers, Houghton Library, Harvard University.
3. WL to JR, 5/19/12, JR papers.
4. Lincoln Steffens, *Lincoln Steffens Speaking* (New York: Harcourt, Brace and Company, 1936), p. 309.
5. JR, "The Harvard Renaissance," p. 3, JR papers.
6. JR, "The Harvard Renaissance," p. 15, JR papers; Granville Hicks, *John Reed* (New York: The Macmillan Company, 1936), p. 34.
7. Robert A. Rosenstone, *Romantic Revolutionary* (Cambridge, MA: Harvard University Press, 1990), p. 85.
8. Charles J. Reed to JR, 3/27/12, JR papers.
9. JR to Edward Hunt, 7/15/12, JR papers.
10. JR to Edward Hunt, 10/21/10, JR papers.
11. Steffens, *John Reed Under the Kremlin* (Chicago: The Walden Book Shop, 1921), p. 10.
12. Steffens to JR, 10/27/12, in *The Letters of Lincoln Steffens,* ed. by Ella Winter and Granville Hicks (New York: Harcourt, Brace, and Company, 1938), p. 311.

Chapter 3

1. John Patrick Diggins, *Up from Communism* (New York: Columbia University Press, 1994), p. 4.
2. Art Young, *On My Way* (New York: Horace Liveright, 1928), p. 20.
3. ME, *Enjoyment of Living* (New York: Harper & Brothers, 1948), p. 16.
4. ME, *Enjoyment of Living,* p. 399.
5. ME, *Enjoyment of Living,* p. 399.
6. ME, "Early History of the Men's League," *The Woman Voter,* 10/12, in *Feminism and the Periodical Press: 1900–1918,* ed. by Lucy Delap, Maria DiCenzo, and Leila Ryan (New York: Routledge, 2006), vol. 2.
7. ME, *Enjoyment of Living,* p. 355.
8. Oswald Garrison Villard to ME, 4/28/13, Oswald Garrison Villard papers, Houghton Library, Harvard University.
9. ME, *Enjoyment of Living,* p. 403.
10. ME, *Enjoyment of Living,* pp. 406–7.
11. The story had been rejected by three magazines before Eastman saw it. Index card tallying rejections (*American, Collier's, Everybody's*), JR papers.
12. ME to JR, 12/12, JR papers.
13. WL to Louis Untermeyer, 6/11/12, 9/27/12, 1/8/13, Louis Untermeyer papers, Special Collections, University of Delaware Library.
14. Young, *On My Way,* p. 281.
15. ME, *Enjoyment of Living,* p. 439.

16. ME, "Knowledge and Revolution," *The Masses,* 2/13, p. 6.
17. ME to Norman Thomas, 5/28/17, ME papers, Lilly Library, University of Indiana.
18. *The Masses,* 7/13, p. 6.
19. ME, *Love and Revolution* (New York: Random House, 1964), pp. 22–23.
20. "A Free Magazine," *The Masses,* 2/13.

Chapter 4

1. "Suffrage Crusaders in Thrilling Pageant Take City by Storm," *The (Washington) Evening Star,* 3/3/13.
2. Doris Stevens, *Jailed for Freedom* (New York: Boni and Liveright, 1920), p. 21.
3. Stevens, *Jailed for Freedom,* p. 10.
4. J. D. Zahniser and Amelia Fry, *Alice Paul: Claiming Power* (Oxford and New York: Oxford University Press, 2014), p. 100.
5. "Suffragette Tells of Forcible Feeding," *The New York Times,* 2/18/10.
6. Mary Walton, *A Woman's Crusade: Alice Paul and the Battle for the Ballot* (New York: Palgrave Macmillan, 2010), p. 64.
7. "Illinois Women Feature Parade," *The Chicago Daily Tribune,* 3/4/13; Rosalyn Terborg-Penn, *African-American Women in the Struggle for the Vote: 1850–1920* (Bloomington: Indiana University Press, 1998), pp. 121–23; Aileen S. Kraditor, *The Ideas of the Woman Suffrage Movement, 1890–1920* (New York: Columbia University Press, 1965), p. 213.
8. Eleanor Booth Simmons, "Novel Suffrage Stunts as Publicity Makers," *The New York Sun,* 2/10/18.
9. Stevens, *Jailed for Freedom,* p. 22.
10. "Suffragists Ask Wilson's Support," *The (Washington) Evening Star,* 3/17/13.
11. Stevens, *Jailed for Freedom,* p. 23.
12. "The Next Work of Congress," *The Suffragist,* 11/22/13, p. 4.
13. "Failure of Vote Means Hatchet," *The Washington Herald,* 12/2/13.

Chapter 5

1. Hutchins Hapgood, "Life at the Armory," *The New York Globe,* 2/17/13.
2. Mabel Dodge Luhan, *Movers and Shakers* (Albuquerque: University of New Mexico Press, 1985), p. 39.
3. MD, *Movers and Shakers,* pp. 92, 118.
4. Hapgood, "The Poet's Arrest," *The New York Globe,* 5/7/13.
5. MD, *Movers and Shakers,* p. 189.
6. JR to WL, 4/28/13, WL papers.
7. *The Masses,* 8/13.
8. JR, "Sheriff Radcliff's Hotel," *Metropolitan,* 9/13, p. 14.
9. JR, "War in Paterson," *The Masses,* 6/13, p. 17.
10. Joyce Kornbluh, ed., *Rebel Voices: An I.W.W. Anthology* (Oakland: PM Press, 2011), pp. 201–2.
11. "Strike Realism Staged in Pageant," *New-York Tribune,* 6/8/13.

12. Kornbluh, *Rebel Voices,* pp. 214, 202; MD, *Movers and Shakers,* p. 204.
13. RB, "Pageantry and Social Art," unpublished mss., RB papers, Rare Books and Manuscripts, Butler Library, Columbia University.
14. JR to WL, 6/12/13, WL papers.
15. MD, *Movers and Shakers,* p. 216.
16. AP, "Report on Congressional Work from January 1 to December 1, 1913," *The Suffragist,* 12/13/13, p. 39; "Suffragists Fear Split on Report," *The Washington Times,* 12/5/13, p. 5; "Will Wait to See President Wilson," *The (Washington) Evening Star,* 12/5/13.
17. Linda G. Ford, *Iron-Jawed Angels* (Lanham, MD: University Press of America, 1991), p. 83; "Miss Paul Ordered to Rest," *The (Washington) Evening Star,* 12/13/13.
18. "Suffragists Here Split with National Leaders," *The (Washington) Evening Star,* 12/19/13.
19. ME, "The Worst Monopoly," *The Masses,* 7/13, p. 6.
20. JR to WL, 9/8/13, WL papers.
21. WL, *A Preface to Politics,* pp. 105, 106.

Chapter 6
1. RB to Prudence Winterrowd, 1/16/13, RB papers. All of these excerpts have been edited slightly for space.
2. RB to Winterrowd, 1/16/13, RB papers.
3. RB to Winterrowd, 4/10/13, RB papers.
4. RB to Winterrowd, 2/5/13, RB papers.
5. RB to Winterrowd, 4/10/13, RB papers.
6. Ellery Sedgwick, *The Happy Profession* (Boston: Little, Brown and Company, 1946), p. 223.
7. RB to AG, 1/19/14, AG papers, Beinecke Library, Yale University.
8. RB to Winterrowd, 4/28/13, RB papers.
9. RB to Arthur Macmahon, 12/23/13, RB papers; Bruce Clayton, *Forgotten Prophet* (Columbia: University of Missouri Press, 1998), pp. 103–4.

Chapter 7
1. RB, "Impressions of Europe, 1913–14," *History of a Literary Radical and Other Essays* (New York: B. W. Huebsch, 1920), p. 264.
2. WL to Felix Frankfurter, 8/2/14, WL papers.
3. WL, *Essays in the Public Philosophy* (Boston: Little, Brown and Company, 1955), pp. 9–10; RB, "War and the Intellectuals," *The Seven Arts,* 6/17, pp. 137, 140.
4. RB, "Impressions of Europe," p. 232.
5. WL and Kenneth McGowan to RB, 3/18/10, RB papers.
6. WL to Louis Untermeyer, 7/31/13, Louis Untermeyer papers.
7. Croly to RB, 6/3/14, RB papers.
8. RB to AG, 9/28/14, AG papers.
9. "Force and Ideas," *The New Republic,* 11/7/14, p. 7.

10. RB to Winterrowd, 1/19/15, RB papers.
11. Arthur Macmahon to John Adam Moreau, 2/18/64, RB papers.
12. RB to AG, 3/13/14, AG papers.
13. RB to Dorothy Teall, 6/14/15, RB papers.
14. Francis Hackett to RB, 11/16/14, RB papers.
15. RB to Mary Messer, 2/7/14, in *Twice A Year*, Spring-Summer 1939, pp. 79–80.
16. RB to AG, "Monday," AG papers.

Chapter 8

1. Francis Hackett, "Where Women Disagree," *The New Republic*, 12/25/15, p. 192.
2. *Baltimore American*, 9/15/14, quoted in "Comments of the Press," *The Suffragist*, 9/19/14, p. 5.
3. Stevens, *Jailed for Freedom*, p. 12.
4. Inez Haynes Irwin, *The Story of the Woman's Party* (New York: Harcourt, Brace and Company, 1921), p. 19.
5. "National Suffrage and the Race Problem," *The Suffragist*, 11/14/14, p. 3.
6. Rosalyn Terborg-Penn, "Discontented Black Feminists," *The Black Studies Reader*, ed. by Jacqueline Bobo, Cynthia Hudley, and Claudine Michel (New York: Routledge, 2004), p. 70; "Agility," *The Crisis*, 1/15, p. 133.
7. Haynes Irwin, *The Story of the Women's Party*, p. 23.
8. *The Boston Transcript*, quoted in "Comments of the Press," *The Suffragist*, 10/3/14, p. 3.
9. "Congressional Election Campaign," *The Suffragist*, 9/26/14, p. 7.
10. Alice Duer Miller, "Are Women People?" *New-York Tribune*, 9/6/14.
11. "Congressional Election Campaign," *The Suffragist*, 10/17/14, p. 5.

Chapter 9

1. *Metropolitan*, 7/14.
2. JR to Carl Hovey, 9/25/14, JR papers.
3. MD, *Movers and Shakers*, p. 257.
4. MD to WL, undated, WL papers.
5. WL to JR, 3/25/14, JR papers.
6. WL to MD, 10/29/14, MD papers, Beinecke Library, Yale University.
7. JR to WL, 11/8/14, WL papers.
8. MD to WL, 12/9/14, WL papers.
9. MD to WL, undated [Saturday], WL papers.
10. WL to MD, 12/11/[14], MD papers.
11. WL, "Legendary John Reed," *The New Republic*, 12/26/14, pp. 15–16.
12. JR, "Almost Thirty," unpublished mss., JR papers, pp. 17–18.
13. JR, "Almost Thirty," p. 20.
14. WL to Oliver Wendell Holmes, 11/23/15, quoted in Steel, *Walter Lippmann and the American Century* (New Brunswick, NJ: Transaction Publishers, 2008), p. 87.
15. JR, "Almost Thirty," p. 18.

Chapter 10

1. "Apology," *The Masses,* 9/14, p. 17.
2. ME, "Fatuous Feebleness," *The Masses,* 2/15, p. 14.
3. ME, "Knowledge and Revolution," *The Masses,* 1/13, p. 7.
4. ME, "Margins," *The Masses,* 3/16, p. 19.
5. ME, "The Revelation," *The Masses,* 10/14, p. 5.
6. ME, "Knowledge and Revolution," *The Masses,* 9/14, p. 5.
7. ME, "Knowledge and Revolution," *The Masses,* 9/14, p. 5.
8. ME, *Enjoyment of Living,* p. 473.
9. ME, *Enjoyment of Living,* p. 491.
10. ME, *Enjoyment of Living,* p. 519.
11. ME, "The Uninteresting War," *The Masses,* 9/15, pp. 5–8.
12. ME, *Enjoyment of Living,* p. 532.

Chapter 11

1. "Capital Aroused, Situation Gravest Yet Faced in War," *New-York Tribune,* 5/8/15.
2. WW to Lord Bryce, 8/19/14, in The Papers of Woodrow Wilson (Princeton University Press), vol. 30, p. 403.
3. "Wilson, in Remarkable Proclamation, Issues a Solemn Warning," *The Washington Times,* 8/18/14; "President Pleads with People to Avoid War Talk Clashes," *The New York Sun,* 8/19/14.
4. "President Resents Negro's Criticism," *The New York Times,* 11/13/14; Stephen R. Fox, *The Guardian of Boston: William Monroe Trotter* (New York: Atheneum, 1971), p. 181.
5. "Mr. Trotter and Mr. Wilson," *The Crisis,* 1/15, p. 119.
6. Colonel Edward Mandell House diary, 11/14/14, Edward Mandell House papers, Manuscripts and Archives, Yale University Library.
7. *PWW,* vol. 33, p. 134.
8. WL to Robert Dell, 6/7/15, in John Morton Blum, ed., *Public Philosopher: Selected Letters of Walter Lippmann* (New York: Ticknor & Fields, 1985), p. 28.
9. RB to AG, 7/24/15, RB papers.
10. Herbert Croly to WL, 8/19/15, WL papers.
11. RB to AG, 7/24/15, AG papers.
12. "Mental Unpreparedness," *The New Republic,* 9/11/15, pp. 143–44.
13. RB to Carl Zigrosser, 9/12/15, in Eric J. Sandeen, ed., *The Letters of Randolph Bourne* (Troy, NY: Whitson, 1981), p. 329; RB, "American Use for German Ideals," *The New Republic,* 9/4/15, pp. 117–18.
14. "The Reality of Peace," *The New Republic,* 10/30/15, p. 322.
15. "President Pleased by Reception Here," *The New York Times,* 11/6/15; "Preparedness Plans Outlined by Wilson," *The Washington Herald,* 11/5/15.

Chapter 12

1. "Socialist Mayor 'Brands' Roosevelt," *The New York Times,* 12/14/11.
2. Zahniser and Fry, *Alice Paul: Claiming Power,* pp. 215, 220.

3. "Ask Suffragettes to Drop New York Work," *The New York Times*, 5/23/15.

4. "The Wrong Time," *The New York Times*, 11/30/15.

5. Haynes Irwin, *The Story of the Women's Party*, pp. 116–21.

6. ME, *Enjoyment of Living*, p. 549.

7. "Editorial Notice," *The Masses*, 12/12, p. 3.

8. ME to the editors of *The Masses*, 3/27/16, ME papers.

9. E. W. Scripps to Kate Crane Gartz, 10/8/16, ME papers.

10. Adaline W. Sterling, "United We Stand," *The Woman Voter*, 1/16, p. 9.

11. CCC to Jane Addams, 1/4/15, Carrie Chapman Catt papers, Manuscripts and Archives Division, New York Public Library; Eleanor Flexner, *Century of Struggle: The Woman's Rights Movement in the United States* (Cambridge, MA: Harvard University Press, 1996), p. 376.

12. Jacqueline Van Voris, *Carrie Chapman Catt: A Public Life* (New York: The Feminist Press at The City University of New York, 1987), p. 44.

13. Amelia R. Fry, *Conversations with Alice Paul* (Berkeley: Suffragists Oral History Project, 1976), p. 326.

14. "Clash of Classes Stirs 'The Masses,'" *The New York Sun*, 4/8/16, p. 6.

15. ME, *Enjoyment of Living*, p. 554.

16. Minutes of Annual Meeting of the Stockholders of *The Masses* Publishing Company, 4/6/16, ME papers.

Chapter 13

1. "Wilson's Decision Waits," *The New York Times*, 1/6/16; "May Not Be Able to Keep Out of War and Maintain Our Honor, Says Wilson," *The New York Times*, 1/30/16.

2. Barbara Gelb, *So Short a Time* (New York: W. W. Norton and Company, 1973), p. 105.

3. JR to Margaret Reed, 4/4/15, JR papers.

4. JR, *The War in Eastern Europe* (New York: Charles Scribner's Sons, 1916), p. 97.

5. JR, *The War in Eastern Europe*, p. 303.

6. WL to Graham Wallas, 1/12/16, WL papers.

7. WL to JR, 2/21/16, WL papers.

8. David Carb to WL, 1/11/13, WL papers.

9. MD, *Movers and Shakers*, p. 298.

10. WL to JR, "Sunday," JR papers.

11. JR to WL, "Monday," WL papers.

12. "Break Is Likely If Sussex Blame Rests on Germany," *The New York Times*, 3/31/16.

13. "Five Americans Lost . . . ," *The Washington Times*, 3/25/16.

14. "U.S. Reports on Sussex Disaster Arouse Grave Official Anxiety," *The Washington Times*, 3/26/16; "Wilson May Lay U-Boat Crisis Before Congress," *The Washington Times*, 3/27/16.

Chapter 14

1. Springfield *State Register,* 4/5/12, quoted in *PWW,* v. 24, p. 296.
2. ME, *Enjoyment of Living,* p. 386.
3. ME, *Enjoyment of Living,* p. 386.
4. ME, *Enjoyment of Living,* p. 387; ME speaking brochure, ME papers.
5. *Pittsburgh Dispatch,* 4/11/12, quoted in *PWW,* v. 24, p. 316.
6. ME, "The Masses at the White House," *The Masses,* 7/16, p. 16.
7. ME, "Negative Pacifism," *The Masses,* 2/15, p. 14.
8. ME, *Enjoyment of Living,* pp. 546, 547.
9. "Mr. Wilson's Great Utterance," *The New Republic,* 6/3/16, p. 102.

Chapter 15

1. "Defense Parade Called Immense," *The Washington Star,* 6/4/16; "Hosts in Chicago on Defense Parade," *The New York Times,* 6/4/16.
2. "4,000,000 Women Start Great Movement in Suffrage Battle," *The Suffragist,* 4/22/16, p. 10.
3. AP, "This Precious Summer," *The Suffragist,* 7/1/16, p. 5.
4. *The New York Sun,* 6/3/16; "Mr. Wilson and the Suffrage States," *The Suffragist,* 6/10/16, p. 4.
5. "Plans for the Woman's Party Convention," *The Suffragist,* 5/13/16, p. 5.
6. *The New York Sun,* 6/8/16.
7. "Socialist Candidate Fails to Register," *The Washington Times,* 11/7/16.
8. "Mrs. Harriot Stanton Blatch to the Woman's Party Convention," *The Suffragist,* 6/17/16, p.
9. Zahniser and Fry, *Alice Paul,* p. 239.
10. Zahniser and Fry, *Alice Paul,* p. 242; Fry, *Conversations with Alice Paul,* Suffragists Oral History Project, Bancroft Library, University of California at Berkeley, 1975, p. 178.
11. "Democratic Excuses," *The Suffragist,* 8/26/16, p. 6.
12. "U.S. Amendment Favored in New Suffrage Plank," *New-York Tribune,* 6/14/16.
13. *The New York Call,* 6/16/16, reprinted in *The Suffragist,* 6/24/16, p. 7.
14. "Small Chance of a Slip-Up in the Convention Program," *The Washington Evening Star,* 6/14/16.
15. "Call Suffrage Plank a Weak Subterfuge," *The New York Times,* 6/17/16.
16. "Will Use $1,000,000 in Suffrage Work," *The New York Times,* 9/8/16; "Women's Hopes High on Wilson's Pledge," *The New York Times,* 9/10/16.
17. "President Wilson Determined Opponent of Federal Suffrage Amendment," *The Suffragist,* 7/29/16, p. 7.

Chapter 16

1. Agnes de Lima to Moreau, 2/9/64, RB papers.
2. Agnes de Lima to AG, undated, RB papers.
3. AG, *Randolph Bourne: Life and Selected Letters,* unpublished ms. in AG papers, p. 9; Dixon Ryan Fox to Blanche Messitte, RB papers.

4. AG, *Day Is Gone* (New York: E. P. Dutton & Company, 1948), p. 136.
5. RB to Van Wyck Brooks, 7/13/16, in *The Letters of Randolph Bourne*, p. 371.
6. RB to AG, 1/21/16, AG papers.
7. RB to Winterrowd, 3/2/13, RB papers.
8. RB, "Trans-national America," *The Atlantic*, 7/16, pp. 86–97 [this and subsequent quotes].
9. Sedgwick to RB, 3/30/16, RB papers.
10. Agnes de Lima to AG, undated, RB papers.
11. RB to Esther Cornell, 12/8/16, RB papers.
12. AG, *Randolph Bourne: Life and Selected Letters*, p. 114; Paul Rosenfeld, *Port of New York* (New York: Harcourt, Brace and Company, 1924), p. 223.
13. Frances Anderson Ewall to Moreau, 10/28/63, RB papers.
14. RB, "A Vanishing World of Gentility," *The Dial*, 3/14/18, p. 234.

Chapter 17

1. Robert Rogers to WL, 6/28/16, WL papers.
2. JR to Amos Pinchot, 8/9/16, Amos Pinchot papers, Manuscript Division, Library of Congress.
3. Bobby Rogers to JR, 1/11/16, JR papers.
4. Mary Heaton Vorse, *Time and the Town* (New Brunswick, NJ: Rutgers University Press, 1991), p. 118.
5. Edna Kenton, *The Provincetown Players and the Playwrights' Theatre, 1915–1922*. Edited by Travis Bogard and Jackson R. Bryer. (Jefferson, NC: McFarland & Company, 2004), p. 2.
6. Robert Károly Sarlós, *Jig Cook and the Provincetown Players* (Amherst: University of Massachusetts Press, 1982), p. 14.
7. Louis Sheaffer, *O'Neill: Son and Playwright* (New York: Cooper Square Press, 2002), vol. 1, p. 356.
8. Susan Glaspell, *The Road to the Temple* (Jefferson, NC: McFarland & Company, 2005), p. 203.
9. May, *The End of American Innocence*, p. 249.
10. Sheaffer, *O'Neill*, vol. 1, p. 252.
11. Sheaffer, *O'Neill*, vol. 1, p. 350.
12. Glaspell, *The Road to the Temple*, p. 207.
13. Glaspell, *The Road to the Temple*, p. 207.
14. ME, *Enjoyment of Living*, p. 564.
15. Kenton, *The Provincetown Players and the Playwrights' Theatre, 1915–1922*, p. 26.
16. Vorse, *Time and the Town*, p. 126.
17. *The Masses*, 11/16, back cover.
18. ME, *Enjoyment of Living*, p. 565.

Chapter 18

1. Steel, *Walter Lippmann and the American Century*, p. 102.
2. RB diary, 9/2/16, RB papers; "Full Text of Mr. Wilson's Speech Accepting the Nomination of President," *The New York Times*, 9/3/16.

3. WL to Graham Wallas, 8/29/16, *Public Philosopher: Selected Letters of Walter Lippmann*, p. 58.

4. WL, "The Case for Wilson," *The New Republic*, 10/14/16, p. 263.

5. *Reminiscences of Walter Lippmann*, p. 92.

6. "Praise Wilson Leadership," *The New York Times*, 10/17/16.

7. "Campaign Against Democratic Party in Equal Suffrage States," *The Suffragist*, 9/30/16, p. 8.

8. AP to Dora Lewis, 9/27/16, in Zahniser and Fry, *Alice Paul*, p. 250.

9. "Last Appeal from Unenfranchised Women," *The Suffragist*, 10/14/16, p. 8.

10. "Women Voters Hear Eastern Appeal," *The Suffragist*, 10/28/16, p. 4.

11. Inez Milholland to AP and AP to Inez Milholland, 10/23/16, in *The National Woman's Party Papers: The Suffrage Years, 1913–1920* (Sanford, NC: Microfilming Corporation of America, 1981).

12. Zahniser and Fry, *Alice Paul*, p. 250.

13. Linda J. Lumsden, *Inez: The Life and Times of Inez Milholland* (Bloomington: Indiana University Press, 2004), p. 163.

14. Lumsden, *Inez*, p. 163.

15. "Call to the Woman Voters," *The Suffragist*, 11/11/16, p. 7.

16. ME, "War and Politics," *The Masses*, 8/16, p. 10.

17. ME, "Sect or Class?" *The Masses*, 12/16, p. 16.

18. ME, "Sect or Class?" *The Masses*, 12/16, p. 16.

19. ME, "Sect or Class?" *The Masses*, 12/16, p. 16.

20. JR to Socialist Party, 10/13/16, Socialist Party of America papers, David M. Rubenstein Rare Book & Manuscript Library, Duke University.

21. Playbill of Provincetown Players, 11/3/17–11/7/17.

22. A. Scott Berg, *Wilson* (New York: G. P. Putnam's Sons, 2013), p. 415.

23. John Milton Cooper, *Woodrow Wilson* (New York: Alfred A. Knopf, 2009), p. 357.

24. Edith Bolling Wilson, *My Memoir* (Indianapolis: Bobbs-Merrill Company, 1939), p. 115.

25. ME, "To Socialist Party Critics," *The Masses*, 2/17, p. 24.

26. "McCormick Joyful at News of Victory," *The New York Times*, 11/11/16; "Democrats Hold Victory Parade," *New-York Tribune*, 11/10/16; WL to Hazel Albertson, 11/10/16, *Public Philosopher: Selected Letters of Walter Lippmann*, p. 58.

Chapter 19

1. William C. Bullitt to Paul S. Reinsch, 1/17/17, JR papers; Robert Lansing to diplomats of Japan, China, India, 1/26/17, JR papers.

2. Granville Hicks, *John Reed*, p. 228.

3. Minute book of Provincetown Players, 2/21/17, Billy Rose Theatre Division, New York Public Library.

4. "The Two Parties After the Election," *The New Republic*, 11/18/16, p. 64.

5. Steel, *Walter Lippmann and the American Century*, p. 108.

6. "Max Eastman is Forbidden Use of Varsity Rostrum," *La Crosse Tribune*, 1/16/17, p. 10.

7. RB to AG, Sunday [1/17], AG papers.

8. RB to AG, Sunday [1/17], AG papers.

9. ME, *Enjoyment of Living*, p. 586.

10. RB to AG, 11/19/16, AG papers.

11. RB to Esther Cornell, 12/8/16, RB papers.

12. AG, *Randolph Bourne: Life and Selected Letters*, p. 112.

13. "Boissevain Memorial Impressive Ceremony," *The Washington Herald*, 12/26/16; Stevens, *Jailed for Freedom*, p. 49.

14. "The Only Tribute," *The Suffragist*, 12/23/16, p. 6.

15. Joseph Tumulty to AP, 1/8/17, *National Woman's Party Papers: The Suffrage Years* microfilm.

16. Stevens, *Jailed for Freedom*, p. 59.

17. Stevens, *Jailed for Freedom*, p. 65.

18. "Scene in the Senate as the President Speaks," *The New York Times*, 1/23/17.

19. House to WW, 1/22/17, quoted in David W. Levy, *Herbert Croly of The New Republic* (Princeton: Princeton University Press, 1985), p. 231.

20. RB, "The Collapse of American Strategy," *The Seven Arts*, 8/17; ME, "Revolutionary Progress," *The Masses*, 4/17, p. 5.

Chapter 20

1. "Pacifists Demand War Referendum," *The New York Times*, 2/5/17.

2. Committee for Democratic Control, "Do the People Want War?," ad in *The New Republic*, 3/3/17, p. 145.

3. RB, "Doubts About Enforcing Peace," unpublished ms., RB papers; *PWW*, vol. 41, p. 305.

4. ME, "Wilson and the World's Future," *The Liberator*, 5/18, p. 19.

5. ME speech to Detroit mass meeting, 4/1/17, ME papers.

6. AP to Joy Young, 2/16/17, AP papers, Schlesinger Library, Radcliffe Institute, Harvard University.

7. Zahniser and Fry, *Alice Paul*, p. 257.

8. *PWW*, vol. 41, p. 388; "Another Leak at Washington," *The Muskogee Times-Democrat*, 1/30/17.

9. Arthur S. Link, *Wilson: Campaigns for Progressivism and Peace, 1916–1917* (Princeton: Princeton University Press, 1965), p. 390.

10. JR, "Whose War?" *The Masses*, 4/17, p. 11.

11. Cooper, *Woodrow Wilson*, p. 382.

12. George Creel, *How We Advertised America* (New York: Harper & Brothers, 1920), p. 5.

13. ME, *Enjoyment of Living*, p. 586.

Chapter 21

1. RB to WL, 2/21/17, WL papers.

2. William James, "The Social Value of the College-Bred," *McClure's*, 2/08, pp. 419–22; Thomas Bender, *New York Intellect: A History of Intellectual Life in New York City* (Baltimore: Johns Hopkins University Press, 1987), p. 228.

3. "Who Willed American Participation?," *The New Republic*, 4/14/17, p. 308.

4. James Oppenheim, "The Story of *The Seven Arts*," *American Mercury*, 6/30, p. 163.

5. Jane Addams to RB, 6/30/17, RB papers.

6. ME to RB, 6/20/17, RB papers.

7. WL, "The White Passion," *The New Republic*, 10/28/16.

8. Steel, *Walter Lippmann and the American Century*, pp. 116–17.

9. Edward G. Lengel, *To Conquer Hell: The Meuse-Argonne, 1918* (New York: Henry Holt and Co., 2008), p. 18.

10. Newton Baker to "Mr. Gifford," 6/1/17, WL papers; Jeffrey O'Connell and Nancy Dart, "The House of Truth: Home of the Young Frankfurter and Lippmann," *Catholic University Law Review*, 1985, p. 82.

11. Crystal Eastman memo, 6/14/17, American Union Against Militarism papers, Swarthmore College Peace Collection.

12. RB, "The Collapse of American Strategy," *The Seven Arts*, 8/17, pp. 417–23.

13. RB, "A War Diary," *The Seven Arts*, 9/17, p. 541.

14. Reminiscences of James T. Shotwell, Oral History Project, Columbia University, p. 78; Lawrence Gelfand, *The Inquiry* (New Haven: Yale University Press, 1963), p. 351.

15. House to WW, 9/20/17, *PWW*, vol. 44, p. 226.

16. WL to House, 9/24/17, Edward Mandell House papers, Manuscripts and Archives, Yale University Library.

17. Minutes of People's Council, 6/21/17, People's Council papers, Swarthmore College Peace Collection.

18. RB, "War and the Intellectuals," *The Seven Arts*, 6/17, p. 146.

19. Paul Shorey, review of *Education and Living*, *The Nation*, 9/6/17, p. 254.

20. Dewey, "The Future of Pacifism," *The New Republic*, 7/28/17, pp. 359, 360.

21. Clayton, *Forgotten Prophet*, p. 230.

22. RB to Horace Kallen, 2/10/17, Horace M. Kallen papers, American Jewish Archives, Cincinnati, Ohio.

23. RB to WL, 8/21/17, WL papers.

24. WL to RB, 8/23/17, WL papers.

Chapter 22

1. ME, "The Religion of Patriotism," *The Masses*, 7/17, p. 9.

2. JR, "Self-Denial Among the Upper Classes," *The Masses*, 7/17, p. 29.

3. ME, "A Separation," *The Masses*, 5/17, p. 14.

4. Arthur Young, "Are Fundamentals Jokes?," *The Masses*, 7/17, p. 24.

5. "A. S. Burleson Dies," *The New York Times*, 11/25/37.

6. George P. West, "A Talk With Mr. Burleson," *The Public*, 10/12/17, p. 986.

7. James Weinstein, *The Decline of American Socialism, 1912–1925* (New York: Monthly Review Press, 1967), p. 90.

8. *PWW*, vol. 43, p. 165.

9. *PWW*, vol. 43, p. 164.

10. Ray Stannard Baker, *Woodrow Wilson: Life and Letters* (New York: Doubleday, Page & Company), vol. 7, p. 165n.

11. Paul J. Murphy, *World War I and the Origin of Civil Liberties in the United States* (New York: W. W. Norton and Company, 1979), p. 67.

12. "The Masses Wins Fight for the Mails," *The New York Times*, 7/25/17.

13. ME, "Bunches of Justice," *The Masses*, 10/17, p. 15.

14. "The Masses Again Held Up," *The New York Times*, 7/27/17.

15. "'The Insolence of Office and the Law's Delay,'" *The Masses*, 10/17, p. 3.

16. ME, "The Post Office Censorship," *The Masses*, 9/17, p. 24.

17. Murphy, *World War I and the Origin of Civil Liberties in the United States*, p. 40.

18. *PWW*, vol. 43, pp. 422–24.

19. JR, "Militarism at Play," *The Masses*, 8/17, p. 18.

20. Murphy, *World War I and the Origin of Civil Liberties in the United States*, p. 94.

21. ME, "Atrocities," *The Masses*, 9/17, p. 13.

22. Murphy, *World War I and the Origin of Civil Liberties in the United States*, p. 123.

23. JR, "The Myth of American Fatness," *The Masses*, 7/17, p. 27.

24. "Enemies Within," *New-York Tribune*, 8/10/17.

25. ME, *Enjoyment of Living*, p. 389.

26. ME to Deshon, 8/19/17, ME papers.

27. ME to Deshon, 8/23/17, ME papers.

28. ME to Deshon, 8/28/17, ME papers.

29. "Fargo Hoots Eastman and Stops Meeting," *The Bismarck Tribune*, 8/29/17, ME to Deshon, ME papers, 8/29/17; ME, *Love and Revolution*, pp. 53–57.

30. "Correspondence," *The Masses*, 11/17, p. 21.

31. "Hard to Draw Line, Wilson Tells Eastman; Things Innocent in Peace Perlilous in War," *The New York Times*, 9/28/17.

32. David Lawrence, "Soft Hand on Censorship is President's Assurance," *The Washington Times*, 9/27/17.

33. WL to House, 10/17/17, House papers.

34. "Court Finds Masses Unfit to be Mailed," *The New York Times*, 11/3/17.

35. "Correspondence," *The Masses*, 10/17, p. 18.

36. Floyd Dell, *Homecoming* (New York: Farrar & Rinehart, Inc., 1933), p. 251.

37. "Max Eastman Held Under $5,000 Bail," *New-York Tribune*, 11/22/17; "7 on 'Masses' Staff Indicted for Sedition," *New-York Tribune*, 11/20/17.

38. ME, "Flavors of Sedition," *The Liberator*, 5/18.

Chapter 23

1. "Russia Rejects a Separate Peace; Action by Soldiers and Workmen After Root Asks for a Firm Stand," *The New York Times*, 6/17/17; Stevens, *Jailed for Freedom*, p. 91.

2. "The Woman's Party Appeals to the Russian Envoys," *The Suffragist*, 6/23/17, p. 1.

3. "Suffs Have New Flag," *The Washington Herald*, 6/22/17.

4. "Mob Led By Woman Rips Suffrage Flags to Bits," *The Washington Times*, 6/21/17.

5. RB to [Joy Young], AP papers.

6. "Prison—and the Reaction," *The Suffragist*, 7/7/17, p. 9.

7. CCC to AP, 5/24/17, Catt papers.

8. Official Bulletin of the Committee on Public Information, 7/3/17, p. 2; "The Picket and the Public," *Woman Citizen*, 6/30/17.

9. "Refuse to Stop Picketing," *The New York Times*, 7/12/17.

10. "Militants Refuse to Stop Picketing," *The Evening Star*, 7/12/17; "Pickets on Duty at White House Again Saturday," *The Evening World*, 7/12/17.

11. Zahniser and Fry, *Alice Paul*, p. 261.

12. Executive Committee minutes, 7/13/17, *The National Woman's Party Papers: The Suffrage Years* microfilm.

13. Executive Committee minutes, 7/13/17, *The National Woman's Party Papers: The Suffrage Years* microfilm.

14. "Pickets 'Obliged to Wilson'; But They'll Picket Again," *New-York Tribune*, 7/21/17.

15. "Suffragettes Lose Banners by Score," *The New York Sun*, 8/16/17; "Sailors Attack Suffragists; Defy Daniels's Order," *New-York Tribune*, 8/16/17; "'Suffs' Buy Gun and 50 Bullets," *The Washington Herald*, 8/16/17.

16. "President Onlooker at Mob Attack on Suffragists," *The Suffragist*, 8/18/17.

17. "Suffragettes Jailed for Picketing," *The Washington Times*, 10/21/17.

18. Ford, *Iron-Jawed Angels*, p. 176.

19. "Seven Months Sentence for National Suffrage Leader," *The Suffragist*, 10/27/17, p. 4.

20. Stevens, *Jailed for Freedom*, p. 215; Zahniser and Fry, *Alice Paul*, pp. 282–83; Florence Brewer Boeckel, "Why They Put Alice Paul in Solitary Confinement," *The Suffragist*, 11/10/17, p. 7.

21. Stevens, *Jailed for Freedom*, p. 177; "Political Prisoners," *The Suffragist*, 11/3/17, p. 8.

22. AP to Grace Henshaw, 7/3/17, quoted in Ford, *Iron-Jawed Angels*, p. 149.

23. "Truce Is Called in Picketing of White House," *New-York Tribune*, 11/16/17, p. 14.

24. Zahniser and Fry, *Alice Paul*, p. 289.

25. Fry, *Conversations with Alice Paul*, p. 225.

26. "Released Pickets Once More in Toils," *The New York Sun*, 11/14/17.

27. Zahniser and Fry, *Alice Paul*, p. 288.

28. "The Prison Notes of Rose Winslow," *The Suffragist*, 12/1/17, p. 6; Stevens, *Jailed for Freedom*, p. 190.

29. "A Note from Alice Paul," *The Suffragist*, 11/24/17, p. 6.

30. Zahniser and Fry, *Alice Paul*, p. 290; "Suffragettes Are Arrested at White House," *The Washington Herald*, 11/11/17.

31. "Suff Pickets Again in Hands of Police," *The New York Sun*, 11/13/17.

32. Ford, *Iron-Jawed Angels*, p. 203.

33. Ford, *Iron-Jawed Angels,* p. 203.
34. "Cat-and-Mouse Remedy for Hunger Striking," *The New York Times,* 11/29/17.
35. Dorothy Day, *The Long Loneliness* (New York: HarperCollins, 1997), p. 79.
36. Sara Hunter Graham, *Woman Suffrage and the New Democracy* (New Haven: Yale University Press, 1996), p. 113.
37. Catt to Mary Gray Peck, 10/23/17, Carrie Chapman Catt papers, Manuscript Division, Library of Congress.

Chapter 24

1. JR, *Ten Days That Shook the World* (New York: Penguin Classics, 2008), p. 37.
2. Albert Rhys Williams, *Journey Into Revolution* (Chicago: Quadrangle Books, 1969), p. 36.
3. JR, *Ten Days That Shook the World,* pp. 103, 85.
4. JR, *Ten Days That Shook the World,* p. 68.
5. JR, "This Unpopular War," *The Seven Arts,* 8/17, p. 407.
6. JR, "Almost Thirty," unpublished ms., JR papers.
7. JR to Bryant, 7/10/17, JR papers.
8. JR to Bryant, 7/15/17, JR papers.
9. JR to Boardman Robinson, 10/16/17, JR papers.
10. Williams, *Journey Into Revolution,* p. 62.
11. JR, *Ten Days That Shook the World,* pp. 83, 73.
12. JR, *Ten Days That Shook the World,* p. 77.
13. JR, *Ten Days That Shook the World,* p. 98.
14. JR, *Ten Days That Shook the World,* p. 100.
15. JR, "Red Russia—The Triumph of the Bolsheviki," *The Liberator,* 3/18, p. 14.
16. Robert Service, *Lenin: A Biography* (Cambridge, MA: Harvard University Press, 2000), pp. 64, 177, 192.
17. JR, *Ten Days That Shook the World,* p. 129.
18. JR, *Ten Days That Shook the World,* p. 129.
19. Rosenstone, *Romantic Revolutionary,* p. 280.
20. JR, "Red Russia—The Triumph of the Bolsheviki," *The Liberator,* 3/18, p. 21; John Reed, "John Reed Cables the Call News of Bolshevik Revolt He Witnessed," *The New York Call,* 11/22/17, p. 1.
21. Williams, *Journey Into Revolution,* p. 41.
22. JR, "Foreign Affairs," *The Liberator,* 6/18, p. 28; *Brewing and Liquor Interests and German and Bolshevik Propaganda* (Washington, DC: Government Printing Office, 1919), vol. 3, p. 565.
23. Bryant, *Six Red Months in Russia* (New York: George H. Doran Company, 1918), p. 235; Hicks, *John Reed,* p. 292.
24. Edgar Sisson, *One Hundred Red Days* (New Haven: Yale University Press, 1931), p. 285.
25. Hicks, *John Reed,* p. 291.
26. Bryant, "Christmas in Petrograd," Granville Hicks papers, Special Collections Research Center, Syracuse University Libraries, p. 3.

27. Sisson, *One Hundred Red Days*, p. 258.

28. Sisson, *One Hundred Red Days*, p. 258.

29. Williams, *Journey Into Revolution*, p. 208.

30. Sisson, *One Hundred Red Days*, p. 287; Eric Homberger, *John Reed* (Manchester: Manchester University Press, 1990), p. 160.

31. Williams, *Journey Into Revolution*, p. 208.

Chapter 25

1. "The Democratic Tide Turns in the Senate," *The Suffragist*, 1/30/18, p. 5; "The Nation Makes an Insistent Demand on the Senate," *The Suffragist*, 1/30/18, p. 9; *The New York Sun*, 1/20/18, special section p. 3.

2. ME, "A Militant Suffrage Victory," *The Liberator*, 3/18, p. 7.

3. Maud Wood Park, *Front Door Lobby* (Boston: Beacon Press, 1960), p. 157; Park, *Front Door Lobby*, p. 153.

4. Eileen McDonagh, "Issues and Constituencies in the Progressive Era: House Roll Call Voting on the 19th Amendment, 1913–1919," *The Journal of Politics*, 2/89; Elizabeth Bass to WW, 5/21/18, *PWW*, vol. 48.

5. Ford, *Iron-Jawed Angels*, p. 235.

6. "Suffragists Certain That the Senate Must Pass National Amendment Soon," *The New York Sun*, 7/7/18.

7. Maud Younger, "Senator Jones Investigates," *The Suffragist*, 8/31/18, p. 7.

8. Flexner, *Century of Struggle*, p. 301.

9. "Wilson Asks Senate to Pass Suffrage Bill," *New-York Tribune*, 10/1/18; "Wilson Talk Saves Party for Women," *The New York Sun*, 10/4/18.

Chapter 26

1. Beulah Amidon to AG, 10/4/48, RB papers.

2. RB to AG, 11/10/16, AG papers.

3. RB, "A War Diary," *The Seven Arts*, 9/17.

4. RB to AG, "Monday," AG papers.

5. Oppenheim, "The Story of *The Seven Arts*," p. 163.

6. John Adam Moreau, *Randolph Bourne: Legend and Reality* (Washington, DC: Public Affairs Press, 1966), p. 193.

7. Oppenheim, "The Story of *The Seven Arts*," p. 163; Van Wyck Brooks, *An Autobiography* (New York: E. P. Dutton and Co., 1965), p. 287.

8. RB, "The Cult of Convention," *The Liberator*, 6/18, p. 38.

9. RB to Sarah Bourne, 10/12/18, RB papers.

10. RB, "Old Tyrannies," *Untimely Papers*, p. 21.

11. Clayton, *Forgotten Prophet*, p. 236.

Chapter 27

1. Young, *On My Way*, p. 293.

2. Dell, "The Story of the Trial," *The Liberator*, 6/18, p. 7.

3. ME, *Love and Revolution*, p. 87; "John Reed Indicted With Shiplacoff," *New-York Tribune*, 9/24/18.

4. ME, *Love and Revolution*, p. 118.
5. "Knit a Strait-Jacket for Your Soldier Boy," *The Masses*, 8/17, p. 42.
6. ME, "Editorials," *The Liberator*, 3/18, p. 7; 7/18, p. 6.
7. ME, "Wilson and the World's Future," *The Liberator*, 5/18, p. 20.
8. ME, *Love and Revolution*, p. 108.
9. "Two Letters," *The Liberator*, 9/18, p. 34.
10. "Two Letters," *The Liberator*, 9/18, p. 34.
11. Roger Baldwin to Harry Dana, 11/21/17, Henry Wadsworth Longfellow Dana papers, Swarthmore College Peace Collection.
12. "Pacifist Professor Gets Year in Prison," *The New York Times*, 10/31/18.
13. Dell to ME, 11/26/53, ME papers.
14. JR, "About the Second Masses Trial," *The Liberator*, 12/18, p. 37.
15. ME, *Love and Revolution*, p. 117.
16. ME, *Max Eastman's Address to the Jury in the Second Masses Trial* (New York: Liberator Publishing Company, 1918), p. 18.
17. "Masses Jury Disagrees," *The New York Times*, 10/6/18.
18. Laurence [illegible] to ME, 12/23/18, ME papers.
19. ME, *Love and Revolution*, p. 121.
20. ME, *Love and Revolution*, p. 123.

Chapter 28

1. Byron Farwell, *Over There: The United States in the Great War, 1917–1918* (New York: W. W. Norton and Co., 2000), p. 206.
2. Farwell, *Over There*, p. 187.
3. Farwell, *Over There*, pp. 216, 213.
4. *Reminiscences of Walter Lippmann*, p. 14.
5. Steel, *Walter Lippmann and the American Century*, p. 142.
6. WL to Faye Lippmann, 10/26/18, WL papers.
7. Colonel House Diary, 10/18/18, p. 10, House papers.
8. Godfrey Hodgson, *Woodrow Wilson's Right Hand* (New Haven: Yale University Press, 2006), p. 188.
9. WL to Faye Lippmann, 10/26/18, WL papers.

Chapter 29

1. Farwell, *Over There*, p. 264.
2. "Lansing Is Swift to Deny Tale," *The New York Times*, 11/7/18.
3. "Wilson Will Tell Quickly of Peace," *The New York Times*, 11/9/18.
4. Dell, *Homecoming*, p. 328; "Tears and Cheers Mingle in New York's Frenzied Acclaim of Peace Report," *New-York Tribune*, 11/8/18.
5. "Truce Electrifies Congress," *The New York Times*, 11/12/18.
6. John Keegan, *The First World War* (New York: Vintage Books, 2000), p. 421.
7. Farwell, *Over There*, p. 234.
8. John M. Barry, *The Great Influenza* (New York: Penguin Books, 2005), pp. 235, 237; Barry, *The Great Influenza*, p. 241.
9. Barry, *The Great Influenza*, p. 276.

10. RB to Van Wyck Brooks, 11/12/18, *The Letters of Randolph Bourne,* p. 424.

11. Merrill Rogers to John Moreau, 12/24/63, RB papers.

12. Robert Morss Lovett, *All Our Years* (New York: Viking, 1948), pp. 151–52.

13. RB to Sarah Bourne, 11/21/18, RB papers.

14. Agnes de Lima to AG, 2/28/49, RB papers.

15. Nicholas Joost, *Years of Transition: The Dial, 1912–1920* (Barre, MA: Barre Publishers, 1967), p. 188; Agnes de Lima to John Adam Moreau, 2/28/64, RB papers.

16. Gregory, *Day Is Gone,* p. 165.

17. Agnes de Lima to AG, 2/28/49, RB papers.

18. Agnes de Lima to John Adam Moreau, 2/9/64, RB papers; Rosenfeld, *Port of New York,* p. 225.

Chapter 30

1. James T. Shotwell, *At the Paris Peace Conference* (New York: The Macmillan Company, 1937), pp. 85–86; Edith Wilson, *My Memoir,* p. 177.

2. Ray Stannard Baker, *A Journalist's Diplomatic Mission: Ray Stannard Baker's World War I Diary.* Edited by John Maxwell Hamilton and Robert Mann. (Baton Rouge: Louisiana State University Press, 2012), p. 271.

3. Heber Blankenhorn, *Adventures in Propaganda* (Boston: Houghton Mifflin Company, 1919), p. 152; WL, *Public Opinion* (New York: Free Press Paperbacks, 1997), p. 8.

4. Herbert Hoover, *The Ordeal of Woodrow Wilson* (Baltimore: Johns Hopkins University Press, 1992), p. 88.

5. *Reminiscences of Walter Lippmann,* p. 17.

6. WL to Newton Baker, 11/12/18, Newton Baker papers, Manuscript Division, Library of Congress.

7. "Make Peace Won by Armies Secure, Wilson's Plea in London Speech," *The Evening World,* 12/28/18.

8. Hayes to Newton Baker, 12/22/18, Newton Baker papers.

9. Baker to Pershing, 7/2/18, WL papers.

10. WL to House, 8/15/18, House papers.

11. WW to House, 8/31/18, Woodrow Wilson papers (microfilm edition) Manuscript Division, Library of Congress.

12. WL Diary, 10/5/17, WL papers.

13. Mezes to Lansing, 10/25/18, Sidney Mezes papers, Manuscripts and Archives, Yale University Library; Sir William Wiseman to Arthur Murray, 9/14/18, Woodrow Wilson papers microfilm.

14. "Notes on the Inquiry," James T. Shotwell papers, Rare Book and Manuscript Library, Columbia University.

15. Hayes to Newton Baker, 12/22/18, Newton Baker papers; WL to Faye Lippmann, 12/20/18, WL papers; "Notes on the Inquiry," James T. Shotwell papers; "Tons of Data Go With Wilson Party," *The New York Times,* 12/4/18; "Experts, Under Guard, Gather Peace Data," *New-York Tribune,* 12/4/18.

16. WL to Faye Lippmann, 12/29/18, WL papers.
17. Ralph Hayes to Carl Boyd, 12/12/18, Ralph Hayes papers, Western Reserve Historical Society; Hayes to NDB, 12/15/18, Newton Baker papers; WL to Faye Lippmann, 12/29/18, WL papers; Felix Frankfurter to WL, 2/19, WL papers; Francis Hackett to WL, 2/21/19, WL papers.
18. WL, *Political Scene,* p. 61.
19. *PWW,* v. 51, p. 500.
20. "Europe Proposes," *The New Republic,* 5/17/19, p. 70.
21. "Joy Among the Philistines," *The New Republic,* 6/7/19, p. 170.
22. WL to Bernard Berenson, 7/16/19, WL papers.
23. "Europe Proposes," *The New Republic,* 5/17/19.
24. "The Tank and the Rosebush," *New-York Tribune,* 6/24/19.
25. WL to Berenson, 7/16/19, WL papers.

Chapter 31
1. JR, *Ten Days That Shook the World,* p. 9.
2. ME, *Heroes I Have Known* (New York: Simon and Schuster, 1942), p. 224.
3. Polly Holliday to John Stuart, 6/17/35, Hicks papers.
4. JR to Lincoln Steffens, 6/29/[18], Lincoln Steffens papers, Rare Book and Manuscript Library, Columbia University Library.
5. Diggins, *Up from Communism,* p. 22; Robert K. Murray, *Red Scare: A Study in National Hysteria* (Minneapolis: University of Minnesota Press, 1955), p. 9.
6. Theodore Draper, *The Roots of American Communism* (New Brunswick, NJ: Transaction Publishers, 2003), p. 16.
7. Draper, *The Roots of American Communism,* p. 137; Reed, "A New Appeal," *Revolutionary Age,* 1/18/19.
8. Benjamin Gitlow, *I Confess* (New York: E. P. Dutton, 1940), p. 25; Letter to Executive Committee of Local New York from 17 members of 17th A.D., Socialist Party minutes, Tamiment Library, New York University Libraries (Reel 10 Series VI:5).
9. Benjamin Gitlow, *The Whole of Their Lives* (Boston: Western Islands, 1965) p. 21; "The Centre Appears," *Revolutionary Age,* 3/29/19, p. 3.
10. Minutes of the Left-Wing Executive Committee, 4/23/19, Theodore Draper papers, Hoover Institution Archives.
11. *The Liberator,* 11/18, p. 2.
12. ME, *Colors of Life,* pp. 13–14; ME, *Love and Revolution,* p. 163.
13. ME, *Heroes I Have Known,* pp. 221–22.
14. Morris Hillquit, "The Socialist Task and Outlook," *The New York Call,* 5/21/18.
15. ME to Florence Deshon, 7/14/19, ME papers.
16. Glaspell, *Road to the Temple,* p. 236.
17. Hicks, *John Reed,* p. 359; ME, "The Chicago Conventions," *The Liberator,* 10/19, p. 7.

18. ME, "The Chicago Conventions," *The Liberator*, 10/19, p. 9; "Complete Report of the Communist Labor Party of the United States," 9/9/19, *Surveillance of Radicals* microfilm, reel 10.

19. Draper, *The Roots of American Communism*, p. 178; ME, "The Chicago Conventions," *The Liberator*, 10/19, p. 5.

20. New York State Joint Legislative Committee to Investigate Seditious Activities, *Revolutionary Radicalism* (Albany, NY: J. B. Lyon, 1920), vol. 1, pp. 810, 801.

21. "Complete Report of the Communist Labor Party of the United States," 9/9/19, *Surveillance of Radicals* microfilm, reel 10.

22. Elizabeth Gurley Flynn, *I Speak My Own Piece* (New York: Masses and Mainstream, 1955), p. 271.

23. JR, "A New Appeal," *Revolutionary Age*, 1/18/19, p. 8. (Draper, *The Roots of American Communism*, p. 137).

24. Gitlow, *The Whole of Their Lives*, p. 29.

25. Report by Sgt. John Dillon and Inspector Leonard Arnold, 1/4/19, *Surveillance of Radicals* microfilm, reel 12, frame 34.

26. Malcolm Cowley, *Exile's Return* (New York: The Viking Press, 1967), pp. 66, 70.

27. Gitlow, *The Whole of Their Lives*, p. 29.

28. *Surveillance of Radicals* microfilm, reel 33, frames 682, 695, 853.

Chapter 32

1. David Glassberg, *American Historical Pageantry* (Chapel Hill: University of North Carolina Press, 1990), pp. 225, 231.

2. "New Year's Day Protest," *The Suffragist*, 1/4/19, p. 7; "The Watchfire," *The Suffragist*, 1/11/19, p. 6.

3. "Impressions from the District Jail," *The Suffragist*, 1/25/19, p. 12.

4. Nancy F. Cott, *The Grounding of Modern Feminism* (New Haven: Yale University Press, 1987), p. 62.

5. "The Demonstration of February 9," *The Suffragist*, 2/22/19, p. 10.

6. "Suffragists Burn Effigy of President," *New-York Tribune*, 2/10/19; "Suffs Burn Wilson Effigy; 65 Arrested," *The New York Sun*, 2/10/19; "Eleven Suffragists From Here in Jail," *The Evening Public Ledger*, 2/10/19; "Suffragists Burn Wilson in Effigy; Many Locked Up," *The New York Times*, 2/10/19.

7. "Suffrage Wins in House by 42," *The New York Sun*, 5/22/19; "House Votes for Suffrage, 304–89," *New-York Tribune*, 5/22/19.

8. Haynes Irwin, *The Story of the Woman's Party*, p. 417.

9. Executive Committee minutes, 7/11/19, *National Woman's Party Papers: The Suffrage Years* microfilm; "Suffragists Rejoice," *The Suffragist*, 6/14/19, p. 9.

10. JR, "Red Russia," *The Liberator*, 3/18, p. 14.

Chapter 33

1. WL to House, 7/19/19, House papers.

2. "Ovation to the President," *The New York Times*, 7/11/19.

3. Joseph Tumulty, *Woodrow Wilson as I Know Him* (Garden City, NY: Doubleday, Page and Co., 1921), p. 435.

4. Cooper, *Woodrow Wilson,* p. 521; William Cochran to Tumulty, 9/11/19, *PWW,* vol. 63, p. 198.

5. *The Bullitt Mission to Russia: Testimony Before the Committee on Foreign Relations, United States Senate, of William C. Bullitt* (New York: B. W. Huebsch, 1919), pp. 101–4.

6. "Treaty's Friends in a Panic Over Lansing's Stand," *New-York Tribune,* 9/14/19; "Held League to be Utterly Useless, Says W.C. Bullitt," *New-York Tribune,* 9/13/19; "Revelations From One of Mr. Wilson's Appointees," *The New York Sun,* 9/14/19; "Mr. Bullitt's Disclosures," *The New York Times,* 9/15/19.

7. WL to Ralph Hayes, 8/6/19, WL papers; "Treaty Action by Senate May Come at Once," *The Washington Herald,* 8/14/19.

8. Hiram Johnson to WL, 8/28/19, WL papers.

9. WL to Hiram Johnson, 9/9/19, WL papers.

10. WL to Hiram Johnson, 9/9/19 WL papers.

11. Tumulty, *Woodrow Wilson as I Know Him,* p. 441.

12. "Address at Pueblo, Colo., September 25, 1919," *Addresses Delivered by President Wilson on His Western Tour,* (Washington, DC: Government Printing Office, 1919), pp. 359–60.

13. *PWW,* vol. 63, pp. 501, 510.

14. *PWW,* vol. 63 pp. 518–19, 641.

15. *PWW,* vol. 63, pp. 521, 527.

16. *PWW,* vol. 63 p. 488.

Chapter 34

1. PWW vol., 64, p. 504.

2. Cameron McWhirter, *Red Summer: The Summer of 1919 and the Awakening of Black America* (New York: Henry Holt and Company, 2011), pp. 13, 74.

3. W.E.B. Du Bois, "Returning Soldiers," *The Crisis,* 5/19, p. 13.

4. Claude McKay, "Sonnets and Songs," *The Liberator,* 7/19, pp. 20–21.

5. Ann Hagedorn, *Savage Peace: Hope and Fear in America, 1919* (New York: Simon & Schuster, 2007), p. 276.

6. "Oust 5 Socialists; Will Compel Party to Purge Itself," *The New York Times,* 4/2/20, p. 1.

7. Paul J. Murphy, *The Meaning of Free Speech* (Westport, CT: Greenwood Publishing Company, 1972), p. 25.

8. WL to Johnson, 1/8/20, WL papers.

9. WL to NDB, 1/17/20, WL papers.

10. Hagedorn, *Savage Peace,* pp. 329, 369; Kenneth Ackerman, *Young J. Edgar: Hoover and the Red Scare, 1919–1920* (New York: Carroll & Graf, 2007), pp. 64, 66, 116, 119, 157.

11. Murray, *Red Scare,* p. 251.

12. Murray, *Red Scare,* pp. 248, 253.

13. John Dewey, "The Discrediting of Idealism," *The New Republic,* 10/8/19, pp. 285–87.
14. Lewis Mumford, "Patriotism and Its Consequences," *The Dial,* 4/19/19, p. 406; "Books in Brief," *The Nation,* 4/17/20, p. 523.
15. RB, "Below the Battle," *The Seven Arts,* 7/17.
16. F. Scott Fitzgerald, *This Side of Paradise* (New York: Charles Scribner's Sons, 1920), pp. 228–29.

Chapter 35

1. "Report John Reed Shot in Finland," *The New York Evening World,* 4/9/20; "Report Reed Put to Death," *The New York Times,* 4/10/20; "John Reed Executed in Finland, Is Report," *New-York Tribune,* 4/10/20.
2. "John Reed Alive and Well, Finland Officially Reports," *New-York Tribune,* 4/16/20.
3. J. Edgar Hoover to Colonel A. B. Cox, 8/14/20, *Surveillance of Radicals* microfilm, reel 33, frame 887; State Department press release, 9/11/20; Lt. Col. William Colvin to General C. E. Nolan, Director of Military Intelligence, 4/27/20, *Surveillance of Radicals,* reel 33, frame 645.
4. Bryant, "Last Days with John Reed," *The Liberator,* 2/21, p. 11; JR to Bryant, 5/13/20, JR papers; MacAlpine ms. in JR papers; Eadmonn MacAlpine to Hicks, 12/26/34, Hicks papers; "Report John Reed Caught in Coal Bunker of Ship in Finnish Port with False Passports," *The New York Times,* 3/18/20; "John Reed, Communist Editor, Captured on Way to Sweden," *New-York Tribune,* 3/18/20.
5. JR to Bryant, 5/3/20, JR papers.
6. *Surveillance of Radicals,* reel 33, frame 795 [report dated 5/27/20].
7. JR to Bryant, 6/7/20 telegram, JR papers; Hollyday telegram to War Department, 6/5/20, in *Surveillance of Radicals,* reel 33, frame 804; MacAlpine ms., in JR papers; Hicks, *John Reed,* p. 385.
8. Hollyday telegram to War Department, 6/5/20, *Surveillance of Radicals,* reel 33, frame 804; Emma Goldman to Lillian Wald, 11/4/20, Lillian Wald papers Rare Book and Manuscript Library, Columbia University; Emma Goldman, *Living My Life* (New York: Alfred A. Knopf, 1931), pp. 738, 849, 735.
9. Corey to Hicks 12/30/35, in Hicks papers; "Agreement for the Unification of the American Communist Party and the American Communist Labor Party," 1/12/20, *Surveillance of Radicals,* reel 33, frame 807; Draper, *The Roots of American Communism,* p. 187.
10. JR, "Soviet Russia Now," *The Liberator,* 12/20, p. 10.
11. ME, *Heroes I Have Known,* p. 231.
12. Proceedings of the Second Congress of the Communist International, p. 86.
13. JR, *Ten Days That Shook the World,* p. 8.
14. JR, "A New Appeal," *The Revolutionary Age,* 1/18/19, p. 8.
15. Bryant, "Last Days with John Reed," *The Liberator,* 2/21, p. 11.
16. Lewis Corey to Hicks 12/30/35, Hicks papers.

17. Steffens, "The Boy from Oregon," *Partisan Review*, 12/33.

18. Alfred Rosmer, *Lenin's Moscow*. Translated by Ian Birchall. (London: Pluto Press, 1971), p. 93.

19. John Riddell, ed., *To See the Dawn: Baku, 1920—First Congress of the Peoples of the East* (New York: Pathfinder, 1993), p. 361.

20. Rosmer, "John Reed in 1920," unpublished ms., Max Shachtman papers, Tamiment Library, NYU, p. 19; Balabanova, "John Reed's Last Days," *Modern Monthly*, 1/37.

21. Riddell, *To See the Dawn*, p. 88; ME, *Heroes I Have Known*, p. 233.

22. Rosmer, *Lenin's Moscow*, p. 95.

23. Bryant, Russia notebook, 10/27/20, Louise Bryant papers, Manuscripts and Archives, Yale University Library; Bryant, "Last Days with John Reed," *The Liberator*, 2/21, p. 11.

24. JR, outline for "The Tides of Men," JR papers; Corey to Hicks, 12/30/35, Hicks papers.

25. JR, "The World Congress of the Communist International," *The Communist*, no. 10, p. 4; Patrick Quinlan to Hicks, n.d., Hicks papers.

26. Bryant, "Last Days with John Reed," *The Liberator*, 2/21, p. 11.

27. JR, *The War in Eastern Europe*, pp. 48, 104.

28. Corey to Hicks, 12/30/35, Hicks papers.

29. Bryant, "Last Days with John Reed," *The Liberator*, 2/21, p. 11; Bryant to Margaret Reed, 10/20/20, JR papers.

30. "Memory of John Reed to be Honored Tonight," *The New York Call*, 10/25/20, p. 1.

31. "Workers Cheer Cause for Which Reed Died," *The New York Call*, 10/26/20, p. 1.

32. ME, "John Reed," *The Liberator*, 12/20, pp. 5–6.

Chapter 36

1. Haynes Irwin, *The Story of the Women's Party*, p. 474.

2. *The Woman Citizen*, 9/4/20, p. 364.

3. *The Suffragist*, 9/20, p. 193.

4. Mildred Morris, "Fight for All Rights Still Facing Women, Declares Alice Paul," *The Washington Times*, 8/19/20.

5. "Suffrage Proclaimed by Colby, Who Signs at Home Early in Day," *The Evening Star*, 8/26/20; "Colby Proclaims Woman Suffrage," *The New York Times*, 8/27/20; "With Neither Dear Charmer," *The New York Times*, 8/28/20.

6. Emma Bugbee, "Woman's Party Will Work for Feminism Only," *New-York Tribune*, 2/19/21; Crystal Eastman, "Alice Paul's Convention," *The Liberator*, 4/21, pp. 9–10.

7. William Pickens, "The Woman Voter Hits the Color Line," *The Nation*, 10/6/20, pp. 372–73; Terborg-Penn, "Discontented Black Feminists," p. 69; Terborg-Penn, *African-American Women in the Struggle for the Vote, 1850–1920*, p. 163.

8. "Negro Women Want Vote," *Washington Evening Star*, 2/12/21; Freda Kirchwey, "Alice Paul Holds the Strings," *The Nation*, 3/2/21, p. 332.

9. Cott, *The Grounding of Modern Feminism*, p. 308.

10. Cott, *The Grounding of Modern Feminism*, p. 308.

11. Cott, *The Grounding of Modern Feminism*, p. 308.

12. Leila J. Rupp and Verta Taylor, *Survival in the Doldrums: The American Women's Rights Movement, 1945 to the 1960s*. (New York: Oxford University Press, 1987), p. 154; Terborg-Penn, *African American Women in the Struggle for the Vote, 1850–1920*, p. 156.

13. Alice Paul, "Editorial," *The Suffragist*, 1–2/21 p. 7.

14. ME, "The New International," *The Liberator*, 7/19, p. 30.

15. ME, *Love and Revolution*, p. 240.

16. ME, "Dogmatism Again," *The Liberator*, 5/21, p. 8.

17. ME, "The Free Press," *The Liberator*, 5/21, p. 5.

18. ME, "Clarifying the Light," *The Liberator*, 6/21, pp. 5–7.

19. H. L. Mencken, "Diagnosis of Our Cultural Malaise," *The Smart Set*, 2/19; Van Wyck Brooks, *An Autobiography*, p. 641.

20. Eastman claimed that Brooks and Daniel Aaron had misunderstood him, that he didn't mean "discipline" in the way that Stalin later meant it. See Aaron, *Writers on the Left*, pp. 50–55, and ME, *Love and Revolution*, p. 239; ME, *Love and Revolution*, p. 229.

21. ME, "Lenin," *The Liberator*, 4/20, p. 6.

22. ME, "An Opinion on Tactics," *The Liberator*, 10/21, p. 6; ACLU, *The Fight for Free Speech*, 1921, p. 4; *Annual Report of the Attorney General of the United States for the Year 1920* (Washington, DC: Government Printing Office, 1920), p. 176.

23. ME, "A Significant Picture," *The Liberator*, 2/20, p. 5.

24. "Eastman Denies Rift With Miss Deshon," *The New York Times*, 2/6/22; Marie Howe to ME, 2/6/22, ME papers.

25. Deshon to ME, 10/20, ME papers.

26. WL to S. K. Ratcliffe, 8/10/20, in *Public Philosopher: Selected Letters of Walter Lippmann*, p. 136.

27. "Wilson Advises Senators," *The New York Times*, 3/9/20.

28. Dr. Edwin A. Weinstein says outright that the effects of Wilson's stroke prevented him from finding a solution to the treaty negotiations. See Edwin A. Weinstein, *Woodrow Wilson: A Medical and Psychological Biography* (Princeton: Princeton University Press, 1981), p. 363.

29. WL to S. K. Ratcliffe, 8/10/20, in *Public Philosopher: Selected Letters of Walter Lippmann*, p. 137.

30. WL, "Hail and Farewell," *Vanity Fair*, 4/21, pp. 29–30.

31. WL to Graham Wallas, 11/4/20, in *Public Philosopher: Selected Letters of Walter Lippmann*, p. 137.

32. Dewey, "Public Opinion," *The New Republic*, 5/3/22, p. 286.

33. WL, *The Phantom Public* (New Brunswick, NJ: Transaction Publishers, 2006), p. 15.

Epilogue

1. Cowley, *Exile's Return*, p. 72.
2. It wasn't limited to the 1910s: Some NWP members used racist arguments to build support for Title VII. See Carl Brauer, "Women Activists, Southern Conservatives, and the Prohibition of Sex Discrimination in Title VII of the 1964 Civil Rights Act," *The Journal of Southern History*, 2/83, p. 43.
3. Pauli Murray, Title VII memo, 4/14/64, Pauli Murray papers, Schlesinger Library, Radcliffe Institute, Harvard University, p. 9.
4. Pauli Murray, *Song in a Weary Throat* (New York: Harper & Row, 1987), p. 358.
5. ME, *Love and Revolution*, p. 627.
6. ME, *Reflections on the Failure of Socialism*, pp. 19, 24.
7. ME, *Reflections on the Failure of Socialism*, p. 46; William L. O'Neill, *The Last Romantic: A Life of Max Eastman* (New York: Oxford University Press, 1978), p. 225; William F. Buckley, Jr. to ME, 8/3/54, ME papers.
8. ME to Buckley, 11/28/58, William F. Buckley papers, Manuscripts and Archives, Yale University Library.
9. O'Neill, *The Last Romantic*, p. 274.
10. Alden Whitman, "Max Eastman Is 'Sorry' for Today's Rebels," *The New York Times*, 1/9/69.
11. Alden Whitman, "Max Eastman Is 'Sorry' for Today's Rebels," *The New York Times*, 1/9/69.
12. Monograph report on Russian conditions, 5/17/21, reel 33, frame 858 in *Surveillance of Radicals* microfilm; Military intelligence to J. Edgar Hoover, 6/10/21, reel 33, frame 853 in *Surveillance of Radicals* microfilm; Angelica Balabanova, "John Reed's Last Days," *The Modern Monthly*, 1/37, p. 3.
13. ME, *Heroes I Have Known*, p. 237.
14. Angelica Balabanova, "John Reed's Last Days," *The Modern Monthly*, 1/37, p. 5.
15. Author interview with Luis Valdez, January 2017.
16. "The Man Who Stands Apart," *Time*, 12/22/58, p. 59.
17. "Walter Lippmann, columnist, dies at 85," *Chicago Tribune*, 12/15/74, p. 1.
18. Harold J. Laski to Oliver Wendell Holmes, Jr., 3/23/31, in *Holmes-Laski Letters: The Correspondence of Mr. Justice Holmes and Harold J. Laski*. Edited by Mark Dewolfe Howe. (Harvard University Press, 1953), p. 1311.
19. WL, "The War and the Election," *Newsweek*, 12/5/66, p. 23.
20. Herblock, "Of the Problems of Vietnam Policy: The War on Lippmann," *The Washington Post*, 5/7/67; Steel, *Walter Lippmann and the American Century*, p. 576.
21. Hugh Sidey, "The Oval Office vs. the Attic," *Life*, 5/19/67, p. 44; Steel, *Walter Lippmann and the American Century*, p. 579; Herblock, "Of the Problems of Vietnam Policy: The War on Lippmann," *The Washington Post*, 5/7/67.
22. Charles Marsh, *The Beloved Community* (New York: Basic Books, 2005), p. 1.

Index

About the Author

JEREMY MCCARTER is the co-author of the #1 *New York Times* bestseller *Hamilton: The Revolution,* with Lin-Manuel Miranda. He wrote about culture and politics for *New York* magazine and *Newsweek,* and spent five years on the artistic staff of the Public Theater in New York. He studied history at Harvard and lives in Chicago.

jeremymccarter.com

About the Type

This book was set in Caslon, a typeface first designed in 1722 by William Caslon (1692–1766). Its widespread use by most English printers in the early eighteenth century soon supplanted the Dutch typefaces that had formerly prevailed. The roman is considered a "workhorse" typeface due to its pleasant, open appearance, while the italic is exceedingly decorative.